C210102

CW00384337

NOTTINGHAMSHIRE
MISCELLANY

NOTTINGHAMSHIRE
MISCELLANY

Michael Smith

Acknowledgements

Several people have helped me in writing this book. I should like to express my particular gratitude to:

Nick Smith for advice and assistance with digital photography.
The staff at DB Publishing for their advice, support and encouragement and for bringing the work to fruition.
The staff at the following libraries without whom the research could not have been completed:
Eastwood Library
Ilkeston Library
Nottingham Local Studies Library
Nottingham University Library (Hallwood and King's Meadow sites).

First published in Great Britain in 2011 by
The Derby Books Publishing Company Limited,
3 The Parker Centre, Derby, DE21 4SZ.

© Michael Smith, 2011

ISBN 978-1-85983-817-4
Printed and bound by Melita Press, Malta.

CONTENTS

Introducing Nottinghamshire

✳ Nottinghamshire is an East Midlands county which borders on Derbyshire, Leicestershire, Lincolnshire and South Yorkshire.

✳ It covers an area of 2,160sq km or 834sq miles.

✳ Nottinghamshire sits on coal measures up to 3,000ft thick. These are overlaid by sandstone and limestone in the west and clay in the east. The north of the county is part of the York Plain. The centre and south west of the county, around Sherwood Forest, features undulating hills with ancient oak woodland.

✳ The River Trent runs through Nottinghamshire for more than 50 miles. Its flood plain is more than two miles wide in places and the county has suffered some disastrous floods in the past.

✳ Other rivers which flow through the county include the Soar, the Leen and the Maun. The River Erewash marks the boundary between Nottinghamshire and Derbyshire for much of its length.

✳ In 2008 the population was estimated to be 1,068,900. Of this over half live in the conurbation of Greater Nottingham.

✳ The average house price in Nottingham in 2010 was £105,000.

✳ The average salary in Nottingham was £22,695 in 2010.

✳ The city of Nottingham has a population of 288,700 although the Nottingham Urban Area has a population of 667,000. It is the seventh-largest urban area in the United Kingdom, ranking between those of Liverpool and Sheffield.

✳ According to the 2001 census people in Nottingham recorded their religion as follows:

Christian	559,689
Buddhist	1,159
Hindu	2,162
Jewish	808
Muslim	3,516
Sikh	2,308
Other	1,461
No Religion	119,562

✳ Nearly a quarter of Nottingham's population is under 20.

✳ The other main towns in the county are Mansfield (87,500), Kirkby-in-Ashfield (27,000), Sutton-in-Ashfield (45,000), Newark-on-Trent (26,700), Worksop (43,500) and Retford (21,000).

✳ About a fifth of the population live outside these areas, mostly in smaller (under 10,000 population) towns and villages. The density of population within the county is about 3.6 persons per hectare, ranging from over 35 in urban areas to below three persons per hectare in rural areas.

✳ Nottinghamshire has a diverse economy and is home to a number of world famous companies in the fields of healthcare, pharmaceuticals, precision engineering, textiles and clothing and professional services. Since the decline of some of the more traditional industries new companies have arrived here including Experian and Capital One as well as government agencies including the Inland Revenue.

✳ Nottingham County Council is the largest employer in the county with over 27,000 employees.

✳ Nottinghamshire Constabulary was created in 1840 with an establishment of a Chief Constable, eight superintendants and 33 constables. It merged with the Retford police in 1854 and Newark Borough Police 1947. In 1968 it amalgamated with Nottingham City Police to form Nottinghamshire Combined Constabulary. On 1 April 1974 it was reconstituted as Nottinghamshire Police under the Local Government Act of 1972.

✳ Nottinghamshire Police is made up of around 2,500 uniformed and plain clothes police officers, 110 police community support officers and almost 500 special constables and other volunteers. The force is organised into four divisions, each headed by a chief superintendant, known as the area commander. The divisions are Bassetlaw, Newark & Sherwood, Mansfield & Ashfield, Nottingham City and South Nottinghamshire. Each division is sub-divided into a number of neighbourhood policing areas each of which is headed by a Neighbourhood Policing Inspector. Local policing is complemented by a range of support units and departments which operate across the force area. These include crime investigation, roads policing and a scientific support unit as well as dog and mounted sections. The headquarters of Nottinghamshire Police is at Sherwood Lodge, Arnold.

✳ The NHS is, at present, undergoing a period of reorganisation and restructuring. Currently the Nottinghamshire County Primary Care Trust plans, and pays, for health services for 660,000 people in Ashfield, Broxtowe, Gedling, Mansfield, Newark & Sherwood and Rushcliffe. It has a budget of over £1,000,000,000 and delivers services through around 250 GPs, 85 dental practices, 144 pharmacies and 92 opticians.

✤ The Queen's Medical Centre in Nottingham is the largest hospital in the UK and the largest teaching hospital in Europe. Opened by the Queen in 1977 it has more than 1,300 beds and employs more than 6,000 people. In April 2006 it merged with Nottingham City Hospital to form the Nottingham University Hospitals NHS Trust.

✤ Other major hospitals in Nottinghamshire include Newark Hospital, Kings Mill Hospital, Ashfield Health Village and Mansfield Community Hospital.

✤ Nottinghamshire is home to two outstanding universities; Nottingham Trent and Nottingham University. Both have campuses in Nottingham and elsewhere in the county.

✤ Over 45,000 full time students attend Nottingham's two universities of which more than 34,000 live within the city boundary. This is equivalent to one in eight of the city's population.

✤ Nottingham was placed top in a Moneywise survey of the quality of life in 67 British towns and cities carried out in 1990. The report declared; 'Nottingham is a wonderful place with a pleasant environment, many attractions and a bustling environment'. It was 'THE place to live…Good local healthcare, low street crime, a low rate of vandalism, affordable housing and good hospitals make the Queen of the Midlands Britain's best City'.

✤ A more balanced description is contained in the conclusion to the Nottingham City Profile, published in 1991 which stated, 'It is the commercial, retailing and administrative centre of the East Midlands with a busy and attractive city centre. Adjacent to the city is the Lace Market, both an important Conservation Area, with one of the finest collections of 18th and 19th-century buildings, and an Industrial Improvement Area which is the home of the city's clothing, textiles and fashion industry…The city, however, also has significant problems…There are high areas of extreme disadvantage, which have disproportionately high rates of unemployment, low income, poor health and social problems.'

✤ Nottinghamshire's countryside provided the inspiration for two of England's greatest writers, Lord Byron and D.H. Lawrence. The ancestral home of Byron at Newstead Abbey is owned by the County Council and is open to the public. The birthplace of D.H. Lawrence at Eastwood is now a museum and heritage centre.

✤ The grand country estates in the Dukeries area of North Nottinghamshire are now available for the enjoyment of the general public, they include Clumber Park and Rufford Abbey.

✤ The county boasts three professional football teams; Nottingham Forest, Notts County and Mansfield Town and the Trent Bridge Cricket Ground regularly hosts both county and international test matches. Other sports are well catered for with the National Ice Centre in Nottingham and the National Watersports Centre at Holme Pierrepont. For race-goers there are courses at Nottingham and Southwell.

✳ The National Trust has two significant properties in the county; Mr Straws House in Worksop and Southwell Workhouse.

✳ The ethnicity of the county is 94.1 per cent White, 2.5 per cent South Asian and 1.5 per cent Afro-Caribbean.

✳ People living in parts of Nottinghamshire have their own distinctive dialect. This is particularly noticeable in the Erewash valley area around Eastwood. The author D.H. Lawrence wrote some of his dialogue in the local dialect.

✳ Nottingham receives around 300,000 million overseas visitors each year.

✳ The highest point in the county is Strawberry Bank in Huthwaite.

✳ Annual rainfall in Nottinghamshire is between 641–740mm (25–29in).

✳ The average temperature in the county is 8.8–10.1 degrees Celsius (48–50 degrees farenheit).

✳ Nottinghamshire receives between 1,321 and 1,470 hours of sunshine each year.

✳ Nottinghamshire is divided among seven district councils. They are Ashfield, Bassetlaw, Broxtowe, Gedling, Mansfield, Newark and Sherwood and Rushcliffe. The City of Nottingham was part of Nottinghamshire between 1974 and 1988 but is now a unitary authority.

✳ Nottinghamshire is served by a number of railway companies. The main railway in the county is the Midland Mainline which links London St Pancras Station to Sheffield via Nottingham. The recently opened Robin Hood Line links Nottingham with Worksop and serves several other villages in the county. The East Coast Main Line from London Kings Cross serves the eastern Nottinghamshire towns of Newark and Retford.

✳ The M1 motorway runs north-south through Nottinghamshire connecting the county with London, Leeds and many other towns and cities. Most of the stretch through Nottinghamshire has been recently widened. The other major road in the county is the A1. This follows the path of the historic Great North Road for much of its route through the county. Many improvements to the road have been carried out in recent years and further major work was being undertaken at the time of writing.

✳ Nottingham is a highly accessible city with three junctions of the M1 within 10 miles of the city centre.

✳ Nottinghamshire is served by the East Midlands Airport just outside the county in Leicestershire. It was originally owned by a consortium which included Nottinghamshire County Council. Robin Hood Airport lies within the historic boundaries of the county but is just inside South Yorkshire.

✳ Nottingham Airport is located at Tollerton a few miles from the city. It is home to a flying school.

✳ A number of local bus companies operate within Nottinghamshire including Trent Barton, Stagecoach, TM Travel and Nottingham City Travel.

✳ Nottingham City Transport is the principal bus operator in Greater Nottingham. It has a fleet of 340 buses which provide a comprehensive network of services across the city, seven days a week. Its 800 drivers operate the 340 buses over 81 routes and make over two million trips each year. The company uses over 8.7 million litres of fuel each year in order to cover over 240,000 miles each week.

✳ Nottingham is also served by a modern tram system. Opened in 2004 at a cost of £229 million, it is operated by a consortium comprising the company Transdev and Nottingham City Transport. The current line starts at Nottingham station, to the south of the city centre and extends north, passing the Lace Market, Nottingham Trent University, Forest Recreation Ground and terminating at Hucknall.

Modern Tram, part of the Express Transit System.

✤ Nottingham has been designated one of six science cities in the UK. It is committed to becoming an international location for scientific excellence, and already has a track record of medical and scientific innovation. Ibuprofen, the MRI scanner, the Vertical Take Off and Landing (VTOL) engine used in the Harrier jump jets, and Speedo's cutting edge LZR swimsuit were all developed in Nottinghamshire.

✤ In September 2010 research by the Campaign for Better transport rated Nottingham as the least car dependent city in England with London, and Brighton and Hove, in second and third places respectively.

✤ Approximate Distances from Nottingham (by Road)

Place	Miles	Place	Miles
Aberystwyth	154	Barnstable	231
Berwick-on-Tweed	219	Birmingham	50
Bodmin	274	Bournemouth	182
Brighton	175	Bristol	138
Cambridge	84	Cardiff	153
Carlisle	182	Chelmsford	125
Colwyn Bay	128	Coventry	48
Derby	16	Doncaster	44

The Nottingham Skyline with Green's Mill in the distance.

Place	Miles	Place	Miles
Dover	186	Exeter	213
Falmouth	300	Filey	100
Fleetwood	138	Folkestone	200
Gloucester	103	Guildford	143
Harwich	151	Hastings	186
Hounslow	132	Huddersfield	63
Kendall	137	Kings Lynn	80
Leeds	67	Leicester	25
Lincoln	36	Liverpool	97
Llandudno	138	London	123
Luton	93	Mablethorpe	77
Manchester	70	Middlesbrough	128
Morecambe	125	Newcastle-upon-Tyne	156
Northampton	57	Norwich	124
Nuneaton	41	Oxford	94
Penzance	322	Perth	325
Peterborough	54	Plymouth	256
Preston	100	Ramsgate	190
Salisbury	152	Sheffield	37
Stoke-on-Trent	50	Swansea	172
Taunton	181	Tenby	215
Torquay	235	Truro	300
Weymouth	199	York	78

Nottinghamshire through Time

Prehistoric Nottinghamshire

* Swamps covered Nottinghamshire 300 million years ago. Creatures which lived there at the time included giant dragonflies with a wingspan of over 2ft and carnivorous fish ranging up to 5ft in length.

* Devils toenails are the nickname given to the fossilised remains of a type of oyster which lived 200 million years ago on the sea bed. They can be found on Jurassic outcrops, one of which lies in South Nottinghamshire from Clifton to the Vale of Belvoir.

* Woolley Mammoths roamed over Nottinghamshire 20,000 years ago. A tusk was found in gravel workings near Newark and a molar tooth was discovered in Wilford in 1928. Both items are now in the Natural History Muscum at Wollaton Hall.

* Cresswell Crags is one of the most important Palaeolithic (Old Stone Age) sites in Britain. Straddling the Nottinghamshire-Derbyshire border, two of the five most significant caves on this site, Church Hole and Boat House, are situated on the Nottinghamshire side of the border. Neanderthal man arrived here around 43,000BC just before the last glaciation. At this time the area was also home to bears, bison, lions, wolves and woolly rhinoceroses. After the retreat of the glaciers modern man made his home in the caves.

* Stone Age hunters roamed over Nottinghamshire and Neolithic axes have been found at a number of locations including Kirkby, Kelham, Oxton and Mansfield.

* During the Bronze Age farmers began to sow patches of emmer wheat and other crops in the fertile alluvial soil of the Trent Valley.

* A Bronze Age hoard comprising 16 socketed axe heads, four socketed spear heads and a pallstaff were found in Great Freeman Street, Nottingham in 1860.

* A variety of weapons, including valuable swords have been found in the Trent at Fiskerton, Newark, Holme Pierrepont, Clifton, Attenborough and elsewhere. These were votive offerings deposited to appease or influence the gods.

* During the Iron Age or Celtic period Nottinghamshire was inhabited by the Coritani tribe. Their territory covered not only the present county of Nottinghamshire but also large parts of Lincolnshire and Leicestershire. They issued their own coins and examples can be found in a number of local museums.

Iron Age Hut.

✤ The North of Nottinghamshire was the territory held by the powerful tribe of the Brigantes and was probably something of a frontier area. Brigantian coins have been discovered in Nottinghamshire.

✤ Iron Age hill forts have been identified in Nottinghamshire at Hollinwood Hill, Arnold, Lonely Grange near Oxton and Combs Farm.

✤ Three Iron Age dug out boats were discovered in a quarry at Holme Pierrepont in 1967 where they had been left stranded when the course of the river changed sometime before 115BC.

Roman Nottinghamshire
✤ The Fosse Way, a major Roman road, cuts across the south-eastern wolds from Six Hills to Newark on Trent.

✤ Nottinghamshire had no major Roman settlements, but a chain of small military forts followed the line of the Fosse Way.

✤ The largest of these forts was at Margidumnum (Castle Hill, East Bridgford). Founded around AD50 it grew into a small town.

✤ The foundations of a building, thought to be a Roman temple was discovered at Thrumpton in the 19th century and two Roman altars have been unearthed at Littleborough.

✤ The Romans built bridges over the Trent at East Stoke and Cromwell.

✢ Evidence of a number of villas has been discovered in the county at places such as Barton-in-Fabis, Car Colston, Cromwell, Epperston, Mansfield Woodhouse, Southwell, Styrrup and Thurgarton. The villa at Mansfield Woodhouse was a substantial residence with attractive plasterwork, coloured tiles and a hypocaust.

✢ Romano British farmsteads have been discovered at Broxtowe and Tuxford.

✢ Pigs of lead have been discovered in Nottinghamshire. Lead was transported from mines in Derbyshire via the Trent into the Humber.

✢ A skeleton was discovered close to the site of the villa at Southwell which had been pierced by iron studs through the shoulders, ankles and heart.

Saxon and Viking Nottinghamshire

✢ Nottinghamshire lay within the Saxon Kingdom of Mercia whose capital was at Repton in neighbouring Derbyshire.

✢ The first mention of Nottingham (as Snottengaham) appears in the *Anglo Saxon Chronicle* in AD867.

✢ The remains of a Saxon warrior were discovered in 1893 in a gravel pit near Aslockton. He had been buried in an east-west position and the remains of a straight two edged sword and a lance head were found close to the body.

✢ An Anglo Saxon bronze broach was discovered at Tuxford in 1865.

✢ Saxon cremation cemeteries containing urns of ashes have been discovered at Holme Pierrepont, Kingston-on-Soar, Netherfield, Newark and Sutton Bonington.

✢ Archaeologists have discovered the remains of a Saxon fish weir set into the banks of the River Trent close to Colwick.

✢ Nottingham was occupied by a Danish army in 867 and it became one of the five fortified towns of the Danelaw. The others were Derby, Leicester, Lincoln and Stamford.

✢ Scandinavian place names include elements such as by, thorpe, thwait and beck.

✢ The Scandinavian word gata (anglicised to gate) provides evidence of Danish settlement in a number of Nottinghamshire towns. Examples include Fisher Gate, Lister Gate, Hounds Gate and Warser Gate in Nottingham while in Newark we find Appleton Gate, Balderton Gate and Barnby Gate. Elsewhere Retford has Bridge Gate and Church Gate. In Mansfield Stockwell Gate and West Gate hint at their Viking origin.

Stapleford Cross.

✳ A Viking sword was discovered during excavations at Farndon Church and was, for many years, preserved in the vestry there.

✳ The Danes divided Nottinghamshire into eight administrative areas called wapentakes, the equivalent of Saxon hundreds. Originally these were Lida, Oswardebec, Broxtowe, Bassetlaw, Newark, Bingham, Thurgarton and Rushcliffe.

✳ In AD918 King Edward the Elder besieged Nottingham as part of his campaign to reconquer the Danelaw. After its surrender he improved its defences and left a combined Anglo-Danish garrison in occupation.

✳ As Christianity spread though Nottinghamshire a number of simple Saxon crosses were erected throughout the county. One of the best examples is at Stapleford.

✳ The first bridge over the Trent at Nottingham was built by Edward the Elder around AD920.

✳ Nottingham was re-occupied by a Viking army in AD938 but only four years later the Saxon King Edmund I drove the Danes back as far as the Humber.

✳ Later, in the 10th century, extensive estates, mainly around Southwell, were granted to successive Archbishops of York. A minster was created at Southwell and in 950 the whole of the county was transferred to the diocese of York.

✳ A mint was established at Nottingham during the reign of King Athelstan.

Nottinghamshire and the Norman Conquest

✳ Edward the Confessor died in January 1066 and was succeeded by Harold Godwinson. It seems likely that men from Nottinghamshire were present in the army which fought against William I at the Battle of Hastings.

✳ In 1067 William I passed through Nottingham on his way to crush the rebellion in the North. It was at this time that he ordered William Peverel to construct a castle on a rocky outcrop to protect the town and defend the passage along the River Trent.

✻ The *Domesday Book* compiled in 1086 provided the first detailed picture of the county.

✻ Apart from Nottingham the only other town in the county at the time of the Domesday survey was Newark. The town was the property of Bishop Remigius and had a total population of around five hundred. As well as a mill and a fishery 10 churches are mentioned along with eight priests.

✻ Mansfield was a substantial manor. At the time of Domesday it had a population of around 600, a mill, a fishery and two churches.

✻ Motte and bailey castles were constructed during the Norman period at a number of places including Bothamsall, Egmanton and Laxton. Many of these were simple earth and timber structure and were never rebuilt in stone.

✻ The Normans constructed a number of stone churches and fragments of Norman stonework can be found in churches across the county.

✻ The only church in Nottingham during the early Norman period was St Mary's. This is mentioned in the *Domesday Book* and lay within the King's lordship. Before the end of the 11th century the parish Churches of St Peter and St Nicholas had been built.

✻ In addition to churches the Normans also founded a number of abbeys and priories in Nottinghamshire. These religious houses were built at Beauvale, Blythe, Broadholme, Felley, Lenton, Newstead, Mattersley, Rufford, Shelford, Thurgarton, Wallingwells, Welbeck and Worksop. The largest and richest of these was the Cluniac Priory at Lenton.

✻ Sherwood Forest was probably created before the Norman Conquest, although it was not used by Edward the Confessor. In 1086 it comprised around 160 square miles and covered around 20 per cent of the county.

Mediaeval Nottinghamshire

✻ During the Civil War between Stephen and Matilda considerable fighting took place in Nottinghamshire. Adulterine castles were built at Cuckney and possibly elsewhere in the county.

✻ The prosperity of Nottingham and Newark during the Middle Ages was closely linked to their importance as inland ports on the River Trent.

✻ A new bridge across the Trent was built at Nottingham during the reign of Henry I.

✻ King John died of dysentery at Newark Castle in October 1216.

✻ King Edward I held a parliament at Clipstone in 1290.

* Queen Eleanor of Castile, the wife of Edward I died at Harby on 27 November 1290.

* A thriving Alabaster carving industry existed in Nottingham during the 13th and 14th centuries. Alabaster was obtained from Chellaston, only a few miles away in Derbyshire. It was then transported to Nottingham where it was carved into religious images for use in churches and monastic houses throughout England and even abroad.

* Nottingham sent two burgesses to represent the town at the Model Parliament summoned by Edward I in 1295. A Parliament was held in Nottingham in 1336.

* The mediaeval wool industry brought considerable prosperity to Nottinghamshire. This was based chiefly in Nottingham and Newark.

* During the mediaeval period over 30 towns in Nottinghamshire were granted market rights

* Lenton Fair, established in 1300 was the largest cloth market in Nottinghamshire.

* A Jewish community existed in Nottingham in the 13th century. They lived in a ghetto between Castle gate and Hounds gate and had their own synagogue in Lister gate. Local merchants borrowed money from the Jews and this may have contributed to the growth of anti Semitism in the town. In 1290 all Jews were expelled from the kingdom by Edward I.

* A number of moated manor houses existed in Nottinghamshire at this time. A document of 1459 provides evidence that the manor house at Lambley was built of timber and plaster, roofed with slates and had four rooms on the ground floor and three rooms on an upper storey; it stood on a mound that was surrounded by a moat. A wooden bridge over the moat connected the house to a large outer courtyard where there were extensive outbuildings. In the north of the courtyard there were stables and a new barn; to the south a bakery, hall for husbandry and a brewhouse; to the west, another barn, a granary, dovecote and gatehouse.

* In 1463 Nottingham approved a series of new measures against prostitutes, brothels and disorderly houses. It was decreed that an alehouse would be considered disorderly if it stayed open after 9pm.

* Edward IV visited Nottingham on a number of occasions during the period 1469–71 and ordered the construction of a great octagonal tower at the castle. This was completed by his brother, Richard III.

* Richárd III was at Nottingham when he received news that Henry Tudor had landed with an army in Wales. It was from Nottingham that he marched out to Leicester, defeat and death at the Battle of Bosworth Field.

Tudor Nottinghamshire

- Henry VII was in Nottingham on 14 June 1487. He attended the Corpus Christi service in St Mary's Church before marching off to defeat a Yorkist army at the Battle of Stoke. Among the local gentry who fought on the side of the king were William Pierrepont, Edward Stanhope and Henry Willoughby.

- Dame Agnes Mellors, the widow of mayor Richard Mellors founded what is now Nottingham High School in 1513. It was originally sited on Stoney Street near St Mary's Church.

- Henry Norris, lord of the manors of Stoke Bardolph, Gedling and Carlton, was one of those accused of undue intimacy with Anne Boleyn, the wife of Henry VIII. He was convicted of treason and executed in 1536.

- John Leyland visited Nottingham in 1540 and described the town as 'welle buildid for tymber and plaster and standeth stately on a clyminge hille'.

- In 1562 plans were made for a meeting at Nottingham between Elizabeth I and Mary Queen of Scots though the meeting was later postponed and never took place.

- During the reign of Elizabeth I the men of Nottinghamshire were regularly mustered for service in war or for defence against a possible Spanish invasion.

Speede's Map of Nottingham, 1610.

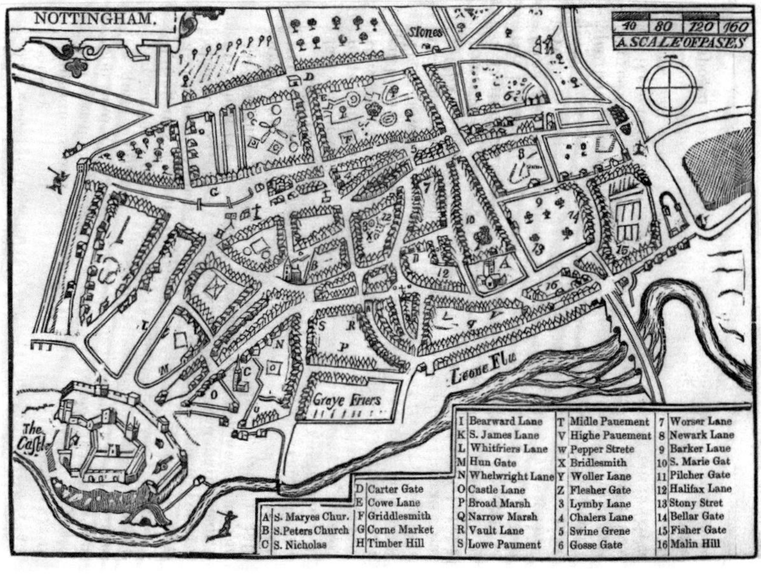

✤ In 1567 the shrievalties of Nottingham and Derbyshire were separated after having been combined under one Sheriff since at least 1066.

✤ In 1569, 700 Nottinghamshire men were recruited to help crush the rebellion of the Northern Earls of Northumberland and Westmorland.

Stuart Nottinghamshire

✤ James I passed through Nottingham in 1603 on his journey from Edinburgh to London for his coronation.

✤ Nottingham brick, made from the clay of Mapperley plains, began to be a common building material from the early years of the 17th century gradually replacing timber structures.

✤ The Civil War between King and Parliament began at Nottingham on 22 August 1642 when Charles I raised his standard there. It fell down a few days later. When the king marched away, the town became a Parliamentary stronghold.

✤ Newark became the Royalist headquarters in Nottinghamshire and the town and castle withheld three sieges from Parliamentary forces before the King ordered its surrender.

✤ Charles I surrendered to the Scots at the King's Arms in Southwell on 5 May 1646. This has since been renamed the Saracens Head.

Civil War re-enactment near Newark.

* The Minster at Southwell suffered considerably during the Civil War. The nave was used not only for stabling horses but also as a military store. Lead was stripped from the roof (possibly for musket balls) and local residents began removing stone and timber for their own use.

* The last Civil War battle in Nottinghamshire was fought at Willoughby in July 1648. It was a sharp engagement in which the victorious parliamentarians lost 30 men and the royalists 44 gentlemen of quality.

* Two Nottinghamshire Members of Parliament, John Hutchinson and Gilbert Millington, sat on the special court which tried the King. During the Commonwealth period two Royalist plots took place within the county.

* General George Monk and his army passed through Nottingham and Newark on 2 January 1660 on his way to London where he began the process which resulted in the restoration of the monarchy.

* After the Restoration 38 puritan clergymen were deprived of their livings under the terms of the Act of Uniformity.

Nottinghamshire in the 18th Century

* John Wesley, the founder of the Methodist Church made the first of 28 visits to the town on 11 June 1741. After meeting in members homes for some years the Methodists went on to establish chapels at Nottingham (1774), Newark (1776), Worksop (1780), Retford (1786) and Mansfield (1799).

* The widespread enclosure of the open fields took place in Nottinghamshire during the 18th century. Common land was lost and many smallholders became landless labourers as a result.

* Richard Arkwright established a cotton spinning mill powered by horses at Hockley in 1769. He later moved to Cromford in Derbyshire where he established the world's first water powered cotton mill in 1771.

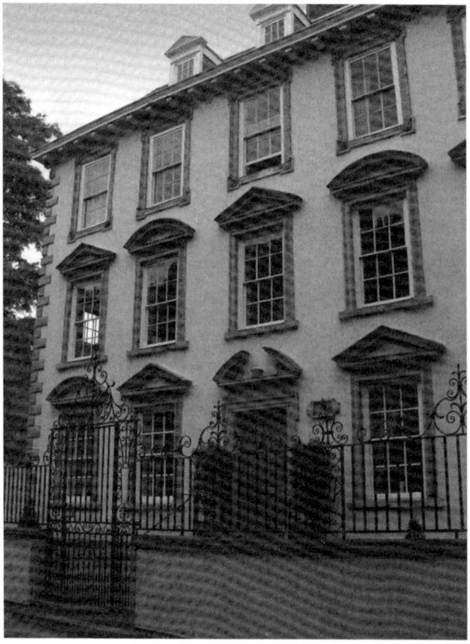

Georgian Town House in Castle Gate Nottingham.

✤ By the end of the century there were eight cotton mills in Nottingham itself with others spread throughout the county at places such as Arnold, Basford, Cuckney, Fiskerton, Gamston and Langwith.

✤ Nottinghamshire was the centre of Luddite activity in the early years of the 19th century.

✤ At the county assizes on 17 March 1812, two luddites were sentenced to 14 years transportation and a further three to seven years each.

✤ The 18th century saw the building of a number of elegant town houses in places such as Nottingham, Newark and Southwell.

Nottinghamshire in the 19th Century

✤ The census of 1801 shows that the population of the county at that time was 140,350. Most people still lived in the countryside and there were only six towns with a population greater than 2,000. These were Nottingham (28,801), Newark (6,730), Mansfield (5,988), Worksop (3,263), Sutton-in-Ashfield (2,801) and Southwell (2,305).

✤ The first railway into Mansfield was opened in 1819 to bring coal trucks from Pinxton. These were drawn by horses up to Kirkby and then travelled downhill on their own weight. On market days the line also carried passengers in horse drawn vans.

✤ The Diocese of Southall was created in 1884. It covers 847 square miles and includes the whole of Nottinghamshire and a few parishes in South Yorkshire. It changes its name to the Diocese of Southall and Nottingham in 2005. The main reason for this was to help people understand its locality within the UK.

✤ A horse drawn tram service was introduced at Nottingham in 1878. The service between St Paul's Church and Trent Bridge was gradually extended to other parts of the town. The system was purchased by the City Council in 1897 and was electrified in 1901.

✤ Nottingham Castle Museum and Art Gallery was opened in 1878 and was the first Museum of Fine Art in England outside the capital.

✤ In June 1897 Nottingham was granted city status in commemoration of Queen Victoria's Diamond Jubilee.

Modern Nottinghamshire

✤ The population of Nottinghamshire in 1901 was 514,578.

✤ In May 1913 suffragettes burnt down the Nottingham Boat Club.

✣ During World War One the Sherwood Foresters Regiment expanded to 33 battalions, of which 20 served overseas. Altogether, around 140,000 men, nearly all from Nottinghamshire and Derbyshire served in the Regiment. 11,409 of these made the ultimate sacrifice. Their names appear on War Memorials in towns and villages throughout the county.

✣ A German Zeppelin attacked Nottingham in September 1916. Huge explosive and incendiary bombs were dropped which damaged buildings in Lister Gate, Castle Gate and Broad Marsh. Three people were killed.

✣ In September 1924 Nottingham City Council purchased Wollaton Hall and Park for £200,000.

✣ The boundaries of Nottingham were extended in 1933 by adding Bilborough and Wollaton as well as parts of Bestwood Park and Colwick. A further boundary extension took place in 1951 when Clifton and Wilford were incorporated into the city.

✣ The River Trent Pleasure Steamer, Empress, was sunk in 1940 while on its second crossing to Dunkirk to rescue British troops.

✣ In May 1941, during what became known as the Nottingham Blitz, 159 people died as a result of German bombing. The worst hit areas were the Meadows, Sneinton and St Ann's.

✣ Shortly after World War Two a survey of the St Ann's district of Nottingham found that there were substantial numbers of people who earned wages so low that they were constantly on the threshold of poverty. The report cited a pipe maker at Stanton ironworks, a soap processor at Boots, a coalminer employed at the National Coal Board and a store keeper at Raleigh Cycles.

✣ Nottingham's famous statue of Robin Hood was unveiled in May 1952.

✣ The construction of Maid Marian Way in Nottingham during the 1950s and 1960s resulted in the destruction of a number of Georgian buildings, including the 17th-century Collins Almshouses.

✣ The 1960s saw the withdrawal of a number of passenger services and the closure of railway stations in various parts of the Nottinghamshire. Mansfield became the largest town in the UK without a passenger train service.

✣ BBC Radio Nottingham went on air for the first time in January 1968.

✣ The 1970s saw improvements in shopping facilities with the opening of the Broadmarsh and Victoria shopping centres.

✳ Local government reorganisation in 1974 created a number of new and enlarged district councils and resulted in the disappearance of civic authorities such as Arnold UDC, Eastwood UDC, and Warsop UDC, all created in 1889.

✳ During the national miners' strike of 1984–85 the Nottinghamshire miners voted against strike action and eventually decided to break away from the NUM and form the Union of Democratic Mineworkers.

✳ Nottingham Tent University was created in March 1993.

✳ In June 1995 the first London style taxi appeared in Nottingham.

✳ The latter years of the 20th century saw a decline in the fortunes of important employers such as Raleigh Cycles and Players Cigarettes.

✳ Many new and exciting buildings were constructed in Nottingham in the first decade of the 21st century. These included the Nottingham Contemporary, parts of Nottingham University's Jubilee Campus and several industrial and commercial buildings.

✳ Nottingham's new tram system linking the city with Hucknall opened in 2004.

✳ Following the 2010 General Election, Kenneth Clarke, MP for Rushcliffe, was appointed Lord Chancellor and Secretary of State for Justice.

Domesday Nottinghamshire

✤ The *Domesday Book* is the first detailed record of the various settlements in Nottinghamshire. The vast majority of towns and villages in Nottinghamshire were named and surveyed in this great document and it remains one of the most useful sources of information for anyone studying the history of their area. It was compiled in 1086 on the orders of William the Conqueror who instructed his commissioners to ask the following questions:

What is the name of the manor?
Who held it at the time of King Edward and who holds it now?
How many ploughs does the lord have and how many do the tenants have?
How many villagers, smallholders and slaves are there?
How many freemen are there?
How much woodland, meadow and pasture is there?
How many mills and fisheries are there?
What has been added or taken away from the estate?
What was it worth in 1066 and what is it worth now?

✤ The return for Colwick follows this template and is typical of the entries for Nottinghamshire.
Land of William Peverel
In Colwick Godric had 7 bovates of land taxable. Land for 1 plough. William Peverel has 1 plough in lordship and 7 villagers and 6 smallholders who have 3 ploughs. A priest and a church; 2 slaves; 1 mill, 5s; half a fishery; meadow, 30 acres; underwood, 15 acres. Value before 1066, 20s; now 40s. Waland holds it.

✤ The *Domesday Book* shows that there were at least 76 churches in Nottinghamshire by 1086 but there were almost certainly more. Built in timber and stone, very little evidence of these pre-conquest churches exist today.

✤ Of 128 pre-conquest land holders only some 25 survived in 1086, their holdings much reduced.

✤ Some of the most important settlements in Nottinghamshire today are mentioned in the *Domesday Book* including Nottingham. Newark and Southwell. Most place names used in Domesday are still recognisable today but others have changed considerably. Some of those which we might find difficult to recognise include Cledreston (Lenton), Odesach (Hodsock) and Chinemarlie (Kimberley).

✻ A full list of all the settlements which existed in 1086 together with their original names are listed below:

Adbolton – Alboltune
Annesley – Aneslei
Askham – Ascam
Averham – Aigrun
Babworth – Baburde
Barnby in the Willows – Barnebi
Barnstone – Bernestune
Basford – Baseford
Beckingham – Bechingham
Besthorpe – Beestthorpe
Bilby – Billebi
Bingham – Bingeham
Blythe – Blide
Boleham – Bolun
Bothamsall – Bodmescel
Bradmore – Brademere
Bridgeford (East and West) – Brugeford
Broadholme – Brodeholm
Broxtowe – Brochelestou
Bulcote – Bulecote
Bunny – Bonei
Burton (West) – Burtone
Calverton – Calvreyone
Car Colston – Colstone
Carlton in Lindrick – Carletone
Caunton – Calnestone
Clarborough – Claureburg
Clifton – Cliftone
Clown – Clune
Coddington – Cotintone
Colston Basset – Coertone
Cossal – Coteshale
Cotgrave – Godegrave
Cottam – Cotune
Cropwell Bishop – Crophille
Cuckney – Cuchnai
Danethorpe – Dordentorp
Drayton (East and West) – Draitone
Eakring – Echeringhe
Eaton – Etune
Edwinstowe – Edenstou
Elkesley – Elchesleig
Elton – Ailetone
Everton – Evretone
Farnsfield – Farnesfeld
Finningley – Feniglei

Alverton – Aluritone
Arnold – Ernehale
Aslockton – Aslachetone
Awsworth – Eldesuorde
Balderton – Baldretune
Barnby Moor – Barnebi
Barton in Fabis – Bartone
Bassingfield – Basingfelt
Beeston – Bestune
Bilborough – Bileburg, Bileburch
Bilsthorpe – Bildestorp
Blidworth – Blideworde
Bole – Bolun
Bonington – Bonnintone
Boughton – Buchetone
Bramcote – Bruncote
Brinsley – Brunescleia
Broughton (Upper) – Brotone
Budby – Butebi
Bulwell – Bulwelle
Burton Joyce – Bertune
Bycarr Dike – Bigredic
Carburton – Carbertone
Carlton in the Willows – Carletone
Carlton on Trent – Carentune
Chilwell – Chideuuelle
Clayworth – Clauorde
Clipstone – Clipestune
Clumber – Clumbre
Collingham (North and South) – Colingeham
Colwick – Colewic
Costock – Cortingestoches
Cotham – Cotes, Cotun
Cromwell – Crunewelle
Cropwell Butler – Crophille, Crophelle
Dallington – Dallintune
Darlton – Derlwetun
Dunham – Duneham
Eastwood – Estwic
Edwalton – Edwoltone
Egmanton – Agemuntone
Elston – Elvestune
Epperstone – Eprestone
Farndon – Farendune
Fenton – Fentone
Fiskerton – Fiscartune

Flawborough – Flodberge
Flintham – Flinteham
Gedling – Ghellinge
Girton – Gretone
Gonalston – Gunnuelvestune
Granby – Granebi
Greasley – Griseleia
Gringley on the Hill – Gringeleia
Grove – Grave
Harby – Herdebi
Harworth – Hardeworde
Hawkesworth – Hochesworde
Hayton – Ettone
Hempshill – Hamessel
Hockerton – Ocretone
Holme Pierrepont – Holmo
Hoveringham – Horingeham
Inkersall – Wirchenfeld
Kersall – Cherueshale
Kilvington – Chelvingtune
Kingston on Soar – Chinestan
Kirby in Ashfield – Chirchebi
Knapthorpe – Chenapetorp
Kneeton – Chinivetone
Lamcote – Lambecote
Langar – Langare
Laxton – Laxintune
Lenton – lentune
Linby – Lidebi
Lound – Lund
Mansfield – Mamesfeld
Maplebeck – Mapleberg
Markham (West) – Westmarcham
Martin – Martune
Misson – Misna
Morton – Mortune
Muskham (North) – Nordmuskham
Newark – Newerche
Newton – Niuuetune
Normanton on Soar – Normantone
Normanton on the Wolds – Normantone
Nottingham – Snotingeham
Ollerton – Alretun
Ordsall – Ordeshale
Orston – Oschintone
Ossington – Oschintone
Owthorpe – Overtorp
Papplewick – Paplewic

Fredborough – Fladeburg
Gamston – Gamelstune
Gibsmere – Gipsmare
Gleadthorpe – Gletorp
Gotham – Gatham
Grassthorpe – Grestorp
Grimston – Grimestone
Gringley (Little) – Grenelei
Gunthorpe – Gulnetorp
Harwell – Herewelle
Haughton – Hoctun
Hawton – Holtone
Headon – Hedune
Hickling – Echelinge
Hodsock – Odesach
Horsepool – Horspol
Hucknall Torkard – Hochenhale
Kelham – Calun
Keyworth – Caworde
Kimberley – Chinemarelie
Kinoulton – Chinelton
Kirklington – Cherlinton
Kneesall – Cheneshale
Lambley – Lambeleia
Laneham – Lanun
Langford – Landeforde
Leake – Leche
Leverton – Cledretune
Littleborough – litelburg
Lowdham – Ludeham
Manton – Mennetune
Markham (East) – Marcham
Marnham (High and Low) – Marneham
Mattersely – Madressig
Misterton – Ministretone
Morton (Great) – Nordermortune
Muskham (South) – Muscham
Newthorpe – Neutorp
Normanton – Normentone
Normanton on Trent – Normentune
Norwell – Nortwelle
Nuthall – Nutehale
Ompton – Almentun
Ordsall (South) – Suderdeshale
Osberton – Osbernestune
Overthorpe – Torp
Oxton – Ostone
Plumtree – Pluntre

Radcliffe on Trent – Radeclive
Ragnall – Ragenhil
Ranby – Ranebi
Ratcliffe on Soar – Radeclive
Retford (West) – Redford
Ruddington – Roddintone
Salterford – Saltreford
Saxondale – Saxeden
Scarrington – Scarintone
Scrooby – Scrobi
Serlby – Serlebi
Shelton – Sceltone
Skegby – Scachebi
Southwell – Sudwelle
Stanford on Soar – Stanford
Stapleford – Stapleford
Staythorpe – Startop
Stoke (East) – Stoches
Strelley – Straleia
Styrrup – Estirape
Sutton in Ashfield – Sutone
Sutton on Trent – Sudtone
Teversall – Tevreshalt
Thorney – Torneshaie
Thorpe – Torp
Thurgarton – Turgarstune
Tollerton – Troclavestune
Toton – Tovetune
Tuxford – Tuxfarne
Walkeringham – Wacheringham
Warborough – Wareberg
Warnall – Watenot
Weston – Westone
Wheatley – Wateleie
Widmerpool – Wimarspol
Wilford – Wilesforde
Willoughby on the Wolds – Willebi
Winthorpe – Wimuntorp
Wiverton – Wivretune
Woodborough – Udeburg
Wysall – Wisoc

Radford – Redeford
Rampton – Rametone
Ranskill – Raveschel
Rempstone – Repestone
Rolleston – Rollestone
Rufford – Rugforde
Saundby – Sandebi
Scaftworth – Scafteorde
Screveton – Scvrevetone
Selston – Salestune
Shelford – Scelford
Sibthorpe – Sibetorp
Sneinton – Nonintone
Spalford – Spaldesforde
Stanton on the Wolds – Stantun
Staunton – Stantun
Stoke Bardolph – Stoches
Stokeham – Estoches
Sturton le Steeple – Estretone
Sutton – Sudtone
Sutton on Soar – Sudtone
Syerston – Sirestune
Thoresby – Turesbi
Thoroton – Torvertune
Thrumpton – Turmodeston
Tithby – Tiedebi
Torworth – Turdeworde
Treswell – Tireswelle
Walesby – Walesbi
Wansley – Wanddeslei
Warsop – Waresope
Welham – Wellun
Whatton – Watone
Whimpton – Wimentum
Wigsley – Wigesleie
Willoughby – Wilgebi
Winkburn – Wicheburne
Wiseton – Wisetone
Wollaton – Olvestone
Worksop – Werchescope

✢ At the time of the Domesday Survey Nottinghamshire was divided into eight wapentakes: Bassetlaw, Lythe, Newark, Oswaldbeck, Bingham, Broxtowe, Rushcliffe and Thurgarton.

✢ Most entries for Nottinghamshire settlements follow a similar format, but there are a few which provide a little more information or are unusual in

some respect. These include:
  A blind man at Warsop
  'Censars' at Gonalston. These were people who held their land by paying an
  individual cash rent rather than by work for the lord of the manor
  A 'Frankus Man' at Langar. This was probably a Frenchman
  Gardens at Gamston, Saundby and Willoughby
  An orchard at Nottingham
  Honey payments at Arnold and Dunham
  Payments of salt at Saunderby
  A quarry at Whatton producing mill-stones
  Two moneyers at Nottingham
  Slaves are mentioned at a number of places including Colwick, Stoke
  Bardulph, Bilborough and Laxton
  Salt payments are recorded at Saundby
  Men at arms are mentioned at Bassetlaw

✤ Fisheries are mentioned at a number of places. Most are connected with rivers,
  particularly the Trent as at Laneham, Newark, Norwell and South Muskham. In
  1973 a mediaeval fish weir was discovered at Colwick. This comprised six rows
  of oak and holly posts forming a V, the neck of which pointed downstream.
  Experts believe that this construction allowed for the eels to be ensnared during
  their annual migration. Eels were a delicacy at this time and 200 of them were
  listed at West Burton. Away from the Trent at Gringley-on-the-Hill 1,000 are
  mentioned. It is believed that these were bred in artificial ponds.

✤ Previous Saxon landowners are meticulously listed. Many of these have
  fascinating names such as Wulfmer, Wulfgeat, Grimkell, Fredigris and
  Leofthnot.

✤ Different classes of people are mentioned in the *Domesday Book* including
  freemen, villagers (or villeins), smallholders (or bordars) and slaves.
    Freemen were free peasants with no formal obligations of labour to the lord
    of the manor. In Nottinghamshire they accounted for around 32 per cent of
    the population.
    Villagers were the wealthiest and most numerous of the unfree peasants. They
    often had substantial farms of around 30 acres but owed the lord two or three
    days work each week. In Nottinghamshire they made up 45 per cent of the
    population.
    Smallholders, or bordars held much less land than the villagers and earned a
    living as blacksmiths, carpenters and other craftsmen. They accounted for
    around 31 per cent of the population in Nottinghamshire at this time.
    Slaves had no property rights and could be bought or sold.

✤ Ferries are mentioned at Fiskerton and Southwell. At Gunthorpe, higher up on
  the Trent there was a toll and a boat, probably a ferry boat, rendering 30s 8d.

�֎ Nottingham had a population of between one thousand and two thousand people. The list of properties within the town include 48 merchants' houses, 25 knights' houses and a mint. A church in the King's lordship is also mentioned.

✷ Measurements in the *Domesday Book* include furlongs, bovates, caracutes, acres, virgates and leagues. They may be calculated as follows:

Furlong – 660ft
Caracute – No exact modern equivalent but often calculated as 120 acres
Bovate – One eighth of a caracute
Acre – 4,840sq yd. Originally an area of land one furlong (660ft) long and one chain (66ft) wide. This may have been the approximate area of land that an ox team could plough in a day.
Virgate – About a quarter of a caracute
League – A measurement of length, about a mile and a half

✷ Values are expressed in a variety of terms including pounds, shillings, pence and marks. Old English currency lasted for over a thousand years until 1971 when the UK changed to a decimal currency. Prior to this the pound contained 20 shillings, each of 12 pence, abbreviated as £(ibrae), s(olidi) and d(enari). A silver mark had a value of 13s 4d making 3 marks to £2.

✷ Different types of land are mentioned including land for ploughs, woodland, meadow, pasture and waste. Land for ploughs is what we would now describe as arable land. It was ploughed and used to grow wheat, barley, oats and beans. The average size of a Domesday plough team was eight oxen. In some entries half a plough is recorded meaning that the team was shared with another manor nearby. Pasture was where animals, such as sheep, cattle, goats and horses, grazed all year round. Meadows, often bordering on streams, were cut for hay and used for grazing. Woodland usually lay in small compact areas and was used for grazing pigs and for firewood. Waste was land that was not fit for farming for some reason.

✷ The population of Nottinghamshire in 1086 has been calculated to be about 30,000 people.

✷ Fifty-five priests are mentioned as living in Nottinghamshire. A few of these are individually named including Ernwy at Normanton-by-Southwell, Norman at Elston and Ernwin at Flintham.

✷ Churches are mentioned in connection with at least 72 places in Nottinghamshire. There were 10 in Newark although one or more of these may have been in its two berewicks of Balderton and Farndon.

✷ Apart from Nottingham, Newark is the only other borough mentioned in Nottinghamshire. In 1086 it had a population of around 400 with 10 churches and eight priests.

✤ The total number of settlements mentioned in the *Domesday Book* for Nottinghamshire appears to be 297 including the boroughs of Nottingham and Newark. This figure must be treated with some caution, because when two or more adjoining villages bear the same basic name today it is not always clear whether more than one settlement existed in the 11th century.

✤ Mills are mentioned in connection with at least 81 places in Nottinghamshire. It is difficult to be sure of the total number because mills sometimes appear in composite entries covering a number of places. These mills would have been water mills, since windmills were not introduced into England until the 14th century.

✤ A millstone quarry where millstones are dug is mentioned at Whatton and valued at three silver marks.

Important Nottinghamshire Landowners Listed in the *Domesday Book*

✤ King William was the major landowner in the county and personally held manors, or a share in land, in over 50 different places in Nottinghamshire.

✤ The Archbishop Thomas of York held land in various parts of the county. His most important holding in Nottinghamshire was at Southwell, which had a population of around 600 at this time and an annual value of £40 15s. Six men at arms and three clerics are recorded as well as two mills, a fish pond and a ferry. He was one of the committee appointed to check the work of the Domesday surveyors.

✤ Bishop Remigius of Lincoln also held land throughout the county. His most important possession was the town of Newark which had a population of around 500 at this time. Ten churches and eight priests are also mentioned. The Bishop also benefitted from a mill and a fishery at Newark.

✤ The Bishop of Bayeaux held five manors in Nottinghamshire at Cotham, Barnby-in-the-Willows, Coddington, Rolleston and Screveton. A fierce warrior, he was William's half brother and fought at the Battle of Hastings.

✤ The Abbey of Peterborough was a major land holder in Nottinghamshire with over 70 manors. William had granted considerable lands to the church, which had supported his invasion and throughout the Kingdom the Church owned around a quarter of all the land in 1086.

✤ Roger of Bully was the founder of Blythe Abbey. He held huge possessions around his headquarters at Tickhill. In Nottinghamshire he held over 130 areas of land.

✤ William Peverel is thought by some to have been the illegitimate son of William the Conqueror, but this is unlikely. He was certainly a trusted favourite and held vast areas of land throughout the kingdom. In Nottinghamshire he held land in no less than 49 manors stretching from Barton-in-Fabis in the south of the county to Sibthorpe in the north-east. He also had income from 48 merchants houses and 12 horsemen's houses in Nottingham. He was also granted the important feudal fief known as the Honour of Nottingham and was ordered by the King to construct a castle there.

- Walter of Aincourt was a considerable landowner in the county. His most valuable land holdings were Fiskerton where two mills, a fishery and a ferry are listed, and Granby which had a population of around 250 as well as a church, a priest and a mill.

- Geoffrey Alselin held land in 23 different places within the county. His most valuable possessions were Laxton and Stoke Bardolph. The latter was probably an important settlement for it had a population of around 200 as well as a church and a priest.

- Ralph, Son of Hubert was an ancestor of the Freshville and Stuteville families. He held land in 14 different places but churches are mentioned at four of them; Chilwell, Bunny, Kirkby in Ashfield and Wansley.

- Ralph of Limesy was a minor landowner in Nottinghamshire. His most valuable land holding was at Epperstone and Woodborough which was valued at £7. The population was around 300. A priest, a church and four mills are recorded here.

- Roger of Poitou was the son of Roger, Earl of Shrewsbury. He held land in different parts of the county, including valuable holdings at Barton-in-Fabis and Bunny.

- Gilbert of Ghent was a nephew of the Conqueror. He was captured during the great Northern uprising in 1069 but apparently ransomed. He held estates in a number of counties including Nottinghamshire where his most valuable holdings were at Kneesall and Wellow.

- Other minor landowners in Nottinghamshire included Earl Hugh, the Count of Mortain, Geoffrey of La Guerche, Berengar of Tosney, Hugh, Son of Balric, Henry of Ferrers, Robert Mallet, Osbern Son of Richard, Robert Son of William and Ilbert of Lacy.

Pre-Conquest Landowners

- The *Domesday Book* also gives us a fairly clear idea of the names of the Saxon landowners in Nottinghamshire. Information about some of them is rather sketchy, but we do know something about the following:

Earl Harold of Wessex, King of England from January to October 1066.

Earl Tostig; Harold' brother who rebelled against him and was killed at the Battle of Stamford Bridge.

Earl Algar of Mercia was exiled twice during the reign of Edward the Confessor. He died shortly before the conquest. His son was Morcar, Earl of Northumbria.

Earl Morcar was one of the northern earls who was defeated at the Battle of Stamford Bridge. He played an important role in the Isle of Eley resistance in 1070–71.

Countess Godiva was the famous Lady Godiva, widow of Leofric Earl of Mercia. She held only a handful of lands in Nottinghamshire and died around 1080.

Ulf Fensc (of the fens) was a major landholder in Eastern England. Most of his lands in Nottinghamshire passed to Gilbert of Ghent.

Siward Barn was a major land holder in northern England. He submitted to William soon after the Battle of Hastings but later joined the resistance. He joined Hereward the Wake in the Isle of Eley and was captured there in 1071. He remained a prisoner until William's deathbed amnesty in 1087.

Tochi had a hall and a number of properties in Lincoln. Most of his properties in Nottinghamshire and elsewhere went to Geoffrey Alselin.

Castles and Manor Houses

✳ **Newark Castle** Newark was established as a town by King Edward the Elder in the early 10th century. In 1073 Robert Bloet, Bishop of Lincoln, constructed a motte and bailey castle on the site. Following Bishop Robert's death in 1123, Alexander the Magnificent, the new Bishop of Lincoln, rebuilt the castle in stone. This new castle included an elaborate gatehouse which housed a private suite of rooms for the Bishop, an audience chamber and a chapel, stone curtain walls and at least one tower. According to the chronicler, Henry of Huntingdon it was 'a magnificent castle of very ornate construction'. Bishop Alexander did not retain control of the castle for long, however, as he was forced to surrender it to King Stephen in 1139. The castle was restored to the see of Lincoln in 1173. Several mediaeval kings visited the castle. John was here in 1205, in 1211 and in 1215, and at midnight on 19 October 1216 he died here from dysentery, allegedly in the south-west tower of the castle, but more likely in the gatehouse.

Changes and improvements continued to be made over the following centuries. Towards the end of the 13th century substantial rebuilding took place and a new riverside curtain wall was constructed.

The castle location on the banks of the Trent also influenced the design of the castle and a Watergate gave direct access to an undercroft storage area and the castle dungeons. Channels from the garderobes in the walls of the castle emptied directly into the river and slaughterhouses and tanneries sited in such a way that waste could be thrown in and carried downstream. The castle was seized by the Crown following the Reformation, and was garrisoned for a time in 1536 when the Pilgrimage of Grace threatened civil unrest and possible rebellion in the East Midlands. It was not really prepared for its new role at this time for a report to the King complained that the castle had 'scant lodging for 100 men and no water'. From 1560 the castle was leased to a variety of owners who spent considerable sums improving and modernising the castle. Over a period of time it became more of a palace than a fortress. Additional rooms were created by inserting floors in the large open areas, more fireplaces were installed and new, larger windows were provided, including the impressive two storey oriole window which was created to light the great hall. These improvements seem to have made the Castle a residence fit for a King. In 1603 the new King James I stayed here on his way from Scotland to London and Charles I was a regular visitor during the early years of his reign. During the Civil War Newark became a royalist stronghold and the town and castle successfully withstood three sieges. The garrison there only surrendered in 1646 on the direct orders of the King. Parliament ordered the destruction of the castle and parts of the stone buildings were blown up using barrels of gunpowder. The castle was further reduced as local people took away stone to build or repair their homes. A survey of the Manor of Newark in 1649 recorded that the castle was 'soe Ruined that it will never be made habitable, having nothing left but ruinous pieces of Walls'. The further destruction of the castle was, however, resisted and when the Crown sold off most of its Newark estates in 1836 it retained the castle. Between 1845 and 1858 considerable restoration work was undertaken at a cost of £650 under the direction of the architect Anthony Salvin. In 1881, William Gilstrap, a local benefactor, offered to build a library in the grounds and this building (now the Gilstrap Centre) was opened in 1885. To commemorate Queen Victoria's Diamond Jubilee in 1887, the Castle grounds were laid out as public gardens and at the same time a certain amount of consolidation of the ruins was undertaken. During the latter part of the 20th century further maintenance work was undertaken. In 1997 a Heritage Lottery Fund Grant, together with funding from the District Council, and other partners allowed for a £800,000 improvement scheme to be carried out between 1998 and 2000. Paths were resurfaced, thousands of trees and shrubs planted and access to the Castle's walls and dungeons improved, and a new Victorian-style bandstand added. Today the castle ruins and surrounding gardens remain popular with both local people and visitors from all over the world who come to see the 'Guardian of the Trent' or the 'Old Grey Lady' as the castle is sometimes known.

✳ **Nottingham Castle.** The first castle at Nottingham was built soon after the Norman Conquest and was, for five centuries, the principal royal fortress in the midlands. Marching North to crush a rebellion in the summer of 1068 William I passed through Nottingham and ordered the building of a castle there. The task was entrusted to William Peverel who constructed a timber motte and bailey castle using pressed labour from Nottingham and the surrounding area. Because the original motte was built on Castle Rock it was not necessary to wait for the ground to settle before building in stone and by the reign of Henry I a stone shell keep had been constructed. Henry II made frequent visits to the castle and spent considerable sums on strengthening its fortifications and improving the domestic buildings. His successor, Richard I, gave the county of Nottingham to his brother, John, but kept the castle in his own hands. In 1191, however, during Richards's absence on Crusade, John occupied the castle and on his return Richard had to regain it by force of arms. After he became King in 1199, John made frequent visits to the castle and the household accounts record a number of payments, including the sum of 7d, to William the Water bearer for baths taken by the King. During his reign further improvements were made to the fortifications of the castle. John was also responsible for one of the most barbaric acts ever committed at the castle. In 1212 he ordered 28 Welsh hostages to be hanged from the castle walls after the Welsh had taken up arms against him. Henry III further strengthened the fortifications and carried out work to make it a more comfortable residence for himself and his newly married wife (Eleanor of Provence). The Queen's apartments were improved; 'large and fair' windows were inserted in her chamber and its adjacent chapel, her wardrobe was enlarged and provided with a privy chamber for her use. Elsewhere in the castle a stable was constructed in the great bailey, a wall was built around the King's herbary and the mill beneath the castle was rebuilt. Edward I succeeded his father in 1272

Nottingham Castle.

and stayed at Nottingham Castel on several occasions. For most of his reign he was engaged in wars against the Welsh and the Scots and during this period several Scottish noblemen were held in the dungeons beneath the castle. Edward II succeeded his father in 1307 and spent a week at Nottingham soon after his accession. He proved to be a weak and unpopular King and in 1314 he led an English army to an ignominious defeat against the Scots at the Battle of

Bannockburn. At home his reign was marked by misgovernment and bitter quarrels, which led to 10 years of virtual sporadic civil war. He was eventually deposed by his wife Isabella and her lover, Roger Mortimer, who established regency in the name of Prince Edward (later Edward III). The King was brutally murdered, but the regency lasted only three years. In 1330 a Parliament was convened at Nottingham castle and the court took up residence there. Young Prince Edward and his followers made their way secretly into the castle through a passageway cut into the rock. They made their way to the royal apartments where they seized Mortimer and the Queen. Isabella was confined a Castle Rising for the remainder of her life and Mortimer met a traitor's death at Tyburn.

Nottingham Castle continued to play an important part in the history of the nation. Edward III held three parliaments there and at one of them, in 1337, laid the foundations of the mediaeval cloth industry by banning the weaning of foreign cloth by all except members of the royal family. Henry IV found refuge here during rebellions against him and the Welsh leader, Owen Glendower, was held prisoner here after his defeat at Shrewsbury. French prisoners were also held here after the Battle of Agincourt.

Edward IV proclaimed himself King from the Castle and in 1476 ordered the building of new state apartments. The poet Skelton reported that Edward IV made the castle 'a place full royal'. Richard III made the castle his principal residence and military base, and it was from here that he set out for Bosworth Field where his death marked the end of the Plantagenet dynasty. Tudor monarchs allowed the castle to fall into disrepair and in 1603 James I granted it to the Earl of Rutland who proceeded to demolish a number of buildings and sell the materials. Despite the castle's ruined state Charles I came here in August 1642 to raise his standard at the start of the Civil War with Parliament. He remained here only a few days, however, before moving on to Shrewsbury. The castle was later seized for Parliament and Colonel John Hutchinson, a local landowner, was appointed governor. His wife, Lucy, recorded that she found it 'very ruinous and inhabitable, neither affording room to lodge soldiers nor provisions'. Nevertheless, Hutchinson repulsed several attacks and the castle remained a thorn in the side of the Royalists throughout the war. At the end of the war the garrison was paid off and the castle slighted.

In 1674 the ruins were sold to William Cavendish, the first Duke of Newcastle. He cleared the site and erected there a magnificent ducal palace. It provided a stately residence for successive dukes for over a century but it was empty and deserted in 1831 when it was set on fire by a mob protesting at the rejection of the Reform Bill by the House of Lords. It lay derelict for over 40 years until 1878 when it was restored as the City Museum and Art Gallery.

✤ **Annesley Castle** was a timber motte and bailey castle built in the late 11th or early 12th century. A small motte, 3m high and 4m in diameter, was surrounded by an inner and outer bailey. A recent geophysical survey has also identified a third enclosure. In 1220 the regents acting for the young Henry III ordered an enquiry into a strong house at Annesley in Sherwood Forest, recently erected by

Reginald Marc which was said to have been built in such a fashion that it would be a nuisance to the neighbourhood. It seems likely that the castle was soon abandoned in favour of Annesley Hall for a document of 1232 refers to 'the old castle of Annesley'.

✳ **Aslockton Castle** was built in the late 11th or early 12th century on a site now known as Cranmer's Mound. This simple motte and bailey castle comprised a small motte and two rectangular baileys. The site was extensively remodelled during the post mediaeval period as a manor house with formal gardens.

✳ **Bothamsall Castle** was, like Annesley and Aslockton, a simple earth and timber fortress raised during the late 11th or early 12th century. It occupied a high point overlooking the valley of the River Meden and was close to one of Nottinghamshire's arterial roads. There is no evidence of any stone structure on the site and it seems unlikely that it was ever of any major strategic significance.

✳ **Cuckney Castle** was constructed in the 12th century by Thomas de Cuckney. It was almost certainly an adulterine castle raised by Thomas de Cuckney during the conflict between King Stephen and the Empress Matilda. Henry II granted it to Stephen de Falkonberg. It was never more than a simple motte and bailey castle with a wooden keep. The whole site was protected by a substantial ditch.

✳ **East Bridgford Castle** was built on an escarpment on the South bank of the River Trent. A simple motte and bailey castle of the late 11th or early 12th century, it was built specifically to protect a major crossing of the Rover Trent equidistant between the castles at Nottingham and Newark. It was never rebuilt in stone and was probably abandoned before the end of the 12th century. The site today is known as Pancake Hill.

✳ **Egmanton Castle** was a simple motte and bailey castle which was probably raised soon after the Norman Conquest. Also known as Gaddick Hill, the motte is one of the largest and best preserved in Nottinghamshire with a height of 20ft and a circumference of 46ft. Little is known of the history of the castle but it was constructed by the d'Eyvilles as the centre of their Nottinghamshire estates. It stood on the edge of the mediaeval village, close to the parish church and some historians have suggested that its role was as the administrative centre of an agricultural community rather than a strategic castle built for a military purpose.

✳ **Greasley Castle** was never really a castle but fortified manor house. In 1341, just before the Battle of Nevilles Cross, Nicholas Cantelupe was granted permission to fortify or crenelate his dwelling place of Gryseleye. Excavations carried out in 1933 uncovered the base of a round tower about 20ft in diameter. Other evidence suggests that the castle was a square or rectangular building with angle towers. Other fortifications included a defensive moat, walls 5ft thick in parts and an elaborate system of earthen ramparts. Today, remains include the earthworks, moat, fishponds and part of the main walls. In the middle of one of the farmyard buildings an arch and window survive. Gresley Castle was abandoned around 1700 and the site is now a modern working farm.

✤ **Haughton Castle** was constructed soon after the Norman Conquest. The motte is one of the largest in Nottinghamshire, standing 11m high with of a diameter of around 40m at the base. Little is known of the history of the castle but the site was incorporated into the formal grounds of Haughton Hall with ornamental lakes and a duck decoy. The motte was transformed into a prospect mound complete with spiral terrace.

✤ **King John's Palace** A royal hunting lodge at Clipstone is known locally as King John's Palace. Founded in the mid-12th century by King Henry II, the first reference to it appears in the Pipe Rolls for 1164–65, when £20 was spent 'on the king's houses at Clipstone'. It was, at first, a timber construction, but was rebuilt in stone between 1176 and 1180. It was visited by all English kings from Henry II to Richard II and it was particularly popular with John and Edward II. It was ruinous by 1525 and a survey of that year reported 'great dekay and ruyne in stonework, tymber, lede and plaster'. Excavations carried out in the 1950s suggest that this was once a substantial complex of buildings which included a great hall, various chambers, stables, kitchens and a chapel. Today only a few walls remain.

✤ **Kirby-in-Ashfield Castle** stands on Castle Hill overlooking the head of the Erewash valley. It was a small fortified manor house owned by the de Stuteville family and was visited by Edward I in 1292. Documents refer to a substantial hall and kitchens although the layout of the building is still being discovered. The de Stutevilles lost their lands in 1340 and the building was allowed to fall into ruin.

✤ **Kingshaugh Castle** was originally built as a hunting lodge in the 12th century. In 1194, during John's rebellion against his brother (Richard I), the lodge was fortified and earth and timber ring works built. It was at this time that the first reference is found to 'Kingshag' describing it as a fortified 'castrum' or castle. In 1211 King John expended a total of £550 4s 8d for the building on the King's houses and enclosing the park. Further work was carried out in 1212 and 1214.

✤ **Laxton Castle** was constructed soon after the Norman Invasion, perhaps on the orders of Geoffrey Alselin though more likely by his son-in-law, Robert de Caux who made the castle his seat after Alselin's death. Described as the finest motte and bailey castle in Nottinghamshire, the original castle comprised an earthen motte or mound surrounded by a strongly defended inner bailey and a larger less strongly defended outer bailey. The British Archaeological Association has recently described the original defences of the castle noting: 'The greatness of the outer court, the formidable character of the defences of the base of the court, the placement of the keep-moat on the edge of the steep natural escarpment on the northern side, and evidence of guarded trackways to the place all tend to show the importance of Laxton castle in the fighting days of its early existence when feudal lords cared only for what they could get and hold, and had little thought for the rights of their neighbours'. In the early 12th century de Caux was appointed hereditary Keeper of the Royal Forests of Nottinghamshire and Derbyshire. The castle was rebuilt in stone around this time and the new structure included a large shell keep on the motte. This appointment may also have led to further improvements to the castle in order to make it suitable to accommodate royal visitors. In 1408 the Roos family acquired the property. The castle was already a ruin by the 16th century when the family constructed a three-gabled brick manor house which became known as Laxton Hall. Today nothing remains on the site of the castle.

✻ **Lowdham Manor House** was a fortified manor house. It stood on a small motte like feature and was surrounded by a wet moat on three sides and the Cocker Beck stream to the north. It may have been built in the 12th century for King John is known to have stayed here in 1205 and 1207. Archaeologists have discovered mediaeval stonework and late mediaeval pottery on the site.

✻ **Strelley Hall** was originally built as a castle or fortified manor house around AD1200 with later improvements during the mediaeval period. Recent archaeological investigations have revealed a 14th-century tower and a mediaeval hall. The original manor house was also surrounded by a rock cut moat. Although no record of any license to crenellate, this fortified manor house undoubtedly had some of the features of a castle.

✻ **Wellow** Jordan Castle at Wellow is a ring-work castle of the late 11th or early 12th century. The site is isolated from the village of Wellow and it has been suggested that it was originally constructed as the manorial centre of the former parish of Grymston. It is believed that a license to crenelate at Grymston granted to Richard Foliat in 1264 refers to Jordan Castle.

✻ **Worksop Castle** may have been built by Roger de Busli in the late 11th century and it has been suggested that it was probably an urban castle built to monitor the market town of Worksop. It was, at first, a simple earth and timber structure but in the 12th century it seems that a stone shell keep was constructed on the mound by William de Lovetot. By the 16th century the castle had been demolished and the stones used in the building of the priory walls.

Nottinghamshire Monastic Houses

In the Middle Ages religion played a much more important part in people's lives than it does today and thousands became monks or nuns. There were several different orders of monks. The largest was the Benedictine, order which was founded by St Benedict in AD529. Benedictine communities lived a life of prayer, hard work, self discipline and good deeds which Benedict himself had established. The rule also set out a timetable for the monks' day which was divided into three parts; first the work of God carried out through eight daily services in church, second the work of the cloisters which included meditation, writing, translating, copying manuscripts, illuminating them; third, work in the monastic fields and gardens to produce the necessary food and clothing or in the form of craftsmanship in sculpture, carving or metalwork. Benedictine houses were established at Blythe and Wallingwells. Other orders followed a version of the Benedictine Rule. The Cistercian Order acquired vast estates and developed skills not only in farming but also in the construction of mills and water courses for the use of the monastery. The great abbeys of Fountains and Rievaulx were built by the Cistercian Order, as was Rufford Abbey in the area of Sherwood Forest. The Carthusians (who established a Charterhouse at Beauvale) and the Cluniacs (who founded Lenton Priory) also based their rule on that of St Benedict but the Cluniacs devoted much of their time to church services, and the Carthusians lived a very austere and isolated existence. There were also three orders of canons. These were priests who followed the monastic way of life but who also went out preaching and provided clergy for the churches which were appropriated to them. They lived in comparative comfort and were well known for the generosity of their hospitality. Communities of Austin Canons were established at Felley, Newstead, Worksop, Thurgarton and Shelford. The Premonstratension Canons were formed at Premontre in France in 1123. They followed a much more austere way of life than the Austin Canons and wore a white habit. These 'White Canons' established their first English house at Alnwick in 1147. In Nottinghamshire both Broadholme and Welbeck were Premonstratension houses. A third order of canons was the Gilbertines. These had been founded by St Gilbert of Semperingham. Mattersley priory belonged to this order. The Cluniac Order was founded at Cluny in France and grew into one of the most powerful and influential orders in Europe. Lenton Priory, however, was the only Cluniac house in Nottinghamshire. Military orders and communities of friars were also established, and these too were represented in Nottinghamshire.

Abbeys and Priories
✠ **Beauvale Priory** This priory for Carthusian monks was founded in 1343 by Nicholas de Cantelupe of nearby Greasley Castle. The Carthusians lived an

austere life of contemplation and prayer and had little contact with the outside world. Their houses were usually known as charterhouses. Archaeological evidence indicates that the layout of Beauvale priory was similar to other Charterhouses in England and comprised a simple church and prior's house. The Church had two entrances, one for the lay brothers and the other for the monks. Each monk had his own cell or set of rooms where he spent most of his time. At Beauvale there were a total of 14 cells arranged around three sides of the great cloister. Each cell comprised four rooms; a lobby, a living room with a door to the garden, a bedroom and a study. The upper floor was probably used as a workroom. Among the endowments made to the Priory were lands in Selston and Greasley and the Church of Farnham in Yorkshire. They held the right to mine coal in Selston. Some may have been mined directly by lay brothers but they also let some of their pits on lease. In 1397, for example, the prior leased a coal mine in Kirkestallaund to William Moneyasche and others, for a weekly rent of 4s 6d per pit. The prior also seems to have sold coal commercially for there is documentary evidence of payments to Sir John Chaworth for the transport of coal out of the area. The monks lived a life of seclusion. Even the poor were obliged to call at the porter's lodge for alms rather than entering the priory. The monks knew little of the outside world and the secular world rarely troubled them. Even contact with other Carthusian priories was sporadic. It has been said that in the worldly sense the priory had little history. In 1535, however, Beauvale and its prior were thrust into the spotlight. It was in that year that Robert Lawrence, the prior of Beauvale and two other Carthusians, John Houghton, Head of the Carthusian Order in England (and previously a Prior of Beauvale) and Augustine Webster, Prior of Axholme, were hanged drawn and quartered at Tyburn for refusing to accept Henry VIII as head of the English Church. Beauvale Priory survived for a little while but on 18 July 1539 the priory was surrendered to Dr London, one of Cromwell's agents. The last Prior, Thomas Woodcock, who had only been appointed a few months earlier, was granted an annual pension of £25 13s 4d. Eight monks each received £5 6s per annum and two lay brothers were unusually rewarded with pensions of 40s. Little remains of Beauvale today but some work has recently been undertaken by English Heritage.

✢ **Blythe Priory** was founded in 1088 By Roger de Builli, one of William the Conqueror's followers and an important landowner in Nottinghamshire, Derbyshire and Staffordshire. Architectural evidence suggests that the nave of the priory church was completed no later than 1100. This served as the parish church and would have been attended by local townspeople. Blythe was the only Benedictine monastery in Nottinghamshire. The monks there followed the rule of St Benedict, and were sometimes called Black Monks because of the colour of their habit. The founder and later benefactors endowed the priory with lands, money and churches. The foundation charter included the town of Blythe, and the rights to a fair, and market there. Under the terms of the charter the prior was also responsible for the erection and use of a gallows! This involvement in the economic and social life of the local community had a considerable impact on the way in which the priory was managed. The prior fulfilled the role of a feudal lord and estate manager. The regulations relating to the market and fair had to be strictly observed and taxes and tolls collected. Comprehensive records were kept of the lands owned by the priory, and towards the end of the 13th century Prior William Burdon ordered a detailed survey of the priory's tenants and properties. This focus on secular matters also had less fortunate consequences and in 1373 Prior Thomas de Vymond and his followers were accused of breaking into the park of William de Furnival in Sheffield, where they hunted, felled his trees, fished in his free fishery, dug in his quarry and carried off coals and stones as well as deer, hares and conies (rabbits). The location of the priory close to the Castle at Tickhill and on the Great North Road meant that it received large numbers of visitors including merchants, pilgrims and soldiers. Hospitality placed a considerable strain on the finances of the priory and it was brought to the brink of ruin in the early 14th century when Henry II and his entourage stayed here on their way to Scotland. In the 14th century some of the priory's tithes were let out to improve the finances. Apart from financial problems it seems to have been a well-ordered house and the reports of the Archbishops visitations mention only minor breaches of discipline and comments relating to financial and administrative matters. In 1307, for example, the prior was instructed to appoint a cellarer and an almoner and exercise more efficient control over the community. Blythe was never a large house. At the end of the 12th century there were at least 12 monks in addition to the prior but numbers declined in succeeding years. When the Commissioners visited the priory in 1536 they reported four cases of serious sexual offences and one of adultery. Prior Dalton wrote to Cromwell, the Lord Chancellor, pleading that he was too ill to come to London to present his case. When the priory was finally dissolved he received a small annual pension of 20 marks. All that remains of the priory is the church, although the original choir, central tower and transepts were demolished in 1664.

✢ **Broadholme Priory** is unusual as it was one of only two nunneries in the county and one of only two houses for Premonstratension Canonesses in the whole country. It was founded by Agnes de Camville around 1145 and there is some evidence to suggest that it was originally a joint house for men and women. It was only a small establishment with seven or eight nuns under the supervision of a prioress who was chosen by the nuns themselves. The affairs of the nunnery were supervised by the Prior of Newholme who appointed a resident canon to say mass, hear confessions and oversee the spiritual life of the community. In other respects the priory retained a fair degree of independence. Two scandals affected the priory in the 14th century both involving the abduction of women from the priory. Little is known of these incidents and in one case, at least, it may have involved a husband seizing his wife from the protection of the priory. Generally the nuns lived in harmony with the local community, fulfilling their life of prayer, providing alms for the poor and offering hospitality to visitors. In 1383, however, the prioress was forced to appeal to the King for justice when William Wauterson and others attacked the priory, carrying off trees and other goods, assaulting the priory servants and threatening the prioress and her nuns. Broadholme priory was dissolved in 1536 and the last prioress, Joan Angevin, was granted a pension of seven marks. The fate of the other nuns is not known. Nothing remains of the priory, and Manor Farm now stands on the site.

✤ **Felley Priory** was a priory of Augustinian Canons founded by Ralph Britto in 1156, close to the site of an existing hermitage. This small priory was made subject to the larger Worksop priory and remained so until 1260 when it was relieved of any obedience to Worksop in return for an annual payment of twenty shillings. Two priors of Felley, however, went on to become priors of Worksop. The priory appears to have been well ordered throughout its history, although in 1276 the prior was deposed by the Archbishop for having assaulted one of his canons and for other irregularities. At the same time three other canons were disciplined for certain irregularities. The priory struggled with poverty throughout its existence and was valued at only £61 in 1535. A year later the priory was dissolved. The prior was granted a pension of £6 a year but he had to relinquish this when he was appointed to the living of Attenborough.

✤ **Lenton Priory** The Priory of Holy Trinity, Lenton, was founded by William Peverel around 1109. It was the only Cluniac house in the county and was dependent on the mother house at Cluny, and the Abbot of Cluny appointed the prior. It was richly endowed by its founder and later benefactors and by the end of the 13th century was probably the richest in the county. Among other privileges were the right to hold an annual fair lasting 12 days, at which the monks were able to levy tolls on most goods sold at the fair. They also had the right to the first draught of fishes in the fishing of Chilwell. This would have been a valuable privilege at a time when salmon were common in the Trent. Lenton was an important and influential house and some of its priors went on to hold important offices within the church or the state. The most influential was probably Thomas Elmham who was prior between 1414 and 1426. He served both as Vicar general to the Abbot of Cluny for England and Scotland, and Henry V as a royal chaplain. He was with the King at the Battle of Agincourt. Not all priors were so favoured or so fortunate. In 1538 Prior Nicholas Heath, along with one of his monks, was found guilty of verbal treason. They were hanged, drawn and quartered in Nottingham and their remains were displayed at the gate of the priory. Shortly afterwards the priory was suppressed by attainder and the monks cast out without the benefit of any pensions. The priory buildings were soon demolished and little now remains above ground. The important decorated 12th-century font from the monastic church is now in the Church of the Holy Trinity, in Church Street, Lenton.

✤ **Mattersley Priory** was a small priory of Gilbertine canons founded towards the end of the 12th century by Roger de Mattersley who endowed it with property nearby. The Gilbertines were members of the order founded by St Gilbert of Semperingham and was the only monastic order to originate in England, being founded by Gilbert of Semperingham (Lincs) in the mid 12th century. Members of the order were known as canons and were ordained priests as well as following the rule of St Benedict. They wore a black habit and a white cloak. Little is known of the history of the priory. This is partly because it was never a wealthy or populous house and partly because of a disastrous fire in 1279 which destroyed all its records as well as most of the buildings. In 1280 the canons were authorised to appropriate Mattersley Church with most of its income 'in consequence of their poverty through fire'. The priory was also exempted from paying tithes on the priory fisheries, tannery or mills, to the vicar of the church. In 1403 Henry V granted the priory a weekly market at Mattersley and two annual fairs. Despite this, the priory continued to struggle financially. It was never able to attract or support enough canons or lay brothers to farm the priory land directly and much was rented out to local people. At the time of the dissolution there remained only the prior and four canons. They all received pensions and the prior later became headmaster of Malton Grammar School in Yorkshire.

�֍ **Newstead Priory** was founded by Henry II around 1170, although there is some evidence to suggest that it may have been in existence for some years before its royal foundation. The original endowment included not only Ravenshead and Kighill but also the township of Papplewick, with its church and mill, the waterside meadow of Bestwood, and the income from rents. Further endowments of land in Derbyshire and Nottinghamshire were made in the early 13th century. Dedicated to St Mary, this was a house of Augustinian canons who served the churches appropriated to the priory. The obligation to provide hospitality placed a considerable financial burden upon the priory. Royal visitors who included King John as well as Edward I, Edward II and Edward III would all have been entertained at great expense. On a number of occasions the priory fell so seriously into debt that it had to be taken into protection by the Crown. The priory received visitations, or inspections, from both senior members of the Augustinian Order and Archbishops of York, in whose diocese the priory lay. From these we can learn a great deal about life at the priory during the 13th and 14th centuries. In 1252 Archbishop Gray visited the priory and found the canons 'fervid in religion and lovers of concord' but seven years later his successor complained about drinking and general slackness. At the same time the prior was ordered to receive guests with a smiling countenance. In 1261 the financial management of the priory was found to be inadequate and the provincial visitors of the Order drew up regulations for the more rigorous control of the priory's finances. There is also evidence of more serious lapses in the morals of the canons. In 1293 the Archbishop forbade all games of dice and removed the sacrist from his office for insolence and for misappropriating a loan. A few years later the prior was found guilty of incontinence (breaking his vow of chastity) with one woman and of relapsing into incontinence with another. In 1534 the annual value of the priory was calculated to be £167 16s 11 ½ d. This placed it below the £200 limit ordered for the possession of lesser monasteries. Exemption was gained on payment of a substantial fine but the priory was finally surrendered on 21 July 1539. John Blake, the Prior, received an annual pension of £26 13s 4d. Richard Kychun, the sub-prior, was awarded £6 and the rest of the 10 cannons who signed the surrender document received sums ranging from £3 6s 8d to £5 6s 8d. The priory was purchased by Sir John Byron of Colwick for £810. Byron renamed the priory Newstead Abbey and began transforming it into a grand house. The church was demolished apart from the west front, and over the following years the refectory was converted into a drawing room, galleries were built over the cloisters and the dormitory was sub-divided into bedrooms. Today Newstead Abbey is owned by the City of Nottingham and is open to the public.

✻ **Rufford Abbey** was founded in 1146 by Gilbert de Gand, Earl of Lincoln for four monks of the Cistercian order. The first monks came from Rievaulx Abbey in North Yorkshire and Rufford became its fifth and final 'daughter house'. Within one hundred years Rufford Abbey had grown into a substantial working estate comprising not only an impressive abbey church with cloisters, dormitories, refectory and chapter house, but also a large house for the abbot and accommodation for visitors. Agricultural buildings included a mill, bake house, brewery. Rufford Abbey housed both choir monks and larger numbers of lay brethren. These were used mainly to farm the 21 granges or farms which the abbey established in the surrounding area. Sheep farming was a major source of income and wool was traded with Flemish merchants at markets in Nottingham and Newark. The abbey also benefitted from later gifts of land, rents and the right to use timber and grazing in Sherwood Forest. The monks also held a weekly market and fair, and had the right to cut down and sell trees from the forest. Gifts from later endowments added further to the prosperity of the abbey. Their most important acquisition was Rotherham in Yorkshire. By 1283 the abbey appears to have possessed a large part of the town including the rectory. As a consequence they received burial dues, Easter offerings and tithes, as well as rents and the income from a weekly market and annual fair in the town. Little direct evidence of daily life at Rufford survives. The Cistercians were a silent order and conversation was only permitted in the parlour. In addition to the regular routine of prayer and study some of the monks also worked in the scriptorium, copying and illuminating manuscripts. Although most of the monks lived devout and blameless lives there is evidence of lapses of behaviour and occasionally of crime or scandal. When the Commissioners visited in 1536 they alleged that the abbot had broken his vows of chastity with at least two married and four single women. In addition, six out of the 15 monks wished to be released from their vows. At the dissolution the abbey had an annual net value of £80. Thomas Doncaster, the last abbot, was granted an annual pension of £25 but this ceased when he became the Vicar of Rotherham shortly afterwards. Today the house and abbey remains are cared for by English

Heritage. The surrounding park is owned by Nottinghamshire County Council and is open to the public.

✠ **Shelford Priory** was founded by Ralph Haunsley during the reign of Henry II (1154–89) as a house of Augustinian Canons. It was always one of the smaller Nottinghamshire religious houses and less important than the nearby Thurgaton Priory. It was not well endowed, though by careful management it was able to purchase more land and property in neighbouring villages. By the 14th century some of the income of the priory came from the sale of wool. In 1333 two merchants from Newark were granted a license to export wool purchased by them from the prior of Shelford. Little is known of the internal history of the priory though we get brief glimpses from Visitation Reports. There is evidence that standards had declined by the end of the 13th century for in 1280 the following injunctions or corrections were issued: the prior to discard all torpor both in spiritual and temporal affairs; the sub-prior to restrict himself to his office, such as the joint custody of the seal; useless servants in granges to be removed; the rule of silence at stated times and places not to be infringed; worthless persons not to be allowed to eat and drink in the frater; no one to be admitted to the farmer save the doctors; no one to be allowed to drink or eat after compline, save in the presence of the prior and by his express license, or in the case of sickness; the sick to be better treated and fed, and alms (in kind) to be more safely kept; canons not to go out of cloister save for necessity or by express leave of the president; carols and chests with locks to be opened twice a year by the prior in the presence e of a fellow canon, in order that the vice of private property might be expelled; no money to be paid for clothes, but they are allotted out of the common store; no little gifts or letters to be received without license of the president, and these to be applied to the common use; and these injunctions to be read in full chapter at the beginning of each month. Royal accounts also show that King Edward II visited the priory in 1317 and again two years later. Other records show that for some years the priory provided for the poor through the distribution of 'broken meats' and the maintenance of almshouse to support six poor men. It may also have been a place of minor pilgrimage for, at the dissolution, it was noted that the monks there kept a number of relics including the girdle and milk of the Virgin Mary. When Layton and Leigh visited the priory in 1536 they found evidence of both sexual impropriety and superstition. When the priory was closed the Prior, Robert Dixon, received a payment of £16. A manor house stands on the site of the priory and is private property.

✠ **Thurgaton Priory** This priory of Austin Canons was founded by Ralph D'Aincourt around 1140. Dedicated to St Peter it was situated on the outskirts of the village of Thurgarton. It was well endowed and received the income from the manors of Thurgarton and Fiskerton together with the dues from 11 churches. In 1270 Henry III granted to the priory a weekly market to be held on a Tuesday in their manor of Fiskerton and also an annual fair there on the feast of the Holy trinity and on the two following days. By careful management the priory was able to add to its holdings and by the 14th century held substantial lands and property in Nottinghamshire, Derbyshire and Lincolnshire. This provided income in the form of both rents and produce and Thurgaton Priory grew in prosperity. The priory was not, however, without scandal and dissent. In 1284 Archbishop Wickwane issued a decree of imprisonment against one of the Thurgaton canons who had written an abusive pamphlet against him. Visitation records also provide accounts of adultery, assault, extravagance and mismanagement. When Leigh and Layton arrived in 1536 to enquire into the affairs of the priory they alleged that 10 canons were guilty of unnatural offences that the prior had been incontinent with several women and that six others had been guilty of similar offences. Eight canons had expressed a desire to be released from their vows. Despite this catalogue of vice and debauchery, generous pensions were awarded to the whole community. The prior, John Berwick, was granted Fiskerton Hall with chapel, gardens, stable, two meadows, tithes of hay and £40 per annum. The sub-prior received £6 13s 4d and the remaining canons £5 a year. What remains of the priory church now forms part of Thurgarton parish church.

⁕ **Wallingwells Priory** The small priory of St Mary was founded by Ralph de Chevrolcourt for a community of Benedictine nuns. It had an uneventful history and the community there lived a frugal and pious existence. In 1262 Archbishop Godfrey described the nuns as being devout and poor. Later visitations confirmed this judgement and a picture emerges of a pious and well managed community. When the King's commissioners visited in 1536 they found nothing to criticise. Despite this the prioress, Margaret Goldsmith, was forced to pay the considerable sum of £66 13s 4d for a license to continue. A year later, in an attempt to safeguard the priory she leased the priory estates to Ralph Oglethorpe for a period of 21 years. Under this agreement the nuns retained the conventual buildings while Oglethorpe was able to benefit from his management of the priory's estates. If this agreement was a device to prevent seizure it failed for on 14 December 1537 the priory was surrendered to the Crown. The prioress was granted an annual pension of £6 and the eight nuns received pensions in proportion to their seniority. Today nothing remains of the priory buildings.

⁕ **Welbeck Abbey** was founded towards the end of the reign of Henry II (1154–89) by Thomas de Fleming and eventually became the mother house of the Premonstratension order in England. The abbey was endowed with the income from land and churches in the immediate vicinity and from other churches in Derbyshire and Nottinghamshire. Others followed the example of the founder and by 1293 the abbey had an annual taxable income of £140. In 1329 the abbey was granted the manor of Cuckney along with seven nearby hamlets. In return the abbey agreed to provide eight canons to act as chantry priests to celebrate mass daily for the King and his royal ancestry. Welbeck was visited on no fewer that 11 occasions between 1462 and 1500 by Bishop Richard Redman, the Commissionary General of the Order. Generally he found little to criticise but in 1482 he discovered that the canons had pawned the abbey jewels and plate, neglected the fabric and were generally lax in their religious observances. The abbot was also guilty of incontinence and was promptly deposed. It took some time to restore the abbey to good order and discipline but in 1491 Redman found that the abbot was ruling well in both external and internal matters. At his last visit on 22 November 1500 he punished two canons for minor infringements of the rules but his report stated that everything else was in an admirable state; there was unity, concord and love between the head and the members, and no complaints; there was an admirable provision of every kind of grain and cattle and of all necessaries. When Leigh and Layton visited in 1536 they found the annual income to be £280 and debts to be £40, they also alleged that four canons were guilty of moral offences. The abbey was finally surrendered to the Royal Commissioners on 20 June 1538, the abbot and canons receiving pensions or being confirmed in their vicarages.

* **Worksop Priory** The Augustinian priory at Worksop was founded between 1123 and 1140 by William de Lovetot. It was generously endowed and as a result of later endowments and gifts it was by 1291, the third wealthiest house in Nottinghamshire. The lands owned by the Priory were farmed by servants and lay brethren. Sheep rearing was one the abbey's main sources of income although the canons also had the privilege of pasturing 40 cattle in Worksop Park between Easter and Michaelmas. The canons also cultivated liquorice for medicinal purposes. The abbey had a great number of churches in its care including those at Gringley, Misterton, Normanton, Car Colston, Walkeringham, Willoughby, Wysall, and Sheffield (now the cathedral) and these also contributed to the wealth of the abbey. In addition to a life of prayer and conducting services in these churches the canons also worked in the scriptorium writing books and documents, mainly for the use of the community. The most important manuscript from Welbeck is the Tickhill Psalter, a beautiful prayer book containing 482 miniatures illustrating the life of David and other scenes from the Old Testament. The priory also played an important role in giving alms and providing hospitality to travellers. These included royal visitors as well as lesser folk who came to buy and sell at the market and annual fair. The abbey gatehouse was constructed in part to accommodate these visitors. Visitation reports shed some light on the daily life at the abbey. Generally they found only minor failings to correct but in 1280 Archbishop Wickwane issued a number of injunctions including forbidding all sinister and forbidding speech, the entertaining of costly and useless guests, the wasting of alms and leaving the priory without good cause. He also ordered that the sick were to be kindly treated and that silence be strictly observed according to the rule. William Selman, 'a rebellious and quarrelsome canon' and William de Grave and Henry de Marcham, two lay brothers accused of

incontinence were ordered to be punished. The Royal Commissioners arrived in 1536 and found its annual value to be £240. They also reported that they had found four of the canons to be guilty of moral offences and that one canon wished to be released from his vows. Perhaps foreseeing the closure of the abbey the canons began to sell off some of their livestock. The priory was surrendered on 15 November 1538. By this time the valuable silver plate had been seized by Sir George Lawson who wrote to Cromwell explaining that he had 'already committed the custody of them to substantial persons' The prior, Thomas Stokes received a pension of £50 and other canons amounts ranging from £6 to 40s. The nave and aisles of the monastic church were retained as the parish church and is open daily to the public. The priory gatehouse also survived and this too is open to the public from Monday to Wednesday each week.

Friaries

❋ Several orders of friar-preachers were established in Europe in the 13th century. Their aim was to go out into the world to help the poor and diseased and to spread the word of God by means of homely and vigorous preaching. They were popular with the ordinary people and attracted both recruits and benefactions. There were three friaries in Nottinghamshire.

❋ The Franciscan Friary in Nottingham was established around 1230 in a poorly drained area in Broad Marsh on the banks of the River Leen. They were known as Grey friars on account of the grey habit which they wore. The original friary was a simple wooden structure but by the early 14th century the friars had accumulated enough money to build a stone church and other buildings. They were popular preachers and were respected for their good works among the local community. The friary was surrendered in 1539 to Dr London by Thomas Basford, warden, and seven others.

❋ The Carmelite Friary in Nottingham was founded around 1272 by Lord Grey of Wilton and Sir John Shirley on a site between Friar Lane and St James Street, although there is evidence to suggest that they arrived in the town some years before. Little is known of the history of the friary but it was visited by Henry VIII in 1511 who presented them with some small gifts. A few years later in 1532 Richard Sherwood, the Prior, killed one of his friars during a drunken brawl. He was pardoned by the King but would in any case have been able to escape trial by pleading benefit of clergy. When the friary was surrendered to the king's Commissioners in 1539 only the prior and six friars remained in residence. In 1541 the friary was granted to James Sturley, possibly the descendant of one of the original co-founders.

❋ A community of Observant friars was established in Newark around 1499 and was dissolved only 40 years later. These observant friars were a reform group of the Franciscans from which they separated in the early 15th century. King

Henry VIII was a great supporter of this order and when he died he left the Newark Observants the considerable sum of £200. They were, however, less popular with Henry VIII as they denounced his divorce from Catherine of Aragon and several were imprisoned. The Order was suppressed by the King in 1534 and a community of Austin Friars was installed at Newark. The friary was finally dissolved in 1539. The site of the friary is on Appletongate near the town centre. Part of the friary grounds are now a public park.

Military orders

✤ A number of military orders were also created in the Middle Ages. The Knights Hospitallers of St John and the Knights Templar both fought in the crusades but some of the lesser orders such as the Knights of St Lazarus served in hospitals for the sick or hospices for travellers. Two military orders established houses in Nottinghamshire. The Knights Hospitallers established a commandery (the name given to a manor or estate in the charge of a member of the Hospitallers) at Ossington and a camera (or cell) at Winkburn. The Knights Templar had a hospice for travelling knights in the Parish of St Mary in Nottingham.

Hospitals

✤ Mediaeval hospitals were primarily religious rather than medical institutions. Their purpose was care rather than cure; for the relief of the body where possible, but pre-eminently for the refreshment of the soul. By various religious observances the staff sought to elevate and discipline character. They endeavoured, as the body decayed (and many of these hospitals cared for lepers) to strengthen the soul and prepare it for the afterlife. In most cases the master, prior or warden, together with the brethren or sisters who formed the staff, followed a definite religious rule and wore a special habit. It was usual for the staff and inmates to take the three main monastic vows, recite the divine office and be subject to a superior. There were over 700 such hospitals in England and at least 12 in Nottinghamshire.

✤ **Hospital of St Leonard at Newark** Bishop Alexander the Magnificent of Lincoln (1123–48) founded the hospital at Newark. Its dedication to St Leonard and its location on the edge of the town suggest that this was a hospital for lepers. It received a number of generous endowments over the years, and because of its charitable function it was allowed to continue after the dissolution of the monasteries. In 1642 a new building was provided by the Dowager duchess of Exeter to provide accommodation for a master, chaplain and two poor men. This was demolished in 1888 and replaced by four separate houses designed to provide accommodation for two deserving married couples and four single men. These almshouses are still in existence today.

✤ **The Hospital of the Holy Sepulchre** in Nottingham is surrounded in mystery. Little is known about its original foundation but there is documentary evidence of a land gift by Robert St Remy to the pilgrims of Nottingham, enabling them to establish a hospital for poor men. This endowment was confirmed by a charter of Henry II in 1170.

�֍ **The Hospital of St Leonard** We have even less information about this leper hospital which stood just outside the walls on the north side of the town. It appears to have been annexed to the ancient Church of St Michael which was destroyed by fire in the 1341. It was still in existence in 1416 but by the 16th century, and perhaps earlier, the office of master had become a mere sinecure.

�֍ **The Hospital of St John** A hospital dedicated to St John the Baptist was established in Nottingham sometime during the first half of the 12th century. This may have begun as a secular institution but was later recognised by Pope Gregory IX and taken under the protection of the Archbishop of York. The main function of this house was the care of the poor. Documentary evidence suggests that the hospital was served by sisters as well as brethren and that both wore a habit of russet and brown.

�֍ Other hospitals which are known to have existed in Nottinghamshire in the Middle Ages include:
The Hospital of St Mary at West Bar, Nottingham
Plumtree's Hospital, Nottingham
The Hospital of St Mary Magdalen, Southwell
The Hospital of St Leonard at Stoke
The Hospital of St Edmund, Blythe
The Hospital of St John the Evangelist, Blythe
The Hospital of St Mary Magdalen, Gonalston
The Hospital of St Anthony, Lenton

Church and Chapel

✳ Saxon carvings and architectural fragments abound in Nottinghamshire churches with good examples being found at Bilsthorpe, Carlton-in-Lindrick, East Bridgford, Hawkesworth, Hickling, Kneesall, Rolleston, Shelford and Shelton.

✳ 85 Nottinghamshire churches are mentioned in the *Domesday Book*. Some of these would have been built before the Norman Conquest.

✳ There are over 50 Norman church doorways in Nottinghamshire.

✳ The Church of St Mary in the Lace Market is the oldest religious foundation in the city of Nottingham and is also known as St Mary's in the Lace Market.

✳ St George's Church, Netherfield has probably one of the briefest descriptions of all the churches listed in Pevsner's Buildings of England. It simply states, 'A towerless brick church of 1887'.

✳ A crude depiction of St James (with his pilgrim's staff) stands over the doorway into the Church of St James, Papplewick. The carving dates from the Norman period.

✳ Southwell Minister is the mother church of the diocese and acts as the Anglican Cathedral for Nottinghamshire. It is the seat of the Bishop of Nottingham and Southwell.

✳ The *Leaves of Southwell* is an amazing relief carved in the roof of the chapterhouse, passage and vestibule of Southwell Minister. In addition to the most beautiful leaves of maple, oak, hawthorn, vine and buttercup.

St Mary's Church, in the Lace Market Nottingham.

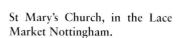

Southwell Minister.

* The Church of St Mary Magdalene, Newark, has been described as one of the finest town churches in the country. Over 220ft long with a 250ft high steeple, it dominates the town and the surrounding countryside.

* The Roman Catholic Cathedral of St Barnabas, Nottingham, was consecrated and opened in 1844 but it was not until 1850, following the restoration of the

Catholic Hierarchy in England, that the church became Cathedral of the new diocese of Nottingham. The first Bishop (Joseph Hendren) was enthroned there in December 1851. Built in the Early English style, the Cathedral is the work of the architect Augustus Welby Pugin who designed a number of Roman Catholic Churches including the nearby St Mary's Church in Derby.

✳ The Church of St John the Baptist at Carlton-in-Lindrick was described by Pevsner as 'the most important late Saxon monument in the county'.

✳ The ruined Church of St Mary at Colston Bassett is a Grade 1 listed building. Its roof was removed in the late 19th century to encourage the use of the new St John's Church which had been built by Squire Millington Knowles of Colston Bassett Hall to commemorate the death of his wife and son. As St Mary's was situated some distance from the village he wanted to build one closer to his home. As a consequence of this St Mary's roof was removed because at that time the Church Commissioners would only allow one church per village.

✳ The parish Church at Plumtree is believed to be the oldest church in Nottinghamshire. It was founded around the year 837 and is mentioned in the *Domesday Book*. Nothing remains of the earliest church, which was probably built of wood, but the underlying stonework dates from Saxon times. The tower is largely Norman and the rest of the church dates mostly from the 14th century, although substantial rebuilding and restoration took place during the Victorian period.

✳ Bunny Church is known as 'the Cathedral of the Wolds'. The church's wide nave and battlements make it appear quite grand.

✳ The Church of St Nicholas, Littleborough, is the smallest church in Nottinghamshire. Dating from the Norman period, and with some Roman tiles in its structure, the nave is only 24ft in length.

✳ The Old Meeting House, Stockwell street, Mansfield is probably the oldest surviving nonconformist chapel in Nottinghamshire. It was built by the Unitarians in 1702 but alterations and additions were made towards the end of the 19th century.

✳ Other interesting nonconformist chapels include the Wesleyan Chapel, Burnby Gate, Newark opened in 1846, Kirby Woodhouse General Baptist Chapel built in 1754, East Leake General Baptist Chapel built in 1786 and the Wesleyan Chapel at Clayworth which dates from 1834.

Bells
✳ One of the bells at St Mary and All Saints at Bingham is believed to have been cast to commemorate the English defeat of the Spanish Armada in 1588.

❉ A local Rhyme describes the sound of the bells in four Nottinghamshire churches:
Calverton crack pancheons
Woodborough merry bells
Oxton ding dongs
Lowdham egg shells

❉ The sanctus bell in St Nicholas Church Littleborough dates from around 1200 and is probably the oldest church bell in the county. It is thought likely that it was cast in the Nottingham bell foundry.

❉ References to the church bells at St Peters in East Drayton have been found in a volume of church accounts. The following entries are typical:

		s. d.
1738	For ale the ringers had	7 8
1757	June 9th. A piece of leather for ye great bell	0 6
	Dec 30. For ale at ye mending of ye bells at ye church	0 6
	For ale at ye Ringers for Christmas and Gunpowder plot	7 6

❉ In 1843 two bells were stolen from the tower of Holy Trinity Church in Kirton. The bells were thrown into a pond where they remained for some time before being carried off and sold. The thieves are said to have lived in the village and stole corn, a flock of geese and other things on an extensive scale; otherwise a bell would be rather a bulky article for the ordinary thief to carry away.

❉ Some church bells are dedicated to parishioners. At St John the Baptist at East Markham the following dedication is to be found on one of the bells: 'Let this bell ring to the GLORY OF GOD and in loving memory of Ann Cowlishaw who passed to her rest 6th April, 1916'.

❉ The single bell in St Helen's, Burton Joyce, was cast from two earlier bells to commemorate the coronation of the present Queen. It is inscribed '1953 Laus de Elizabeth 1953'.

❉ A survey of the older churches in Nottinghamshire made by Revd R.F. Wikinson, Rector of Ordsall, revealed the fact that in 222 towers there were 876 bells. Of this number 58 werc Pre-Reformation, 722 were cast about 1550–1850, and 96 have been added in recent years.

❉ A single bell at Bulcote Holy Trinity is one of the oldest in the diocese. Dating from 1450 it was cast at a mediaeval bell foundry in Leicester. The inscription around the top of the bell is in Latin and reads: AVE MARIA GRATIA PLENA.

❉ In 1919 Tom Lawson, vicar of St Leodegarius, Basford, proposed a memorial to those who had given their lives in the Great War. A counter proposal was made by a sidesman named Samuel Padley who suggested five new bells to add to the three that they already had, to make a peal of eight. After a long and acrimonious dispute Mr Padley won the support of the congregation. At one stage the vicar declared that he was 'sick and tired of Mr Padley and his bell'. The new bells were installed in 1921.

Brasses

�֞ The Annesley Brass in All Saints Church is unusual and in some respects, unique. It shows the figure of William Breton on a hunting expedition accompanied by his hound and is dated 1595. In his left hand he carries a bow while the right holds an arrow which he is about to fit to his bow. No other brass featuring a longbow is known to exist in this country.

✚ The earliest surviving English brass in the county is at Bothamsall and dates from around 1360. Although incomplete it is clearly that of a lady and may represent Margaret Buslingthorpe who died in 1369.

✚ A brass of Dame Millicent Meryng (1419) in the Church of St John the Baptist, East Markham, shows her as a young girl despite the fact that she was married three times

✚ The monumental brass of Alan Fleming (from 1361) in St Mary Magdalen, Newark, is one of the four largest 'Flemish' brasses in England. Fleming was a wool merchant who founded a chantry in the Corpus Christie Chapel in 1349. His wife Alice endowed the Chantry house.

✚ At All Saints Church, Strelley, is a double brass to Sir Robert Strellcy (1487) and his wife, who died at Oxton in 1458. Her brass shows a beautiful example of the butterfly style of headdress popular at the time.

✚ Two brasses of exceptional quality are to be found in the Church of St Leonard, Wollaton. They represent Sir Richard Willoughby who died in 1471 and his wife who died in 1467. He is clad in an elaborate suit of armour, with his crest, an owl, on his helm. His hands are in an attitude of prayer and his sword is worn diagonally. She wears long robes and a heart-shaped headdress of the period. She wears a cross around her neck.

✚ The Church of All Saints, Willoughby-on-the-Wolds, contains a memorial brass from the time of the Civil War. It is inscribed; 'Here lyes the body of Colonel Michael Stanhope who was slain in Wiloughby Field in the month of July 1648 in the 24th year of his age, being a soldier for King Charles the First'.

Churchyards

✚ A Saxon Cross stands in St Helen's Churchyard, Stapleford. It was probably erected around AD700 and is believed to be the oldest Christian memorial in Nottinghamshire. It is over 3m tall and features many interlacing carvings including a symbol of Saint Luke treading on a serpent.

- A plague pit in the churchyard of St John the Baptist at Beeston contains the remains of 138 people who died from the plague in 1593–94.

- A memorial in the form of a stone obelisk dedicated to the local men who died in the Crimean War stands in the churchyard of St John the Baptist, Beeston.

- South Nottinghamshire churchyards adjacent to the Vale of Belvoir are notable for their Swithland slate headstones. They date from the early 18th century and are remarkable for their fine engraving.

- There is an unusual lynch gate at St George's Church, North and South Clifton. It is constructed entirely in iron with a barrel roof, incorporated lettered texts and large iron gates matching the adjacent iron railings.

- The victims of the Chilwell Explosion of 1918 in which 134 people were killed are buried in a collective grave in the churchyard of St Mary's Church, Attenborough.

- In the churchyard of Gedling All Hallows lie the graves of Alfred Shaw and Arthur Shrewsbury. They were famous cricketers who played for England and Nottinghamshire on numerous occasions. Shaw was a bowler and Shrewsbury a batsman. They lie just over the length of a cricket pitch apart. There is also the grave of John Flinders who served as a soldier for 62 years. When he came home to Gedling he found living with his relatives intolerable and went to live in the workhouse because it provided the same regimented routine that he had been used to during his long military career.

- In the south-west corner of the churchyard of St Lawrence, Norwell is an early pedestal sundial of considerable interest. The dial itself is dated 1665 but the pedestal on which it is mounted is dated 1736 and bears the names of two church wardens, Richard Wright and Richard Birkett, who were probably responsible for putting it up.

- The churchyard of St Nicholas Church, Nottingham contains the gravestone of John Attenburrow, the first man in Nottingham to inoculate against smallpox.

Clocks

- The clock at St Mary's Church, Bunny was fixed in 1897 in commemoration of Queen Victoria's Diamond Jubilee. Money was originally collected for a party to celebrate the event but there was a surplus so the vicar at that time, the Revd H. Cooper spent it on providing a clock.

- The church clock at Babworth was made by Sharpe of Retford and is inscribed with the words, 'Watch and pray till he come'.

✣ The wooden frame and ironworks of a derelict clock stand in the south west corner of the nave at Baton in Fabis. The initials I.N. and the date 1735 are said to be inscribed on the oak frame. Apparently it would strike the hour. The clock was possibly made by Richard Roe of Epperstone with the help of the local blacksmith.

✣ The clock at Car Colston, St Mary was erected as a Jubilee Memorial in 1887–88.

✣ The original clock from Plumtree, St Mary had no face or hands but simply chimed the hours. It was made by Richard Roe of Epperstone in 1686 and is currently on loan to the British Horological Institute Museum at Upton.

✣ The clock on the tower of St Mary's Church at East leake was erected by public subscription to commemorate the Coronation of King George V.

Dedications

✣ The Church at Basford is one of only four in the whole country dedicated to St Leodegarius. He was a 7th century Bishop of Autun who became entangled in the politics of the Frankish court resulting in his martyrdom.

✣ The dual dedication of Blythe Church to St Mary and St Martin is unusual and has puzzled historians. Blythe Abbey was dedicated to St Mary but the dedication to Saint Martin is something of a mystery. Some believe that it was a dedication from an earlier church or from one of the now lost chapels. Others have suggested that this new dedication was made to mark the change in status of the church after the Reformation and the closure of the priory.

✣ Dual dedications to Saint Peter and Saint Paul as at Oxton, Gringley-on-the-Hill, Shelford and Mansfield are common throughout the country. According to tradition they were martyred on the same day in AD67. Saint Peter was crucified but Saint Paul, as a Roman citizen, received the privilege of being slain by the sword! They share the same feast day on 29 June each year.

✣ An unusual dedication is that to Saint Cyprian at Sneinton. Cyprian was born sometime in the early 3rd century in North Africa, possibly Carthage. This was part of the Roman Empire and Cyprian received a classical education. After conversion to Christianity he eventually became Bishop of Carthage and an important early Christian writer. During the reign of the Emperor Valerian I he refused to make sacrifice to pagan gods and was beheaded.

✣ Saint Mary is a popular dedication in Nottinghamshire with churches in a number of towns and villages being named after her. Saint Mary is described in the New Testament as the mother of Jesus and was the subject of particular veneration during the Middle Ages. The popularity of this saint declined after the Reformation.

✤ There are also a number of churches dedicated to Saint John the Baptist within the county at places such as Collingham, Colwick, Beeston, Gunthorpe and Stanford-on-Soar. According to the New Testament John went into the wilderness and began baptising his followers including Jesus himself in the River Jordan. He declared that people should repent because the kingdom of heaven was coming. He is best known for the manner of his death. Having been imprisoned by King Herod Antipas he was executed because of a trick. Salome had so delighted Herod by her dancing that he promised to grant her any wish. At the urging of her mother, she asked for the head of John the Baptist. This was promptly presented on a plate. The scene was painted a number of times by various renaissance artists.

Fonts

✤ The Norman font in All Saints Church, Lenton originally belonged to Lenton Priory and is widely regarded as one of the finest in the country. It is almost square in shape and measures 34in by 30in and stands 30in high. A riot of carvings on the four sides depict various scenes from the New Testament. On the North side is an elaborately decorated cross but this is decidedly plain compared with the rest of the font. On the East there are rows of cherubim and seraphim above the four evangelists and a central panel depicting the baptism of Christ by John. The holy spirit, in dove like form, is seen descending and the figure of Christ uplifts his hands in prayer. The south side shows the Crucifixion with a Roman soldier piercing Christ's side with his spear as the soul of the unrepentant thief is devoured by the jaws of a dragon. The West side is divided into four panels, the first of which represents the resurrection of Christ. A second panel provides a narrative of the Entombment and Resurrection. A brutal looking Roman soldier is seen putting on the coffin lid, beneath which lies the shrouded figure of Jesus. The risen Christ stands above with his hands raised in blessing. The third panel shows three women coming to the tomb bearing in their hands spices and ointments. The fourth panel provides a view of the Holy Sepulchre in Jerusalem.

✤ The font at Bramcote parish church (St Michael and All Angels) is a 13th-century stone bowl. Lined with lead it is considered to be one of the most notable Early English fonts in the country. It is decorated with a shallow arcading of pointed arches with a narrow trefoil design above.

✤ Holy Trinity Church at Ratcliffe on Trent has two fonts; one is modern, a gift from Kingston-on-Soar in 1936, but the other is contemporary with the building (late 12th century) and shows marks of the hinges and latches that were used to secure the original wooden cover.

✤ The lower part of the font in St Mary Magdalene Church at Newark dates from the 15th century and has two figures of saints carved into the niches on each side. During the Civil War the shaft was broken and the original bowl destroyed. After Restoration in 1660 the font was repaired at the expense of Nicholas Ridley, a local tailor.

✤ All Saints Church at West Markham contains an interesting Norman font with crudely carved figures under the arcades.

✤ The font at St Mary's Church, Lowdham is thought to be by masons working on the Chapter House at Southwell towards the end of the 13th century. It was unusual for the period in retaining shafts at the base. Instead of arcading the octagonal font, the masons produced a niche which had a richly decorated pediment with foliage.

✤ St Swithun's Church at Woodborough has a Norman tub-shaped font decorated with crosses at the top and bottom with zig-zags in between.

Windows and Glass

✤ The Beauvale Priory Window in the church of Greasley at St Michael contains two roundels of glass depicting St Agatha and St Lucy, said to be from Beauvale Priory and were previously in a window in Beauvale Manor Farm.

✤ Adam and Eve are depicted naked in a 14th-century window in St Michael's Church, Halam.

✤ One of the finest modern church windows in the county is at St Albans, Forest Town.

✤ The church of St Mary Magdalene at Hucknall contains one of the largest collections of windows by the famous artist C.E. Kemp.

✤ The diocesan window in Greasley parish church contains shields bearing the arms of the dioceses of York, Lincoln and Southwell, and roundels depicting the three minsters. The inscription reads: 'From ancient time Nottinghamshire with the Minster of Southwell was included in the Diocese of York. In 1837 the county and its churches were transferred to the Diocese of Lincoln. In 1884 the Diocese of Southwell was created'.

✤ A stained glass window celebrating the bicentenary of the Bramley apple was installed by Barley Studio at Southwell Minster in March 2009.

✤ A millennium window in the church of St Mary Magdalene at Keyworth depicts the four village churches (Anglican, Methodist, URC and Roman Catholic) with a symbol for the Baptists who do not have their own building.

✤ Another good example of modern stained glass is the baptistry window at St Leonard's Church, Wollaton. It was commissioned in 1972 in memory and thanksgiving for the lives of David and Dorothy Chambers. David Chambers was the Professor of Economic History at the University of Nottingham. Made by John Hardman Studios in Birmingham, the window is unusual in that the very thick glass was cut up on an anvil. The various shapes were then rearranged in the chosen design and set in resin.

Lecterns and Pulpits

❊ There is a rare early wooden pulpit dating from around 1400 in Holy Trinity Church, Wysall.

❊ The church of St John of Jerusalem at Winkburn has a rare three decker pulpit with carved panels.

❊ The eagle lectern in the Church of St John the Baptist at Beeston is a copy of one in Sandringham Church. It was donated by Mr C.F. Fellows at Christmas 1875.

❊ Holy Trinity Church at Wysall has the only pre-reformation pulpit in the county. Dating from around 1400 it was discarded when the church was restored in 1872–73 but reinstated in 1909. When cleaned it was found to have had painted figures on the panels but they could not be preserved.

❊ There is an unusual Georgian two decker pulpit and reading desk in Holy Trinity Church, Tythby.

❊ The pulpit in All Hallows at Gedling was made from 16th-century bench ends.

Monuments and memorials

❊ One of the earliest church monuments in the county is at St Andrew's Skegby. This dates from around 1300 and is the figure of a warden of Sherwood Forest carrying his horn. Alongside is his wife, robed in a wimple and gown.

❊ St Edmund's Church, Holme Pierrepont, contains a fine altar tomb to the memory of Sir Henry Pierrepony, Knight in 1615. He is depicted in armour and an attitude of prayer. On the sides of the tomb are a son, four daughters and an infant in swaddling clothes

❊ The tomb of John and Matildas Heiz can be found inside the parish church of St Lawrence in Gonalston.

❊ There is only one wooden mediaeval effigy in the county which is at St Michael's Church at Laxton and is of Adam Everingham's second wife. His first wife lies alongside him in stone.

❊ The Barton monument at Saint Giles church at Holme is in two tiers, with a rotting corpse below and two well-carved effigies above.

✤ At All Saints Church Annesley there is a monument to an unknown man dating from the 16th century. Carved from alabaster the figure is wrapped in a shroud and has been described as sombre and moving.

✤ At St Michael's Church at Averham there is a 14th-century effigy of a bearded man holding his heart in his hands.

Towers

✤ The tower of St Leodegarius Church at Basford collapsed in 1859 just before the church was due to reopen after repairs. A new tower was erected in the Early English style.

✤ The tower of St Bartholomew's Church, Kneesall, built around 1425, is decorated with animals and angels instead of gargoyles.

✤ The lantern tower at St Mary Magdalene, Keyworth, is unique in Nottinghamshire. It is thought that the lantern, occupying one of the highest points in the area may have provided a guide to travellers in mediaeval times.

✤ The spire of St Mary Magdalen at Newark is reputed to be the fifth tallest church spire in the country and is visible for many miles around.

✤ The tower of the church of St John the Evangelist at Carlton in Lindrick is one of the oldest in Nottinghamshire and dates from the 11th century.

✤ A small steeple was added to All Saints Church, Eaton, in 1992 at a cost of £12,000.

✤ The west tower of Saints Peter and Paul Church in Warsop is almost entirely Norman with only the top modified in the perpendicular style.

✤ Only the tower of the church at Bradmore remains after the rest of the church was burnt down in 1705. Later a room was attached to the tower and this continues to be used occasionally for services and social functions.

✤ On the west wall of the clock chamber in the tower of Calverton Parish church are nine Norman carvings illustrating the occupations of the seasons. They include a reaper, a man threshing, a man pruning a vine, a man hoeing and two men dancing with bladders on sticks. Another carving depicts a a man seated at a trestle table. With his hawk beside him, he drinks from a horn, a knife in his hand, with a flagon, a boars head and other foods on the table.

Curiosities

✤ The north and south walls of the bell ringing chamber of St Peter at West Drayton are covered with around 60 'cakes' or 'cheeses'; being large circles painted in red ochre on a black background with initials and dates commemorating weddings between 1777 and 1865.

✻ The bronze crucifix in St Mary's Church Edwinstowe was rescued from a shell hole in France during World War One.

✻ At St Mary Magdalen in Newark there are two 16th-century painted panels of the dance of death on the Markham Chantry. This is believed to be one of only two surviving in the whole of England.

✻ The splendid alabaster tomb of Sir Sampson de Strelley in Strelley Church includes the grisly depiction of a strangled Saracen which lies underneath Sir Sampson's head.

✻ Holy Trinity Church at Ratcliffe-on-Soar has an Edward VII Reformation 'Honest Table' which replaced the stone altar in 1550.

✻ Three small foreign stones are set into the chancel wall at St Patrick's Church, Nuthall. They were given by Mr George Turton following his travels in the Holy Land shortly after World War Two. Each is accompanied by a metal plaque and are labelled 'GETHSEMANE', 'MARS HILL, ATHENS' and 'BETHLEHEM'.

✻ In All Saint's Church, Huthwaite there is a panel to a miner. The inscription reads 'This church was built with stone taken from the deep hard seam of the New Hucknall Colliery and this panel was placed here to the Glory of God by miners and their families to commemorate those who laboured there from 1876 to 1982'.

✻ The church of St Michael and All Angels at Averham had a father and son who held the rectory between them for nearly 90 years.

✻ A kissing stone blessed by Pope Innocent IV (1243–54) is embedded in the fabric of the porch At St Leodegarius Church, Basford. Only 3.5in square, it was passed around the congregation during Mass in the pre-reformation period. It was rediscovered in 1859.

✻ A parish map hangs at the back of the North aisle at Edwinstowe, St Mary. It is a piece of embroidery patchwork and tapestry and was completed in 1996 after four years of work by members of the community.

✻ The late mediaeval choir stalls in St Stephen's Church, Sneinton contain a number of misericords which, when raised, reveal carved figures of:
    a monkey holding a begging cup
    a rat riding a hound and blowing a hunting horn

a goat licking its back
a 'green man'
a lion
a unicorn
a cat with a rat in its mouth
a human head with curled beard and hair

✢ The Wollaton antiphon is a hand written and vividly illustrated book of services. It was given to St Leonard's Church at Wollaton around 1460 but had been produced some years earlier for another (at present unknown) church. Following the Reformation it was kept in the library at Wollaton hall. It remained there for four centuries until it was returned to the Church in 1925. It remained on display for a number of years but is now kept securely by the University of Nottingham Department of Manuscripts and Special Collections. It is only one of about 20 such books still in existence and is thus both very rare and valuable.

✢ At the end of the 18th century the Archdeacon of Nottingham, Sir Richard Kaye, employed a water-colour painter named Samuel Hieronymus to make drawings of several churches. His drawing of St Oswald's Church at Dunham-on-Trent survives in the British Museum.

Country Houses in Nottinghamshire

✳ **Bestwood Lodge** was once a royal residence much used for hunting. Various monarchs stayed here and by the 16th century the Lodge was a substantial building of wood and plaster, covered with slate and tiles and containing 38 rooms. The present Bestwood Lodge was built for the 10th Duke of St Albans in 1862–65. The architect, Samuel Sanders Teulon, has been described by Pevsner as 'one of the most ruthless, insensitive, and original of the High Victorians'. The house was constructed in the Gothic style and was built in brick with stone facings. The Lodge lacked symmetry but it is said that the Prince of Wales was so inspired by the plans of Bestwood that he decided to employ Teulon at Sandringham. The most striking feature of the building was the central hall with its first-floor arcaded galleries. This was top-lit by a lofty octagonal lantern decorated with carvings by Thomas Earp of Robin Hood and his Merrie Men. The Duke was a friend of the Prince of Wales (later Edward VII), who visited Bestwood both for formal events, such as the opening of Nottingham Castle Museum in 1878, and informally on other occasions. His younger brother, Prince Leopold stayed at the Lodge when he opened the University College at Nottingham in 1881. In the latter years of the 19th century the Duke also built the conservatory to the west of the house, a wing which was later extended to provide a half-timbered ballroom with additional bedrooms above, and an orangery beyond. The conservatory was later converted into a drill hall. A disastrous fire occurred in 1893. It was discovered by George Fisher, the estate carpenter, who found the drawing room in flames. Before the fire brigade arrived men and horses were summoned from working on the estate. The loyal tenants and workmen gathered quickly to form a human chain of water buckets and succeeded in controlling the flames. Unfortunately, many of the house's treasures were destroyed as well as a number of valuable paintings. In the early years of the 20th century the lodge was leased to Sir Frank Bowden, the founder of the Raleigh Cycle Company. It eventually ceased to be a private home and was taken over by the army during World War Two. It remained Ministry of Defence property until the mid-1970s when it was converted into the Best Western Bestwood Lodge Hotel.

✳ **Colwick Hall** stands on a site which has been occupied since Saxon times. On the death of William de Colwick in 1362 it passed to the Byron family who held it until 1660 when it came into the possession of the Musters. The present house was constructed for John Musters in 1776. It was built by Samuel Stretton from Nottingham to designs provided by John Carr of York. This new building was built in the Palladian style and comprised an elegant centre, crowned by a pediment, resting on four Ionic pillars. To either side were lofty single storey wings. Inside the house the entrance hall was symmetrically designed with four Spanish mahogany doors and an ornamental fireplace with detailed wood and gold plated cornice work. Similar decoration was evident in other parts of the house and a later visitor praised the moulded architraves, elegant staircase and wonderful fireplaces crafted in multi-coloured marble. Terrible damage was done to the Hall by the Reform Bill rioters from Nottingham in 1831. Mary Chaworth Musters and her daughter had to hide in the shrubberies while the Hall was looted and partially set on fire. She died a few months later from shock. In 1896 the Hall was sold to the Nottingham Racecourse Company and became a public house, part of which was used to accommodate grooms and jockeys. Nottingham Corporation acquired the Hall from the Racecourse Company in 1965. It fell into disrepair but it was restored a few years ago and is now a luxury hotel.

✤ **Holme Pierrepont Hall** is one of the earliest brick buildings in the county. It was built around 1500 by Sir William Pierrepont on the site of an earlier house. The family prospered during the Tudor period and the house was further enlarged and improved. Fine new gardens were laid out in accordance with the fashion of the time. Queen Anne, the wife of James I, stayed here on her journey from Scotland to London and was lavishly entertained by Sir Henry Pierrepont. John Evelyn, the diarist, in 1664 described the Hall as 'a noble place' and in 1724 Sir Thomas Parkyns said the Hall could be seen from High pavement in Nottingham. The family rose to be Duke of Kingston in the 18th century and by this time their principal seat was Thorsby hall in North Nottinghamshire. As a consequence Holme Pierrepont Hall was reduced in size. Charles Meadows revived the estate when he inherited it and was created Earl Manvers. Extensive building work took

Holme Pierrepont Hall.

place in the 1870s. The present north wing, the arcade around the courtyard and the elegant courtyard garden were all created around this time. In the 20th century the house was virtually abandoned between the wars but in 1969 it was purchased by the present owners to prevent the property from leaving the family. Since then they have carefully and sensitively restored the house and grounds. The stucco has been stripped from the exterior, the rooms a have been refurbished and the courtyard garden has been restored. Today the Hall is open to the public for a few days in February and March each year. The house is also a luxury function venue available for weddings and corporate events and is also used for filming and photo shoots.

❋ **Kelham Hall** was originally built in 1730 in the Palladian style. This was largely destroyed by fire in 1857, leaving only the Jacobean-style service wing. It was rebuilt for John Manvers Sutton (MP for Newark) by the architect, George Gilbert Scott, who was also responsible for the Albert Hall and St Pancreas Station in London. The overall design has been criticised. Gilbert Scott was primarily a church architect and restorer and the exterior was loaded with an indiscriminate variety of features. Unfortunately John Manvers Scott could not afford to complete the building of the hall and in 1898 the mortgage was foreclosed and the estate closed. The Hall was sold to the Society of the Sacred Mission and housed the monastic order for the next 70 years. During the 1920s the Great Chapel was constructed (now known as the Dome). The main accommodation buildings at the front of the Hall were completed in 1939 to accommodate the monks and theological students. Its first occupants, however, were a garrison of the 'Blues' cavalry and also Texas and Oklahoma oil men who were involved in drilling for oil at the nearby Eakring oilfield. Since 1974 the Hall has been the Head Office of the Newark and Sherwood District Council. Public tours of Kelham Hall are available from Monday to Friday.

❋ **Newstead Abbey** was originally an Augustinian priory founded during the reign of Henry II. After the dissolution of the monasteries by Henry VIII Newstead was sold to Sir John Byron for £810. He converted the buildings into a country house. The body of the church was demolished and the prior's lodging and great hall were converted to his own use. The refectory became the great chamber (later salon) and the monk's dormitory was split up into separate rooms. Sir John's descendents seem to have made few improvements to the building, being frequently burdened with debt, although some of the upstairs apartments probably date from the Stuart period. The fifth Lord Byron, known as 'the wicked lord' allowed the house to fall into ruin and when he died only one corner of the south-east wing was habitable. The sixth Lord Byron, George Gordon, the poet, succeeded to the estate in 1788. He spent little time at Newstead and eventually sold it in 1817 to Colonel Thomas Wildman, an old school friend. Wildman began a programme of extensive restoration and improvement including the construction of the Sussex Tower at the southern end of the west front. He also carried out extensive work to the grounds. When Colonel Wildman died in 1859, the Abbey was bought by William Webb, an African explorer and friend of Dr Livingstone. Improvements to the building continued and after Webb died in 1899 Newstead passed through successive generations of his family until it was purchased by Sir Julian Cahn, a Nottingham businessman, who presented it to the City of Nottingham in 1931. Today there is much to see and do at Newstead Abbey. All year round visitors can enjoy its stunning grounds. Covering 300 acres the gardens and park feature paths that meander past lakes, ponds and waterfalls. From April to September visitors may also explore the historic house with its mediaeval cloisters, splendid Victorian room settings and even the private apartments of Byron; complete with his personal belongings and the table at which he wrote his poetry.

✤ **Rufford Abbey** was originally a Cistercian monastery founded during the 12th century. Following the dissolution, the buildings were granted to George Talbot, fourth Earl of Shrewsbury, in exchange for estates in Ireland and in consideration of the prompt measures he had adopted to suppress the rebellion in the north, known as the Pilgrimage of Grace. Neither George Talbot nor his son ever lived at Rufford though it may have been used as a hunting lodge. The transformation of the abbey into a country house was really begun by the sixth Earl. His successors also made changes to the house. The seventh Earl, Gilbert Talbot added projecting wings onto the north and south ends of the lay brothers wing of the old abbey, forming some of the country house we still see today. The most impressive room was, however, the Great Hall which was used by Gilbert to entertain James I when he came hunting in Sherwood Forest. In the 17th century the Rufford estates passed to the Savile family who lived here for several generations. In 1633 the then Sir George Savile was raised to the peerage as Viscount Halifax. He carried out further substantial work on the house. In 1660 he constructed the stable block and in 1680 he pulled down what remained of the old monastery and built a new north wing with large reception rooms and a splendid long gallery on the former site of the Abbey Church entrance. The east front was also redesigned. In the 19th century Anthony Salvin, the eminent Victorian architect, was employed to undertake a thorough redesign of the house. His work undertaken at this time included the construction of a Tudor-style entrance porch, steps and balustrade, a clock tower and bell cupola on the south front. A coach house, brew-house and water tower were also built. Shooting parties were regularly held at Rufford during this period and King Edward VII was a frequent visitor. Rufford suffered a steady decline during the first half of the 20th century. In 1938 the estate was broken up and sold. The abbey buildings were mostly demolished in 1956 and the restored ruins and grounds now form the nucleus of Rufford Country Park, owned by Nottinghamshire County Council. Entry to the park, gardens and Abbey is free with just a small seasonal charge for car parking. It is open every day except Christmas day.

✤ **Thoresby Hall** The first Thoresby Hall was remodelled in 1685–87 from a hall built during the reign of Charles I. It was burnt down in 1745 when 'nothing was saved from the ravages of that fire but the writings, plate and some little of the best furniture'. As second hall, designed by John Carr, constructed in red brick with a stone basement and a central feature of four Ionic columns was a more modest affair. The traveller and diarist John Byng compared it with one in St James' Square and in 1772 the grounds gave Horace Walpole 'no temptation to stop'. The present hall was built for the third Earl Manners by Thomas Salvin in the Victorian neo-Tudor style. The frontage was basically E shaped with projecting entry porch and wings, and the overall appearance was that of an Elizabethan mansion. Pevsner compares the central tower with that at Burghley House. The house was open to the public when Earl Manners was not in residence. One visitor was dazzled by the magnificence of the house and described satin-covered walls, tapestry curtains, statuary mantle pieces and gilded ceilings. The same visitor noticed family portraits, ornamental timepieces, fine specimens of Sevres china and a massive vase which had been presented to Lady Manners by the Empress Eugenic in 1854. One of the most remarkable rooms was the Earl's library which contained a spectacular wooden fireplace incorporating carved scenes of Sherwood Forest and beautifully fashioned figures of Robin Hood and Little John. The house contained over 200 bedrooms some of which had substantial dressing rooms attached. The house was provided with a range of workshops and its own gasworks. In the 20th century the house was threatened by subsidence caused by coal mining. The buildings were sold in 1989 to the NCB and after passing through a number of hands it was bought by the Warner Leisure Group. It reopened in 2000 as a 200-room country house hotel.

⁜ **Thrumpton Hall** The original Thrumpton Hall was owned by the Powdrill family who lost their estates as a consequence of their involvement in the Gunpowder plot. Henry Garton, one of the conspirators is said to have hidden in the priest hole there. The present house, a Jacobean mansion constructed in brick and stone, was built between 1609 and 1616 by Gervase Pigot from Weston-on-Trent in Derbyshire. The house was built on an H plan typical of this period and it is thought that the hall may have occupied the whole of the cross wing, now divided into hall and library. Further work was carried out by Gervase Pigot II including external decoration and the installation of a new staircase. Designed by John Webb, a leading architect of the time, it was constructed on the cantilever principle from five different woods all grown on the estate. It was this same Gervase Pigot, High Sheriff of Nottinghamshire in 1669, who encouraged his friend Dr Robert Thoroton, to write the first history of Nottinghamshire. Over the years various minor changes and improvements were made to the house. Further outbuildings and a turreted gatehouse were added around 1830. Today the hall remains in private ownership but is open, by appointment, for visits throughout the year. The Hall may also be hired for weddings and corporate function.

⁜ **Welbeck Abbey** was originally a Premonstratensian house founded in the 12th century though little of the original structure survives. At the dissolution the building passed into private hands and after several changes into those of Sir Charles Cavendish, son of Bess of Hardwick, who leased it in 1597 and bought it outright 10 years later. Members of the Cavendish family converted it into a country house and added a riding house in the 17th century to a design of Robert Smythson.

The house later passed to the Dukes of Portland and the fifth Duke undertook substantial building work. New buildings included a riding school, hothouses and a number of neo-Tudor lodges. Much modernisation took place with the installation of modern plumbing, gas lighting and railway lines to carry food from the kitchens to the Gothic Hall and the dining room. Impressive sunken chambers were constructed including library rooms, a ballroom and a chapel. His successor, the sixth Duke abandoned the plans for a sunken hall and the foundations were converted into a sunken Italianate garden. Further work was undertaken during the 19th century and the house became a centre of Victorian and Edwardian upper class society. The Oxford Wing which contained some of the oldest parts of the building was destroyed by fire in 1900 although most of the contents were saved. The wing had been rebuilt to the design of Ernest George by 1905. After World War Two Welbeck was leased to the Ministry of Defence and was used as an army training college, Welbeck College, until 2005.

✣ **Wollaton Hall** has been described as the most Elizabethan house in the county and one of the most important in England. It was built by Sir Francis Willoughby between 1580 and 1588. He was a wealthy and powerful individual who had made a fortune from the coal mines which he owned in the area. The Ancaster stone which was used to build the house was exchanged for coal from his estates. Despite this the total cost of building the Hall was £8,000. He employed as his architect Robert Smythson who was also responsible for Longleat and Wardour House in

Wollaton Hall.

Wiltshire. Wollaton is distinguished from earlier Elizabethan houses by its spectacular all round symmetry and raised central hall with turreted prospect room above. The ground plan is basically one of a rectangle with four, almost free standing towers in each corner. Smythson's inspiration for this seems to have come from du Cerceau's Premier Livre of 1559, a popular architectural source book of the period and known to have been in Willoughby's library. After completing the house, Smythson remained at Wollaton as agent to the estate, while also designing other major houses including Worksop Manor and Hardwick Hall (in Derbyshire). On his monument in Wollaton Church he is described as 'Architector and Surveyor unto the most worthy house of Wollaton divers others of great account'. The Willoughby's continued to live at Wollaton for several generations. Sir Percival and Lady Bridget Willoughby hosted two royal visits; Queen Ann and Henry Prince of Wales in 1603 and the future King Charles I the following year. Thomas Middleton was created first Baron Middleton in 1712. Later in the 18th century the fifth Lord Middleton chose to live on his wife's estate, Birdsall in Yorkshire, and Wollaton became only a secondary residence for the family. Some modernisation of Wollaton Hall was carried out during the early years of the 19th century and it was at this time that the camellia house in the garden was constructed. Wollaton Hall was sold to Nottingham Corporation in 1926. Part of the estate was developed for housing and a third of the park was turned into a golf course. The house became the city's Natural History museum. Today the house and grounds are open to the public.

Industrial Archaeology

Industrial Archaeology is the study and recording of the remains of industry including mills, mines, railways, factories and machines. Nottinghamshire has a particularly rich industrial heritage dating back to the middle ages. Mining, textiles and brewing were important for many years and by the end of the 19th century they had been joined by tobacco, pharmaceuticals and cycles with Players, Boots and Raleigh becoming internationally known brands. Transport has also been important and the county still has important relics of turnpike roads, canals and railways.

Power

✻ Water power was used to power corn mills from at least the Saxon period and several mills are mentioned in the *Domesday Book*. Later, water power was used in the textile industry in fulling mills and other processes. Despite this, when Richard Arkwright constructed a prototype cotton mill in Nottingham in 1769 he used horses to power his machinery. Later Arkwright and others built a number of water powered cotton mills in the county. A number of windmills also exist in Nottinghamshire. From the 14th to the 18th centuries these were used to grind corn. A number of windmills, watermills and water powered textile stills, still exist in Nottinghamshire. In the 20th century a number of power stations were constructed in Nottinghamshire on the banks of the Trent. A number of water and wind mills as well as power stations can be seen throughout the county. Some of the best examples include:

Green's Mill at Sneinton was built in 1807. It was restored to full working order and attracts around 40,000 visitors each year. Ollerton Corn Mill is a well preserved 18th-century water mill. It remains in working order and, until recently, it ground barley and oats for local farmers. Ratcliffe on Soar power station is one of a number of power stations along the banks of the River Trent which may be viewed from the outside.

Green's Mill, Sneinton.

Brewing

✤ Brewing in Nottinghamshire dates back to the mediaeval period. An important ingredient of beer is malt, which is grain that has been encouraged to germinate under controlled conditions. This process was carried out in malting, where the barley was germinated on the floor before being transferred to kilns for drying. Large numbers of these malting were established in various parts of the county including Nottingham, Newark, Mansfield Retford and Worksop. The first commercial breweries in Nottinghamshire were established in the 18th century and some of the best known included Mansfield Brewery, Hardy's & Hansons at Kimberley and Shipstones and Home Brewery in Nottingham. At Newark, Warwick's & Richardson's, James Hole & Co. and the Trent Brewery were among the most successful. Mergers and takeovers in the 20th century have seen a decline and virtual disappearance of brewing in Nottinghamshire. Relics of this once important industry can be found in maltings, brewery buildings and traditional public houses throughout the county. Museums too tell the story of a number of local breweries. The following are worth seeing:

Hardy Hansons Brewery at Kimberley is a traditional 19th-century brewery which only ceased production a few years ago.

The Millgate Museum at Newark contains a reconstruction of a typical 19th-century working-class pub as well as information about brewing and malting.

Historic public houses such as the Old Trip to Jerusalem at Nottingham and the Saracens Head at Southwell.

A number of old malt houses in Newark.

Textiles

✤ Nottinghamshire's involvement in the textile industry dates back to the Middle Ages when both Nottingham and Newark were important centres of the wool trade. Later, Richard Hargreaves the inventor of the spinning jenny opened a cotton mill in the town and in 1769 Richard Arkwright constructed a prototype cotton spinning mill in Nottingham powered by horses. Later water powered cotton mills were built on rivers and streams throughout the county. The knitting frame was invented in 1589 by William Lee from Calverton and by the 18th century Nottinghamshire was one of the most important centres for framework knitting in the whole

Stocking Frame at the Framework Knitters Museum at Ruddington.

country. The Lace Industry was also important in Nottinghamshire and Nottingham Lace became famous throughout the world. In Nottingham the Lace Market was the commercial, rather than the manufacturing centre of the lace industry, although finishing was carried out in the extensively fenestrated attics of the warehouses.

✴ Important sites relating to the textile industry in Nottinghamshire include the following:

The Anglo-Scotian Mills at Beeston. These large crenellated mills have recently been converted into apartments.

Other cotton mills may be seen in various parts of the county, including Lowdham.

The Lace Market area in Nottingham contains a number of historically significant buildings, many of which have since been converted into offices and university buildings. Perhaps the most impressive is the Adams Building on Stoney Street.

Framework knitters cottages exist in a number of Nottinghamshire villages but particularly at Calverton, Sutton Bonington and Ruddington where there is also a Framework Knitters Museum.

Coal Mining

✴ Coal has been mined in Nottinghamshire for many hundreds of years and there is documentary evidence of coal mining at Cossal and Selston towards the end of the 13th century. By the 16th century the Willoughby and Strelley families were engaged in coal mining in the Wollaton area and Sir Francis Willoughby built Wollaton Hall out of his coal profits. The industry continued to grow and develop and by 1774 a total of 14 collieries were listed in the county near to

places such as Wollaton, Bilborough, Nuthall, Teversall and Eastwood. The development of canals and later railways further stimulated the coal mining industry. Eastwood, which lay on the junction of the Erewash, Cromford and Nottingham canals, became an important mining town during this period. Local mine owners Thomas Walker and Thomas Barber formed Barber, Walker and Co. Ltd and by the end of the 19th century were operating mines at Beggarlee, Bilborough, Hucknall, Moorgreen, Newthorpe, Selston, Strelley,

Brinsley Headstocks.

Underwood and Watnall. Other coal masters such as Thomas North developed mines in the Basford area. He built houses for his workers near the Cinderhill Colliery, one of four which he owned. Coal production within the county increased dramatically in the later years of the 19th century, reaching over 11 million tons per year by 1910. Mining continued to be an important until the second half of the 20th century, but today there are no deep mines remaining in the county. Remains of the coal mining industry can be seen at many places throughout the county including:

Bestwood Colliery Winding Engine. The pit here was sunk in 1872 and the winding engine was commissioned in 1876. When the colliery closed in 1971 the site was transformed into a country park with the engine house and pithead gear a solitary reminder of the once vibrant works. The engine house contains Britain's sole surviving example of a two cylinder vertical winding engine.

The offices of the Barber Walker Company at Eastwood are now the Durban House Heritage Centre which houses an exhibition devoted to the life and times of D.H. Lawrence.

Brinsley headstocks are an interesting example of wooden headstocks reinstalled at their original site.

The restored horse gin and capstan in use at Pinxton Green Colliery is now at Nottingham Industrial Museum at Wollaton Hall.

Tobacco

✤ The tobacco industry was dispersed throughout Britain in the 18th and 19th centuries and there were tobacco factories in Nottingham. The transformation of the industry was, however, led by John Player. Realising that there was a market for ready rolled cigarettes, he bought an existing tobacco factory in Broad Marsh in 1877 for their manufacture. The business grew rapidly and in 1884 the Castle Factory at Radford was opened. John Player died in the same year but the business continued to grow under the direction of his two sons. By the end of the century Players had become one of the largest employers in the East Midlands. Marketing was an important factor in this growth and the then familiar 'sailor' trademark and the introduction of cigarette cards both contributed to this growth in business. The company also realised the danger of foreign competition (particularly from the USA) and Players were one of the founder members of the Imperial Tobacco Company, formed in 1901. A new manufacturing centre (the Horizon factory) was opened in the early 1970s on the outskirts of the city. Increased foreign competition and changes in smoking habits were, however, already having an impact on the tobacco industry. During the 1980s Players closed down a number of their factories in Radford, concentrating production in other parts of the country, and one of their largest factories, on Radford Boulevard, has since been demolished to make way for a new shopping complex. Little remains of Nottinghamshire's tobacco industry but the relatively modern Horizon Factory is still an important feature of the industrial landscape.

Pharmaceuticals

✣ Boots has its roots in the mid-19th century when John Boot opened a small herbalist store on Goose Gate in 1849 from which he prepared and sold herbal remedies. After his death his widow Mary continued trading with the assistance of her son, Jesse, who became a full partner when he was 21. The store continued to flourish and in 1877 Jesse took sole control. He soon expanded the range of products sold to include proprietary medicines and household necessities. Turnover increased rapidly, allowing him to move into larger premises in Goose Gate in 1881. Jesse had ambitions for Boots to be a nationwide chain and his store network grew rapidly. By 1914 there were over 500 stores nationwide. The range of products sold also expanded beyond the traditional chemist's lines and the growing retail side of the business was matched by a growth in the manufacturing of Boots own brand products and research into new pharmaceuticals and chemicals. Sites on Island Street and Station Street In Nottingham, housed the company's growing factories, warehouses, laboratories and offices. The company continued to grow and develop throughout the 20th century. A new manufacturing site was acquired in Beeston and in 1933 the 1,000 Boots store was opened. Research continued to be important, and the company developed a new drug, Ibuprofen, in the 1960s. Today the company is part of an international enterprise and its importance as an employer in the area has much declined. A number of sites associated with the Boots empire may still be seen in the county. These include:

The original store opened by John Boot at No. 6 Goose Gate.

The first large store opened by Jesse Boot is also on Goose Gate. It opened in 1884 and continued trading as a chemist until 1967. The exterior of the building with its original decorative ironwork has been carefully restored.

The most impressive previous store in the city stands on the corner of High Street and Pelham Street. This startling building designed by A.N. Bromley has a beautifully decorated exterior and a miniature clock tower.

A number of modern manufacturing sites including the D10 'Wets' building and the D6 'Drys' building, both designed by Sir Own Williams in the 1930s.

Bicycle Manufacture

✣ Bicycle manufacture started in Nottinghamshire in 1860 when William Campion, a hosier, began making bicycles as a sideline. One of his employees, Thomas Humber started his own company in Stretton Street. In 1875 he opened a new factory in Queens Road near the Midland Station from where he manufactured a range of tricycles with chain transmission, direct steering and wire-spoke wheels. A few years later the company opened another factory in Beeston. The business flourished and expanded into motor manufacturing but in 1908 the company moved to Coventry where it had another factory. The best known cycle company in Nottinghamshire, and perhaps the world was founded in 1887 when Frank Bowden took over a small cycle workshop in Raleigh Street. He renamed the company Raleigh Cycles and was successful in rapidly expanding the business and increasing production. In 1896 the company moved to Radford Boulevard, a site which eventually expanded to over 30 acres, encompassing assembly line factories, warehouses, offices and recreational facilities. By the 1930s Raleigh was also manufacturing motorcycles and even a small three-wheeler car. This diversification was short lived, however, and by 1938 the company had divested itself of all but cycle production which had reached around 500,000 units a year by this time. The company continued to expand and in 1957 an enormous new site was opened on Lenton Boulevard. By this time the company was employing around 7,000 people in the largest and most modern cycle plants in the world. The company was hit badly by increasing foreign competition and the economic downturn of the 1980s and the company was obliged to close down part of their premises in Lenton, including their office block on Lenton Boulevard. Despite attempts to retain production in the UK, Raleigh's Triumph Road factory finally closed in November 2002 after the company decided to switch production to Vietnam, Sri Lanka and Thailand. Little remains of Nottinghamshire's cycle and motor-cycle industries but a number of machines built by various firms in Nottingham can be seen at the Industrial museum at Wollaton Hall.

Roads

✤ Turnpike roads began to be constructed in Nottinghamshire in the 18th century. These were roads which were constructed or improved by a Turnpike Trust. In return they were allowed to charge a toll to all those who used the road. Gates were erected and toll houses were built for the toll-keeper and his family. Evidence of these roads remains in the form of coaching inns, toll houses and bridges. These include:

The Saracen's Head at Southwell.

The toll house at Littleborough.

An early stagecoach can also be seen at Nottingham Industrial Museum at Wollaton Hall along with other early horse-drawn vehicles.

Canals

✤ The first canal to be built in the county was the Chesterfield Canal which ran through Nottinghamshire from Worksop to West Stockwith and was completed in 1777. Colliery owners, keen to transport their coal cheaply and easily to the Trent, promoted the Erewash Canal which opened in 1779 and ran from Langley Mill to Trent Lock near Long Eaton. Others followed over the next 20 years including the Beeston Canal, the Nottingham Canal and the Grantham Canal. For over one century they transported a whole range of goods including coal, pottery, corn, beer and lead. A number of canals are still used for leisure cruising. The River Trent continues to be used as a commercial waterway and warehouses and wharves can still be seen in places such as Nottingham and Newark. Much interesting canal architecture still exists and locks, tunnels, bridges and aqueducts are still in regular use by leisure cruisers. Canal-side taverns now attract holidaymakers rather than boatmen and some lock keepers cottages are now much sought after family homes. Particularly interesting buildings and structures include:

The lock and lock cottage at Trent Lock

Stretches of the Chesterfield Canal at places such as Worksop, Retford and Misterson. (Including locks, bridges and associated buildings)

The Fellows, Morton and Clayton offices (now a pub) and the 1895 warehouse in Nottingham

The Worksop depository on the Chesterfield Canal; built in the early 1800s and used by Pickfords.

Railways

✤ The first railways in Nottinghamshire were horse drawn tramways which were used to transport coal and other goods to the canal. Following the success of the Liverpool-Manchester Railway in 1830 'railway mania' swept the country and a number of railway companies constructed lines in Nottinghamshire. It was at the Sun Inn at Eastwood in 1832 that a meeting was held to discuss the construction of the Midland Counties Railway linking Derby and Leicester with Nottingham. The line opened in 1839 and only a few years later the Midland Counties Railway merged with two others to form the Midland Railway. Before long two other companies, the Great Central Railway and the Great Northern Railway both built lines through Nottinghamshire. Railways remained important until the middle of the 20th century. In the Victorian era

Nottingham Railway Station.

they transformed the lives of millions of people. Cheap travel enabled ordinary people to take day trips and later holidays to the seaside. Later they allowed the newly emerging middle class to commute to work from the suburbs. As in the rest of the country, the railways brought change and benefits such as national newspapers, standard time and fresh food from the countryside. In 1923 the Midland Railway merged with the London and North Western Railway to become the London Midland and Scottish (LMS) while the Great Northern and the Great Central joined together to become the London and North Eastern Railway (LNER). Both were subsumed into British Railways following nationalisation in 1948. A number of branch lines and railway stations were closed in the 1960s but much remains from the 19th century. The number of sites (many still open and in regular use) are too numerous to list but the most interesting and significant include the following:

Worksop Station is an attractive and elegant building, built in grey Steetley stone in what Pevsner describes as a Derbyshire-Yorkshire Jacobean style. It was opened in 1850.

Newark Castle Station is a small building of Italianate design which was opened in 1846. It remains in regular use today.

The Kings Mill Viaduct is the oldest in the county and was built in 1817 to carry the tramroad of the horse-drawn Pinxton and Mansfield Railway.

The Bennerley Viaduct is one of the longest cast-iron viaducts in the country. It was built in 1876–77 to carry the Great Northern line from Nottingham to Derby across the Erewash Valley at Awsworth.

The Redhill Tunnel is in effect two tunnels constructed side by side. The earlier west tunnel was built for the Midland Counties Railway in 1839. The later east tunnel was constructed in 1893 to allow for the widening of the Midland line to Leicester. Both tunnels have impressive castle style entrances of stone at the north end with castellated parapets and flanked by octagonal turrets.

Industrial Museums

✤ Nottingham Industrial Museum at Wollaton Hall contains a wide range of exhibits relating to a number of local industries including coal mining, textiles, engineering and bicycle manufacture.

✤ Ruddington Framework Knitters Museum contains a large number of stocking frames and other early hosiery machinery.

✤ Ruddington Transport Heritage Centre is home to a number of interesting exhibits including locomotives, rolling stock, and motor buses. Special events are held from time to time at which a wide range of motor vehicles are displayed.

✤ Mansfield Museum contains a number of exhibits relating to local industries including coal mining, quarrying, brewing and transport.

✣ Calverton Folk Museum is a small museum housed in four rooms of an 18th-century framework knitters cottage. Exhibits relate to the stocking industry, including a framework knitting machine and a display illustrating the history of framework knitting.

✣ The Millgate Museum, housed in a former warehouse at Newark, contains displays relating to a number of local industries including brewing, printing and the manufacture of agricultural machinery.

Directories, Diaries, Journals and Gazetteers

An anonymous mediaeval writer, possibly a monk from Lenton abbey wrote:
I cannot without lie or shame
Commend the town of Nottingham
The people and the fuel stink
The place is sordid as a sink

Other descriptions of the county include the following:

John Leyland (1540)

Nottingham is booth a large Town and well builded for timber and plaster and styandeth stately on a ...Hille. The market place and street both for the building on the side, for the very great wideness of the street, and the clean paving of it is the most fairest without exception of all England. There be three parish churches; but the Church of St Mary is excellent, new and uniform in work and so many fair windows set in it...Southwards as to the waterside be great cliffs and rocks of stones that be large and very good to build with, and many houses set on the tops of them; and at the bottom of them be great caves where many stones hath been digged out for buildings in the town, and these caves be partly for cellars and store houses...The little river of Leen and the great stream of Trente come near together in the meadow on the south side of the town ; and when any waters come down, much of the vale and meadows there be over flowen.

John Ogilby (*c*.1680)

Nottingham

Nottingham is a very ancient borough town by prescription, and county incorporated by charter, under a Mayor, Recorder, 6 Aldermen, a Sheriff, a Chamberlain, 2 Coroners, a Senior Council of 18 persons, including the Coroners, a Junior Council of 6 persons (who are called the Clothing, and whose number is uncertain), and about 1200 common burgesses. The said Corporation and county is represented in Parliament and in ye town ye assizes for ye county and the common gaole are kept. It is very agreably situate, plentifuly supplied with wood-firing from Shire Wood, near it with good pit coaln from mines not far off, with fish from its Trent and in fine ...with all the conveniences of life. Its chief trade is in weaving hose and it has 3 neat parish churches, 3 markest weekly... and 4 fairs...The market place is very commodious, and ye castle was formerly very strong.

Celia Feinnes (1695)

Newark

Newark is a very neate stone built town the market place is very large and look'd fine, just by it is the Great Church which is ;large and with a very high Spire, there is prayers twice a day in it; there remains the holes in the Church walls that the bullets made which were shot intxo the town in the siege laid to it by the Parliament army in the Civil Wars; the Castle was then demolish'd so that only the ruinated walls remaine which is washed by a very pretty river.

Nottingham

The town of Nottingham is the neatest town I have seen, built of stone and delicate large and long streets much like London and the houses lofty and well built, the Market place is very broad – out of which runs 2 very large streets much like Holborn but the buildings finer and there is a Pyaza all along one side of one of the Streetes, with stone pillars for walking that runs the length of the Streete, which is a mile long; all the streets are of good size all about the town and well pitched.

They make brick and tile by the town; the manufacture of the town mostly consists in Weaving of Stockings, which is a very ingenious art; there was a man that spun Glass and made severall things in Glass birds and beasts, I spun some of the glass and saw him make a Swan presently, with divers coulloured glass he makes Buttons which are very string and will not breake; Nottingham is famous for good ale so for Cellars they are all dug out of the rocks and so are very coole, att the Crown inn is a cellar of 60 steppes down all in the Rock like arch worke over your head, in the Cellar I drank good ale; we were very well entertained and very reasonably at the Blackamore Head.

Daniel Defoe (1726)

Nottingham

Nottingham is one of the most pleasant and beautiful towns in England.

Nottingham, notwithstanding the navigation of the Trent, is not esteemed a town of very great trade, other than is usual to inland towns; the chief manufacture carried on here is framework-knitting for stockings, the same as at Leicester, and some glass and earthen-warehouses; the latter much increased since the increase of tea-drinking; for the making of fine stone-mugs, tea-pots, cups &c. The glass houses, I think are of late rather decayed. As there is a fine market place, so is there a very good market, with a vast plenty of provisions, and those of the best sort, few towns in England exceeding it; to say nothing of their ale, as having reserved it to a place by itself. As they brew a very good liquor here, so they make the best malt, and the most of it in any town in this part of England, which they drive a great trade for, sending it by land carriage to Derby, through all the Peak as far as Manchester, and to other towns in Lancashire, Cheshire, and even into Yorkshire itself.

Southwell

Southwell in the county of Nottingham is about nine miles north east from Nottingham, four miles west from Newark, eight south east of Mansfield and about two south west from the River Trent. The soil of it is rich clay and marle; the air very good and well-watered; the River Greet runs by it. It is a market town and the market day Saturday; it is remarkable for no sort of manufacture.

Mansfield

Hence crossing the forest I came to Mansfield, a market town without any remarkables.

Carl Phillip Moritz (1782)
Nottingham

Of all the towns I have seen outside London, Nottingham is the loveliest and the neatest. Everything had a modern look, and a large space in the centre was hardly less handsome than a London square. A charming footpath leads over the fields to the highway where a bridge spans the Trent. Not far from this bridge was an inn where I ate my midday meal. I could get nothing but bread and butter so I asked them to make it into toast. Nottingham stands on a hill, and, with its high houses, red roofs and church steeples, looks excellent from a distance. At no town in England have I enjoyed so beautiful a prospect.

Costock

There were three inns adjacent to each other in Costock, which, to judge by their exteriors, were dens of the most abject poverty. At the one where I stayed only the landlady was at home. A sick carter and a sick butcher were staying there for the night, which depressed me. During the evening I felt a kind of fever, slept disturbed that night and lay in bed very long the next morning until my landlady woke me saying she was getting worried on my account.

John Byng, Viscount Torrington, 1789
Southwell

Southwell is a well built, clean town. Such a one as a quiet distressed family ought to retire to: Coals, provisions and Religion to be had good and cheap.

Bottesford

Botesford is a long dirty village, has a beautiful Church with a very lofty spire.

J.R. Martin (1844)
Nottingham

I believe that nowhere else shall we find so large a mass of inhabitants crowded into courts, alleys and lanes, as in Nottingham and those too, of the worst possible construction. Here they are clustered upon each other; court within court, yard within yard, lane within lane, in a manner to defy construction – all exceeding right and left from a the long narrow streets above referred to. The courts are, almost without exception, approached through a low arched tunnel of some 30 or 36in wide, about 8ft high, and from 20 to 30ft long, so as to place ventilation or direct solar exposure out of possibility on the space described. The courts are noisome, narrow, unprovided with adequate means for the remove of refuse, ill-ventilated, and wretched in the extreme, with a gutter or surface drain, running down the centre: they have no back yards, and the privies are common to the whole court: altogether they present scenes of a deplorable character, and of surprising filth and discomfort. It is just the same with the lanes and alleys with the exception that these last were not closed at each end like the courts. In all these confined quarters, too, the refuse matter is allowed to accumulate until, by its mass and its advanced putrification, it shall have acquired value as manure; and thus it is sold and carried away by the 'muck-majors' as the collectors of manure are called in Nottingham. The houses in the narrow streets, lanes, courts and yards above described, are for the most part singularly defective, being erected in 'parallel ranks', three stories high, side to side and back to back, with one department in each storey, about 11 ft square, exclusive of a narrow staircase under which is a small closet used for keeping victuals and coals. The lower room is used for ordinary day purposes; the second, generally as a bedroom; and the upper very frequently as a workshop; occasionally both as a work-shop and a bed-room. The outer doors open into the lane, common court or alley, directly, and so as to admit of no privacy when the occupants would leave them open for the admission of air.

John Marius Wilson (*Imperial Gazetteer of England and Wales*) 1870–72

East Retford

East Retford is a well-built town, with a spacious market at the centre, a handsome town hall, a corn exchange and a grammar school. It carries on a considerable trade in horses, cattle, cheese and hops. The industrial establishments include iron foundries and paper mills.

Hucknall

An extensive colliery, employing about 500 men and yielding coal of excellent quality was recently opened. Excellent limestone is quarried and stocking making and lace making are carried on ...The church is ancient and in tolerable condition; and contains the tomb of Lord Byron...There are chapels for Baptists, Wesleyans, Primitive Methodists and New Connexion Methodists, a national school and a charity of about £50 a year.

Kimberley

Framework knitting and coal mining are largely carried on ; and there are two breweries and a large corn mill...The church was built in 1847 at a cost of £2,300... There are chapels for Primitive Methodists and New Connexions Methodists, and a British School.

Mansfield

Mansfield...is surrounded by the vestiges of Sherwood Forest. Silk and cotton mills, iron foundries, brick and tile works and breweries &c, give employment to the inhabitants. The cattle markets and corn markets are important.

Sutton-in-Ashfield

The town stands near the Nottingham and Mansfield Railway, 3½ miles SW of Mansfield; is irregularly built; carries on cotton and thread hosiery manufactures; publishes a weekly newspaper; and has a post office under Mansfield, a railway station, a fine church with lofty spire...four dissenting chapels, a large national school, a provision market every Saturday, and stock fairs on Easter Tuesday and on the second Tuesday of October.

John Bartholomew (*Gazetteer of the British Isles*) 1887

Newark-on-Trent

Newark is connected with the Trent navigation and carries on an immense trade in malt and flour; its corn market is one of the largest in the kingdom. Ironfounding, brassfounding, brewing and the manufacture of boilers and agricultural implements are conspicuous industries. The town has long been known for the manufacture of a special plaster, which alone was used in the erection of the great International Exhibition.

D.H. Lawrence, 1926, recalling the Nottinghamshire of his boyhood

Eastwood

Most of the dwellings of the old-style miners were pulled down, and dull little shops began to rise along the Nottingham Road, while on the down-slope of the north side the company erected what is still known as the New buildings or the Square... planked down on the rough slope of the hill, little four-room houses with the front looking outward into the grim blank street, and the back, with a tiny square brick yard, a low wall and a w.c. and ash-pit looking into the desert of the square.

J.B. Priestley (*An English Journey*) 1933

Nottingham

Such big concerns as Player's, the tobacco firm, Boot's the chemists, and the Raleigh Cycle Company, have their headquarters in Nottingham. The town has some very rough quarters still, but it is developing itself sensibly both in the old parts and the new, the housing estates on the outskirts...Among provincial towns it has always passed for the most frivolous...It was supposed to be a paradise for commercial travellers of the livelier sort. Rumour had it that the place was rich with pretty girls who were anything but prudes. There were goings on in Nottingham. So ran the legend, which turned the place into a sort of industrial Venusberg...Certainly in my tiny experience of it, Nottingham seems gayer, in its own robust Midland fashion, than other provincial towns...There are a great many pubs in the place, and now and then a rough house in one of the vaults down in that old-fashioned quarter, the Poultry...The local accent is noticeable, having the harsh quality of the Northern accent without the leavening and salt of rich dialect: it is in short ugly speech.

Goose Fair

The goose fair I saw was the usual agglomeration of roundabouts, shows and stalls...Any roots this fair had in commerce had withered long ago. Neither had it any concern now with popular sports and pastimes and competitions. It offered the people no opportunity of amusing one another. And the only fairings they could buy there were little plates of peas or winkles, portions of ice cream, or packets of brandy snap. It was now simply an assembly of devices, chiefly mechanical, contrived to attract the largest number of pennies in the shortest possible time.

A football match between Notts County and Nottingham Forest football clubs

I have known games that displayed the finer points of the association football game much better than this one, but for all that it was a good match, clean and fast and exciting. Nearly everything has been done to spoil this game; the heavy financial interests; the absurd transfer and player-selling system; the lack of any birth of residential qualification for the players; the betting and coupon competitions; the absurd publicity given to every feature of it by the Press...

Nottinghamshire Notables

✣ **Thomas Adams** was born in Worksop in 1807. Having learned the lace trade as an apprentice in London he came to Nottingham in 1830 to start his own business. He became very successful and in 1885 he opened his palatial new warehouse, now known as the Adams Building. It employed 6,000 people who enjoyed the a wide range of amenities including a library, schoolroom, rest rooms, a canteen and a chapel. He was a generous philanthropist, donating substantial sums to local educational and religious organisations. He died at his home in Lenton on 16 May 1873.

✣ **Field Marshall, Viscount Edmund Allenby** was born at Southwell in 1861. He was educated at Haileybury College and the Royal Military College at Sandhurst. Commissioned into the sixth (Inniskilling) Dragoons he was posted to South Africa where he took part in the Bechuanaland Expedition of 1884 and later saw service in Zululand. He returned with his regiment to Britain in 1890. After a period involved in training and other duties he entered the Staff College. He was promoted to major and in 1898 joined the third Cavalry Brigade then serving in Ireland as Brigade Major. At the outbreak of the Second Boer War he was returned to his regiment. He gained a reputation as a daring commander and ended the war as a Colonel. Further promotions followed and by the start of World War One he held the rank of Major General. Initially he saw service on the Western Front in command of a cavalry division. Having distinguished himself and his division in the retreat after the Battle of Mons he was rewarded by being made commander of the Cavalry Corps in the newly expanded BEF. In 1915 he commanded V Corps in the Battle of Ypres and in October took charge of the British Third Army. He clashed with Field Marshall Haig and in June 1917 he was sent to Egypt as commander-in-chief of the Egyptian Expeditionary Force. It was here that he really made his name fighting against the Turks. He quickly won the respect of his men by making frequent visits to front line troops and moving his own headquarters nearer to the front line. He also took the bold step of supporting T.E. Lawrence (Lawrence of Arabia) with £200,000 a month to carry on his guerrilla warfare with the support of local Arab tribes. Success soon followed and Allenby captured Jerusalem on 9 December 1917, officially entering on foot two days later out of respect for the Holy City. After receiving reinforcements of Empire troops he defeated the Turks at the Battle of Megiddio in September 1918 and swept onwards. Damascus fell on 1 October, Homs on 16 October and Aleppo on 25 October. Turkey capitulated on 30 October 1918. Allenby was made a Field Marshall in 1919 and in the same year was created Viscount Allenby of Megiddio and of Felixstowe in the County of Suffolk. He remained in the Middle East as High Commissioner for Egypt and the Sudan and was instrumental in the creation of a sovereign Egypt. He retired in 1925 and died very suddenly from a ruptured cerebral aneurysm on 14 May in London. His ashes were buried in Westminster Abbey.

✤ **Richard Arkwright** is generally regarded as the father of the factory system. The inventor of the spinning frame, he was a successful entrepreneur who brought together for the first time machines, a source of power and a labour force. He received financial support for his invention from the Nottingham banker, Ichabod Wright and his first prototype mill was built in Nottingham around 1769. This used horses to power his spinning frames. In 1771 he opened the first water powered cotton mill in the world at Cromford in Derbyshire. His ideas on the manufacturing system spread throughout Britain and the world, and when he died in 1792 his fortune was said to be around £500,000.

✤ **Albert Ball** was a famous and highly decorated World War One fighter pilot. Born in Nottingham in 1897, he was educated at Lenton Church School, Grantham Grammar school and Nottingham High School. At the age of 14 he transferred to Trent College, Long Eaton where he displayed a natural aptitude for anything mechanical. On leaving school in September 1913, with the help of his father he bought an interest in an electrical engineering and brass founding business in Nottingham. Ball, however, like many young men of his class, was fiercely patriotic and at the outbreak of war he joined the Sherwood Foresters. Swiftly promoted to sergeant, he was commissioned on 29 October 1914 and spent the winter in training. Keen to get involved in the fighting he transferred to the North Midland Cyclist Company but when this resulted in another home posting he began to take private flying lessons. He transferred to the Royal Flying Corps and received his wings in January 1916. After a brief period in a reconnaissance role he transferred to 11 squadron, flying single-seater Nieuport Scouts. He was awarded the Military Cross in July and by the end of the year he had become the top-scoring pilot in the RFC. With great skill, courage and determination he often single-handedly took on several enemy aircraft. On one occasion in August 1916 he attacked four enemy formations, one seven strong and another five, before returning with his aircraft riddled with bullets. His courage was recognised with the award of a DFC and bar on the same day. His victories continued after his transfer to 60 squadron, and by the end of September he had a total of over 30 'kills' to his credit. A second bar to his DFC followed in November, making Ball the most highly decorated pilot in the RFC. During a home posting Ball received the honour of Freeman of the City of Nottingham. Returning to combat in February 1917 he was posted to the elite 56 squadron and within a short period of time scored a further 11 victories. He died on 7 May 1917, although the circumstances of his death remain something of a mystery. He attacked a large formation of German fighters and was seen pursuing an opponent into a thunder cloud before crashing to earth in a shallow dive. It seems likely that Ball became disorientated in the cloud, and his engine cut out when the aircraft was inverted. He was dragged from the wreckage of his aircraft and died in the arms

Statue of Albert Ball.

of a local French girl, Cecile Deloffre. The Germans buried him with full military honours in the village of Annoeullin. He rests there today, the only Englishman among many German dead. He was widely mourned, and on 8 June 1971 he was posthumously awarded the Victoria Cross. The citation reads: 'For most conspicuous and consistent bravery from the 25th of April to the 6th of May 1917, during which period Captain Albert Ball took part in twenty-six combats in the air and destroyed 11 hostile aeroplanes, drove down two out of control, and forced several others to land. In these combats Captain Ball, flying alone, on one occasion fought six hostile machines, twice he fought five and once four. When leading two other British aeroplanes he attacked an enemy formation of eight. On each of these occasions he bought down at least one enemy. Several times his aeroplane was badly damaged, once so seriously that but for the most delicate handling his machine would have collapsed, as nearly all the controls had been shot away. On returning with a damaged machine he had always to be restrained from immediately going out on another. In all, Captain Ball has destroyed 43 German aeroplanes and one balloon, and has always displayed most exceptional courage, determination and skill'. The reason for Albert Ball's success as a flying ace was summed up by Air Marshall Sir High Trenchard: 'Ball used to tend his machine like some of us look after our ponies, and almost like some people look after their children. He painted it, oiled it, tested it and cleaned it, not occasionally but consistently. He knew all about the mechanism and he looked after his guns...His reputation was that not only that of a brilliant pilot, but of a thoroughly reliable workman, a man imbued with the necessity for thoroughness, care and detail.' His reputation as a national hero is enduring, and in 2006 he was chosen as one of six VC holders to appear on a set of Royal mail commemorative stamps.

✤ **Robert Blincoe** is believed by many to have been the inspiration for the character of Oliver Twist. Orphaned or abandoned soon after his birth around 1792 he was admitted to St Pancras Workhouse in 1796. At the age seven, tempted and deceived by promises of roast beef and plum pudding, he was one of a number of children who agreed to become apprentices at the cotton mill owned by the Lambert brothers at Lowdham in Nottinghamshire. Told that they would be allowed to ride their master's horses and have silver watches and plenty of cash in their pockets, Robert and his companions were keen to start their new lives. The children made the long journey to Nottinghamshire by horse drawn wagon. Stopping at Nottingham on their way to Lowdham they were allowed to visit the Castle and Sherwood Forest. As they approached Lowdham Mill, however, local people gathered around the wagons and pitied the children with comments such as 'God help the poor wretches' and 'The Lord have mercy upon them'.

On their arrival at the Mill, Robert and his companions were ushered into a long room where they were provided with supper. Shortly afterwards the new arrivals were sent to their beds in the apprentice house where they slept two to a bed, having to share with the smelly unkempt children already there. Woken at five o'clock the next morning Robert had only half an hour to wash under the cold pump and eat his breakfast of black bread and blue milk porridge before starting work. Hours were generally long; 14 hours a day with only short breaks allowed for meals. When the machinery had to be cleaned and overhauled this could increase to us much as 16 hours a day with little opportunity to take any form of refreshment.

Robert described the overseers at the mill as brutal, illiterate, ferocious ruffians who took delight in hitting and teasing the apprentices. He later realised that their task was to keep the children in a 'constant state of exertion' and recalled that when he failed to work hard enough he had to endure the strap or the stick, the cuff or the kick with as much resignation as any of his fellow sufferers. He contemplated suicide but instead attempted to run away. He got as far as Burton Joyce but was apprehended by a local tailor who returned him to the mill. The standard reward for returning a runaway apprentice at that time was five shillings. Robert's reward for his unsuccessful attempt was a beating which left him covered in bruises.

This regime of long hours, hard work, limited diet and brutal discipline took its toll, and by their second year at the mill Robert recalled that his companions from London had lost their plump and fresh appearance and acquired the pale and sickly hue which distinguished factory children from all others. Many of the children suffered minor accidents such as crushed or torn fingers and dislocations, but sometime early in 1801 a girl called Mary Richardson was caught up by her apron and drawn into the machinery. Robert heard her bones break while she was screaming and the machinery only stopped when it was jammed by her almost lifeless body. The poor girl survived but remained a cripple for the remainder of her life. Conditions at Lowdham Mill later improved and became better than those at many similar mills throughout the country. The pauper apprentices there were kept decently clad, had a better suit reserved for Sundays and holidays and were occasionally allowed a little time to play in the open air. They were taken to goose fair each year and the youngest was given sixpence in money. They went fairly regularly to Lowdham Church on Sundays and were not confined within the walls as was the case at most other mills where parish apprentices were immured. Their food latterly was good, and evenly cooked. Their bedding, though coarse, was clean. It came as something of a shock, therefore, when, in 1804, Lowdham Mill was closed down. Robert, along with most of the other pauper apprentices were transferred to Litton Mill in Derbyshire where conditions were even worse than those at Lowdham, the food was awful and beatings took place on a regular basis. Eventually, in 1813, Robert completed his apprenticeship. He worked as an adult operative until 1817 when he set up his own small cotton spinning business. In later life he told his story to John Brown, a journalist from Bolton. It was published in various forms including as a pamphlet and was used as part of the propaganda campaign to improve the condition of child labourers in the cotton mills.

✤ **William Booth**, the founder of the Salvation Army was born on 10 April 1829 at 12 Nonintone Place. At the age of 13, following his father's bankruptcy, he went to work as an apprentice to a local pawnbroker. This made him aware of the poverty, and poor living conditions suffered by many people at the time. He was inspired to become a Christian and spent some time evangelising in the Nottingham area. Following the completion of his apprenticeship he moved to London, again to work as a pawnbroker. He joined the local Methodist Church and later decided to become a minister. He married Catherine Mumford in 1855 and spent several years travelling around the country preaching to all those who would listen. He increasingly came to feel that he should be doing more to work with the poorest members of society. He resigned his position as a Methodist Minister and in 1865, together with his wife, he founded the Whitechapel Christian Mission in the East End of London to help feed and house the poor. In 1875, after struggling for some years, the mission was reorganised along military lines as the Salvation Army. Ministers became known as officers and Booth was their General. William Booth wanted Salvation Army services to be lively and enjoyable. Joyous singing, instrumental music, clapping of hands and an invitation to repent, were all features of their meetings. They were strong supporters of the temperance movement and were sometimes subject to violence and abuse. The Church of England was at first hostile to this new movement and members of the Salvation Army were sometimes imprisoned for their open air preaching. Gradually support and respect for the Salvation Army began to grow. During his lifetime William Booth spread the work of the Salvation Army to over 50 different countries including the USA, Australia and India, and he himself was received by Kings, Princes and Presidents. He composed hymns, published a regular magazine and wrote a number of books. His book, *In Darkest England and the Way Out*, published in 1890 became an immediate best seller and has been reprinted several times, most recently in 2006. In 1905 he was made a freeman of the City of Nottingham. Today his birthplace is a museum and part of the William Booth Memorial Complex. He died in 1912 and is buried in the non-denominational Abney Park Cemetery in Stoke Newington.

✣ **Jesse Boot** began his working life in his mother's herbalist shop at 6 Goosegate which was already successful as working class people could not afford to consult a doctor at this time. He worked hard to learn the essentials of the business and became a full partner at the age of 21. The store continued to flourish and he eventually took full control of the business. He expanded the range of products he sold to include proprietary medicines and household necessities and adopted a strategy of buying stock in bulk and selling his goods much more cheaply than his competitors. In February 1877 he launched a campaign in the *Nottingham Daily Express*, advertising 'Patent Medicines Retail at Wholesale Prices'. This dramatically increased his weekly takings from £20 to £100. It was also in this year that he took sole control of the business. Increased turnover allowed him to move into larger premises in Goosegate. This was followed by yet more shops and then in 1884 the opening of the first shops outside the city, in Lincoln and Sheffield. In the same year he employed his first qualified pharmacist to dispense medicines and oversee the recruitment of others. Boot had always manufactured some of his own remedies but in 1885 he began to lease space in various factories close to Nottingham's Midland Station. This unrelenting hard work took its toll and in 1886 he was forced to take a holiday in Jersey in order to recuperate. Here he met and fell in love with Florence Rowe, who worked in her father's bookshop in St Helier. After something of a whirlwind romance the two were married on 30 August 1886. Florence proved to be a real asset to the business and was later responsible for building up 'no 2 department' (stationary, books, fancy goods, pictures and so forth) within the company's shops. She also acted as personnel manager for all women employed in the company's shops, warehouses and factories. With renewed enthusiasm Jesse now began to create a national chain of shops. He believed strongly in the importance of shop display, advertising and packaging and established his own building, shop-fitting and printing departments to provide for his expanding network of shops. He now began to take over other chains of shops and his empire grew rapidly. Ten stores in 1890 rose to 251 in 1901 and 560 in 1914. The range of products also expanded beyond traditional chemist's lines and the larger stores even included cafés and subscription libraries. The growth in the number of retail outlets was accompanied by a growth in manufacturing of Boots own brand products and research into new pharmaceuticals and chemicals. Sites on Island Street and Station Street were acquired to house Boots growing factories, warehouses, laboratories and offices. Suffering from declining health Jesse sold the business for £2.2 million in 1920 and retired to Jersey. Generous gifts to the Liberal Party resulted in honours including a knighthood and a baronetcy. He became a generous benefactor to his native city. His most lasting legacy was University College, later to become the University of Nottingham. He provided both the land and a substantial contribution to the building costs as well as overseeing much of the design of the buildings and overall layout of the campus. Because of his ill-health he was unable to attend the royal opening ceremony in July 1928 but the speeches were relayed to him in a private room and afterwards King George V

Reconstruction of an Early Chemist's Shop.

and Queen Mary took tea with him. His philanthropy was rewarded with a peerage and a few months later he proudly assumed the title of Lord Trent of Nottingham. He maintained a close interest and involvement in University College until his death in 1931.

✱ **Richard Birkin** was an important lace manufacturer. He was one of a number of pioneers who transformed William Lee's simple framework knitting machine from a cottage industry into an industrial process. Born in Derbyshire, he moved to Nottingham in 1825, where he bought his first lace manufacturing in a small building in Gladstone Street, New Basford. His business prospered and by the 1850s he was a successful and well respected businessman. He was elected Mayor of Nottingham on a number of occasions and lived at Aspley Hall.

✱ **Frank Bowden**, the founder of the Raleigh Cycle Company was born in Bristol in 1848. Ill health forced him to cut short a successful legal career in Hong Kong. After returning to Britain he was advised to take up cycling for the good of his health. He was so impressed with the cycle that he bought he went to visit the manufacturers. This was the firm of Angois, Woodhead & Ellis, whose workshops were in Raleigh Street, Nottingham. Bowden became a financial backer and two years later in 1889 the Raleigh Cycle Company was incorporated. Shortly afterwards he gained a controlling interest in the company. Bowden made a significant contribution to Raleigh's success introducing new and innovative manufacturing methods and promoting the brand through extensive advertising campaigns. As an active cyclist himself, he was also one of the first English manufacturers to recognise the potential benefit of pneumatic tyres and variable gears. In 1903 Bowden founded the Three-Speed Gear Syndicate Ltd which became the Sturmey Archer Gear Company in 1908. Frank Bowden became an important figure in the local community. He was a JP for Nottingham and in 1915 received a baronetcy for converting Raleigh Cycles into a munitions factory during World War One. He died at his home, Bestwood Lodge, Nottingham on 25 April 1921.

Bust of Lord Byron.

✣ **George Gordon**, sixth Lord Byron is probably the most glamorous and infamous of all English poets. Born in 1788 his father died when he was three, with the result that he inherited his title from his great uncle in 1798. The ancestral home at Newstead abbey was in a ruined and dilapidated state so he and his mother came to live at Burgage Manor in Southwell. While there he cultivated the friendship of Elizabeth Pigot and her brother John and the three of them staged two plays for the local community. Elizabeth encouraged him with his writing and his first collection of poems, 'Fugitive Pieces' were printed by Ridge of Newark at the corner of the Market Place. The local museum still displays the printing press which was used to print 'Figitive Pieces' and 'Hours of Idleness' (1807). In 1809 he moved into Newstead Abbey and took his seat in the House of Lords. Later in the same year he embarked upon a two year Grand Tour, visiting Portugal, Italy and Greece. On his return he wrote the first two cantos of Childe Harold's Pilgrimage which were received with much critical acclaim. Byron became famous overnight. In 1812 he embarked upon a scandalous affair with a married woman, Lady Caroline Lamb, who later described him as 'mad, bad and dangerous to know'. Other affairs and liaisons followed along with an expensive and lavish lifestyle. In 1824, Byron's half sister Augusta gave birth to a daughter, almost certainly Byron's. The following year he married Annabella Milbank, with whom he had a daughter. Byron treated his wife badly and the two separated in 1816. Facing mounting pressure as a result of a failed marriage, scandalous affairs and mounting debts Byron left England never to return. He spent the summer at Lake Geneva with Percy Bysshe Shelley, his wife Mary and Mary's half sister Claire Claremont, with whom Byron had a child. The following year he left for Italy where he was to spend the next six years. In 1819, while staying in Venice, he began an affair with Teresa Guiccioli, the wife of an Italian nobleman. It was also during this time that he wrote some of his best known works including 'Don Juan'. In July 1823 Byron joined the Greeks in their struggle for independence from the Turks. Before he could see much action he contracted fever and died at Missolonghi in April 1824. His body was returned to Nottinghamshire, where he lies among his ancestors in Hucknall Church.

✳ **George Green** is famous as a 19th-century mathematician. Born in Nottingham in 1793, he was the only son of a baker also called George Green who, in 1807, built a brick windmill on a hill at Sneinton. At the age of eight he was sent to Mr Goodacre's Academy in Nottingham. After only four terms, however, George Green senior removed his son and set him to work in the bakery as he had learned all the mathematics that his masters could teach him. He continued to work in the bakery and later the mill until the death of his father in 1829. He then leased the mill and used his time and money to concentrate on the study of mathematics. In 1823 he joined the Nottingham Subscription Library and five years later published at his own expense 'An Essay on the Application of Mathematical Analysis to the Theories of Electricity and Magnetism'. This brought him to the attention of a number of important and influential people and he was encouraged and persuaded to seek a place at the University of Cambridge. Here he published a number of papers on wave theory. He was elected fellow of Gaius College in November 1839 but shortly after his health began to fail and he died at Nottingham on 31 May 1841. His work provided the foundation for much important research by later scientists and mathematicians working in fields such as nuclear physics, quantum mechanics and super-conductivity. In his last paper on light he helped define the principles which eventually led to the development of fibre optics and indirectly to the growth of the modern communications industry. He is commemorated by a plaque in Westminster Abbey and the George Green Library at the University of Nottingham is named after him.

✳ **James Hargreaves**, the inventor of the Spinning Jenny was born in Blackburn but fled to Nottingham to escape the wrath of fellow spinners who feared that his machine would put them out of work. He established a small cotton mill in the town and continued working there until his death in 1778.

✳ **Thomas Hawksley** was a Victorian civil engineer. Born at Arnold in 1807, he designed the waterworks for the Trent Waterworks Company which was to provide clean water for the city for almost 70 years. His design provided a supply at a constant high pressure which prevented any contamination from entering the mains. This was so successful that when many other towns suffered from outbreaks of cholera in 1848–49, Nottingham escaped. As a result Hawksley was asked to supervise water projects throughout the country. Upgrades in a number of places including Derby, Leicester, Leeds and Sunderland were all overseen by Hawksley. His fame spread and he was honoured in Sweden, Denmark and Brazil for solving their water distribution and storage problems. In Britain he was elected president of the Institute of Civil Engineers, Institute of Mechanical Engineers and Institution of Gas Engineers. In 1878 Thomas Hawksley was elected as a Fellow of the Royal Society. He died in 1893.

✳ **John Russell Hind** was born in 1823. The son of a Nottingham lace manufacturer, he developed an interest in astronomy from an early age and became a regular contributor on astronomical subjects to the Nottingham Journal. As a young man he was employed at the Greenwich observatory and later took charge of the observatory in Regent's Park. He is credited with the discovery of 10 asteroids, two comets and 15 variable stars. He wrote four books and contributed numerous articles on astronomy. He later became secretary and afterwards president of the Royal Astronomical Society. On his retirement the government awarded him an annual pension of £200

✣ **Thomas Hine** was one of Nottinghamshire's most influential 19th-century architects. His most famous work is the Adams Building which was originally a textile factory, lace warehouse and salesroom built for the lace manufacturers, Messrs Adams Page. Other buildings for which he was responsible include several churches, a number of railway stations and the monument to Lord George Bentinck in Mansfield. He took an active interest in antiquarian matters and published a book entitled 'Nottingham Castle; a Military Fortress, a Royal Palace, a Ducal Mansion, a Blackened Ruin, a Museum and Gallery of Art'. He was responsible for laying out the Park as a building estate, and many of its houses were built under his direction. He died in 1899.

✣ **Richard (Dick) Iliffe** working with his colleague Wilf Bagguley started to compile a collection of old Nottingham photographs in 1940 and 20 years later established the Nottingham Historical Film Unit. As a result of his work a number of books showing images of Nottingham in the Victorian and Edwardian Era have been published. He died in 1983.

✣ **William Lee** invented the framework knitting machine in approximately 1589. Some have suggested that this same William Lee was the vicar (or curate) of Calverton but there is no reliable evidence to support this. The first known reference to Lee and his knitting frame appears in an agreement between William Lee and George Brooke dated 6 June 1600 in which it was stated that: 'William Lee hath by long study and practice devised and invented a certain invention or artificiality of being a very speedy manner of working and making in a loom or frame all manner of works usually wrought by knitting needles as stockings, waistcoats and such like...' George Brook was a wealthy courtier and a useful patron, but in 1603 he was charged with treason and subsequently executed. Despite repeated attempts, Lee failed to obtain a patent for his invention and sometime around 1610 he took his machine to France where attempts were being made to manufacture luxury goods such as silk. Here he achieved some success but died soon afterwards. His brother, James, brought the knitting frame back to London and made a number of improvements which enabled finer fabric to be produced. Despite this the use of the knitting frame was slow to be adopted and by the mid-17th century there were probably fewer than 100 machines in use throughout the kingdom. A Company of Framework Knitters was formed in London and incorporated by charter in 1657 and again in 1664. The charter of 1664, granted by Charles II enabled the hosiery trade to be controlled and regulated by masters, whom engaged apprentices for a period of seven years and trained them to become journeymen. The strict controls imposed by the company, however, led some hosiery manufacturers to leave the capital and establish themselves in Nottinghamshire, Derbyshire and Leicestershire. By 1700 there were over 7,000 frames at work in Nottinghamshire and the neighbouring counties.

✵ **Robert Lowe** was one of the most successful and outstanding politicians of the Victorian age. During his parliamentary career he held a number of offices including Secretary of the Board of Control, Vice-President of the Board of Trade, Paymaster General, Vice President of the Committee of Council on Education, President of the Board of Health, Chancellor of the Exchequer and Home Secretary. Born at Bingham in 1811 he was educated at Winchester School and University College Oxford. As vice-president of the Board of Education he announced the Revised Code of Education which introduced the system of payment by results for school teachers. He introduced competitive examinations into the Civil Service and as Chancellor of the Exchequer he reduced income tax from 6d to 3d in the pound. He later served as Home Secretary and was created Viscount Sherbrook in 1880. When he died in 1892 his obituary in the *Times* described him as 'one of the striking figures of English life'.

✵ **John Player** arrived in Nottingham in 1859. He found work initially as a drapers assistant before establishing a business on Beastmarket Hill acting as an agent for lace thread and for Prentice & Company's agricultural manures and seeds. His next door neighbour was Ann Whiteley, a milliner and although a widow and 10 years his senior he married her on 16 August 1862. The couple had two sons. Player soon added tobacco to his other lines. At that time tobacco was sold loose from jars, and weighed and handed over in screws of plain paper. Player soon realised that customer loyalty to a particular brand was strong and he began to pre-pack his blends. Before long tobacco took over as the main business of the shop. The business was so successful that in 1877 Player purchased an existing tobacco factory in Broad Marsh. This had been established by William Wright in 1823 and produced pipe-smoking and chewing tobacco as well as hand-made cigarettes. By the time Player took over the business it was employing 150 people and producing enough tobacco to supply local needs. Player, however, wanted to both expand the business and create his own brands. The first name to be registered was Gold Leaf, in 1877, when he first began to manufacture under his own name. In the same year he also registered his first actual trademark, the familiar image of Nottingham Castle. John Player's marketing methods were so successful that he was able to buy an extensive site at Radford, an area which was largely undeveloped at the time. With customary foresight he built three factory blocks, the nucleus of the 30 acres of factories and offices that were to grow on the site. Since only one block was needed immediately the other two were hired out for lace making until such time as they would be needed for the expansion of the tobacco business. The Castle Tobacco Factory was opened in April 1884 but John Player did not live to see his plans come to fruition. He died a few months later at the tragically early age of 45. The company he founded went on to become one of Nottingham's major employers and through advertising and sponsorship, one of the best known brands in the world.

✢ **Stella Rimington** was the first female Head of MI5. Born in Nottingham in 1935, she attended Nottingham Girls High School. After university she worked at Worcestershire County council Archives before moving to the India Office Library in London in 1962. She joined the Security Service part time in 1965 and rose to become the Director General. She retired in 1996 and was made a Dame Commander of the Bath in the same year. Since her retirement she has become a non-executive director of Marks and Spencer and published her autobiography, *Open Secret*. She has also written a number of best selling espionage thrillers.

✢ **Charles Shaw** was the first press photographer to employed by the *Nottingham Guardian* in the early years of the 20th century and claimed to have taken the first aerial photograph in 1907. In 1930 he left the *Nottingham Guardian* and joined the *Nottingham Evening News* where he wrote the Newsman's Notebook under the pen name of The Scribe. He died in August 1959.

✢ **Paul Smith,** the world famous fashion designer was born in Nottingham in 1946. He left school in 1961 without any qualifications and was forced to take a job as an errand boy in a Nottingham clothing warehouse. He became interested in art and fashion through making displays for the clothing warehouse and taking charge of warehouse buying. He opened his first shop on Byard Lane in 1970.

✢ **Sir Francis Willoughby,** a descendant of the builder of Wollaton Hall became a founder member of the Royal Society in 1662. One of the most distinguished naturalists of his age he travelled abroad and was vulnerable to a recurring fever. He died aged 37 in 1672. His most famous work entitled *Ornithologia libri tres* was published after his death in 1676 and marks the beginning of scientific ornithology in Europe.

✢ **Abel Smith** was a great-great-grandson of Queen Victoria through her youngest son, Prince Leopold, Duke of Albany. After a military career he settled at Blidworth Dale House, Ravenshead where he became a successful farmer. He was High Sherriff of Nottinghamshire from 1978 to 1979 and was Vice Lord Lieutenant of Nottinghamshire from 1991–99. He died in 2004.

Rebels, Reformers and Revolutionaries

✻ **Jeremiah Brandreth** was the leader of Britain's last revolution and one of the last men to be beheaded in this country. Born at Wilford, he later moved to Sutton-in-Ashfield where he lived with his wife and two children and earned a meagre and uncertain living as a framework knitter. There were also rumours that he had served for some time in the army or the militia. There was a great deal of poverty and unemployment among framework knitters at this time and many were suffering real hardship. Luddite attacks on machinery had taken place in the area and it is believed that Brandreth had previously been involved in Luddite activities. There was also a secret revolutionary committee in Nottingham. It was led by William Stevens, a needle-maker, and was one of many throughout the country which talked a great deal but generally did nothing. It was through this committee that Brandreth met William Oliver, a government spy and agent provocateur and agreed to co-operate in a plan to join with other groups throughout the country to march on London and overthrow the government. Brandreth was deputed to lead the contingent from Pentrich, a village in nearby Derbyshire. He met to brief his followers at the White Horse Inn where he promised them £100, a pound of bread, a pint of spirits and a quart of ale when they reached Nottingham. The ill fated uprising began on the night of Monday 9 June 1817 at Hurt's Barn, to the west of South Wingfield. It was from here that

Brandreth and his ragged band set off towards Nottingham. As they marched they called at the cottages of farm labourers demanding guns and recruits. In some cases men were bullied or cajoled into joining the enterprise but others avoided being 'pressed' in this manner. At the house of Mrs Mary Hepworth at Wingfield Park, a window was broken and a single shot was fired killing Robert Walters a servant. Marching on they arrived outside the Butterley Iron Works, expecting to seize arms and win more recruits. Instead they were bravely confronted by George

Jeremiah Brandreth.

Goodwin, the company's agent. He told them to disperse or they would all be hanged. Some did slip away but the remainder marched on towards Nottingham in the heavy rain. The ragged band of revolutionaries continued to dwindle as the expected support failed to materialise and only about 40 remained when a detachment of hussars routed them a Giltbrook. Some were immediately rounded up but others fled across the fields and hedgerows. With a price on his head Brandreth made a desperate attempt to escape. He made his way to Bristol where he twice tried to board a ship bound for America. He was recognised and had to keep running. Eventually he gave up hope of trying to leave the country and attempted to return to his wife and family. He never reached home and was arrested at Bulwell. The conspirators were imprisoned in the County Gaol at Friargate in Derby until they could be brought to trial. They were eventually brought before a special commission at Derby in October, presided over by Sir Richard Richards, the Chief Baron of the Court of Exchequer. Here it was charged that 'Thomas Bacon...Jeremiah Brandreth... otherwise known as the Nottingham Captain...William Turner...together with a great multitude of false traitors...to the number of five hundred and more, arrayed and armed in a warlike manner, that is to say with swords, pistols, clubs bludgeons and other weapons... did then with great force and violence parade and march in a hostile manner in and through divers villages, places and public highways...and did there and then maliciously and traitorously attempt and endeavour by force of arms to subvert and destroy the Government and Constitution of this realm...' After a trial lasting about two weeks Jeremiah Brandreth along with Thomas Bacon and William Turner, the other ringleaders, were sentenced to be hanged drawn and quartered though the sentence was later commuted by the Prince Regent to hanging followed by beheading. The rest of the convicted revolutionaries were sentenced to varying periods of imprisonment and transportation.

�֍ **Thomas Cranmer** was certainly a reformer and some would argue that he was also a revolutionary, for he played a major role in the break with Rome and the creation of the Church of England. Like many revolutionaries he paid for his views and actions with his life and he was executed at Oxford in 1556. Born in Aslockton in 1489 he was educated locally and at Southwell Grammar School. He was given a fellowship to Jesus College Cambridge which he had to relinquish when he married the daughter of a local tavern keeper. She died in childbirth at which point he was re-accepted by the College and devoted himself to study. He took holy orders in 1523. He entered Royal Service in 1527 and joined the English diplomatic mission to the Emperor Charles V in Spain. On his return he was honoured with a half-hour interview with the King who presented him with gifts of gold and silver rings. By the time of the controversy over the divorce of King Henry from his wife Catherine of Aragon, Cranmer had risen to an influential position. It was Cranmer's suggestion that the matter be resolved by reference to the university theologians throughout Europe rather than the Papal Court and it was on the basis of Cranmer's research that the King began to question Papal authority. On 30 March 1533 he was appointed

Archbishop of Canterbury. Almost immediately he declared Henry's marriage to Catherine null and void and four months later married him to Anne Boleyn. He was to deal with all of Henry's marital difficulties and was also responsible for declaring void the marriage to Anne Boleyn, and arranging the divorce from Anne of Cleves. Despite becoming Head of the Church of England Henry VIII was theologically conservative and few reforms were introduced during his reign. Cranmer did, however, support the translation of the Bible into English and in 1545 wrote a litany which is still used in the church. When Edward VI came to the throne he was able to promote further reforms. He wrote and compiled the first two editions of the Book of Common Prayer and with the assistance of several Continental reformers to whom he had given refuge he set out new doctrines in areas such as the Eucharist, clerical celibacy, the role of images in places of worship and the veneration of saints. After the death of Edward VI he supported Lady Jane Grey as his successor. Her reign, however, lasted only a mere nine days and when the Roman Catholic Queen Mary came to the throne he was charged with heresy and treason. After a long trial and imprisonment he was persuaded to recant his views. Despite this, he was sentenced to be burnt to death at Oxford on 21 March 1556. He famously thrust his right hand into the fire declaring, this was the hand that wrote it (his recantation) therefore it shall suffer first!

✤ **Feargus O'Connor**, the radical politician and Chartist leader was Member of Parliament for Nottingham from 1841 to 1843 and has a statue to his memory in Arboretum Park. Born in Ireland he campaigned against the imposition of tithes and the power of the church. In 1832 he was elected Member of Parliament for Cork after advocating the repeal of the Act of Union and the abolition of tithes. He also demanded political reform including universal suffrage and the introduction of a secret ballot. He was deprived of his parliamentary seat in 1835 after failing to meet the property qualifications and embarked upon a tour of the country making radical speeches. In 1837 he established a weekly newspaper, the Northern Star which supported the reform of Parliament. This was a huge success and within two years was selling over 48,000 copies each week. He soon emerged as one of the leaders of the Chartist Movement. They took their name from their six point charter which demanded universal suffrage, annual parliaments, secret ballots, abolition of the property qualification, equal constituencies and the payment of MPs. Huge petitions in support of their demands were presented to Parliament in 1839 and 1840 but were rejected on each occasion. Chartist organisations sprung up all over the country. In support of their campaign they organised petitions and protest meetings and in some areas they held weekly lectures and reading classes. On occasions they could resort to violence. On 18 January 1840 Nottingham chartists attempted to seize the town hall. Two years later the authorities received reports that they were arming themselves. This was followed by rioting and as a result around 400 demonstrators found themselves in the Nottingham House of Correction. Around 50 of them were eventually sentenced to between two and six months imprisonment with hard labour. In 1847, O'Connor was elected MP for Nottingham, becoming the first and only Chartist Member of Parliament. In April 1848 he presided over the last great Chartist demonstration on Kennington Common in south London. It was intended to march across London and present a third petition to Parliament but the government acted quickly to prevent disorder. Armed troops and special constables barred the way and the petition was taken by a convoy of cabs. The petition too proved to be something of a damp squib for instead of the five million signatures claimed by the Chartists it contained less than two million and many of these were forgeries with Queen Victoria and Mr Punch featuring prominently. In the years which followed, Chartism fell into a period of decline and the last convention was held in 1858. O'Connor's behaviour became more and more irrational. In 1852 he was declared insane and sent to an asylum in Chiswick. He died on 30 August 1855. Although an apparent failure Chartism laid the ground for the formation of the early trade unions and with the exception of annual parliaments, all their demands had been accepted by 1918.

Roundhead Rebels

The people of Nottinghamshire, like those in other parts of the Midlands, had divided loyalties during the Civil War and it was not uncommon for members of the same family to take opposing sides. Although Nottinghamshire was on the whole Royalist, the people of Nottingham supported Parliament. By contrast Newark-on-Trent was a Royalist stronghold. Five leading Parliamentarians in Nottinghamshire were also signatories to the King's death warrant.

✤ **Francis Hacker** was born in East Bridgford in 1618 though the family later moved to Colston Bassett. He was regarded as a fine soldier and militia commander who was engaged chiefly in fighting in Leicestershire. He was taken prisoner in November 1643 but was released just a few weeks later in exchange for a Royalist colonel. Captured again in 1645 he was held for some time in Belvoir Castle. In 1648 he commanded the left wing of Colonel Rossiter's victorious Parliamentary forces at Willoughby. At the end of the war Hacker was given responsibility for taking charge of the King during his trial in London. He was one of those who signed the death warrant, and on 30 January 1649 he accompanied the King to the scaffold. Over the next few years Hacker remained a staunch supporter of Cromwell and was given command of the militia in Nottinghamshire. He was briefly a Member of Parliament during the reign of Richard Cromwell but contributed little. Following Charles II's return from exile he was arrested and put on trial. He made no attempt to deny his involvement in the death of the King but claimed that he was merely following legitimate orders. He was found guilty and executed on 19 October 1660. It was reported that he went to his death with dignity and courage.

✤ **Colonel John Hutchinson** was born at Owthorpe Hall in 1615. His father was a Member of Parliament and a supporter of the rights of the Commons. After studying law at Cambridge John Hutchinson lived for a while in London. There he met and married Lucy, the daughter of Sir Allen Apsley, the Lieutenant of the Tower of London. After three years of marriage the couple returned to the Hutchinson family home at Owthorpe. Here they lived quiet and happy lives until the outbreak of the Civil War. Hutchinson was appointed Parliamentary Governor of Nottingham and defended the town with great vigour during the early years of the conflict. He enforced strict discipline, and drunkenness, swearing and unruly behaviour were punished by imprisonment. He treated his enemies with honour, however, and even entertained some of his Royalist prisoners to supper. He was elected Member of Parliament for Nottingham in 1646 and thereafter spent much of his time in London where he was joined by his wife and children. Following the King's trial he was the 13th to sign the death warrant. His wife later wrote that he prayed for guidance before proceeding to 'signe against the King'. Following Cromwell's disillusion of Parliament the Hutchinsons returned to Owthorpe. They rebuilt the hall and laid out extensive gardens with trees, canals and fishponds. There followed a period of quiet contentment during which the Colonel spent his time in hawking, playing his viol and educating his children. He escaped punishment following the Restoration but in 1663 he was accused of being implicated in the 'Northern Plot' against Charles II. After several months of imprisonment he died of fever in Sandown Castel in Kent. His widow brought the body back to Owthorpe for burial in the church.

* **Henry Ireton** is considered by many to have been one of the finest commanders on the Parliamentary side in the Civil War. Born at Attenborough in 1611, he studied law at Trinity College Cambridge but chose not to pursue that career. He joined the Defence Committee in Nottingham and later rose rapidly through the ranks of the Parliamentary army. He fought at Edgehill and then at Gainsborough under Oliver Cromwell. He was wounded and taken prisoner at the Battle of Naseby but escaped and took part in the siege of Bristol in 1645. The following year he married Cromwell's daughter Bridget. A close bond of friendship developed between the two men in the years which followed. Ireton could be merciless when military necessity demanded it. After the siege of Gloucester he demanded the deaths of Sir Charles Lucas and Sir George Lisle as part of the terms of surrender and personally supervised their execution. He was one of those who was keen to hold the King accountable and enthusiastically accepted his commission as one of the judges appointed to try him. Having found his sovereign guilty he added his own name and seal to the death warrant. Ireton served under Cromwell in Ireland where he became Lord Deputy but died of swamp fever in Limerick in 1651. His body was brought back to England where it was buried with great ceremony in Westminster Abbey. Following the Restoration Ireton's body along with those of Cromwell and Bradshaw were exhumed and taken to Tyburn where they were hanged until sunset. Their heads were then displayed on pikes outside Westminster Hall while their bodies were buried in a deep pit.

✴ **Gilbert Millington** was born in 1584 and lived at Felley House, near Annesley. He represented Nottingham in the Long Parliament but his relationship with Colonel John Hutchinson, the Governor, was far from cordial. Lucy Hutchinson reported that at the age of 60, following the death of his first wife, he married a flirtish alehouse wench of 16. Not surprisingly this caused considerable consternation and outrage among the local puritan community. He was one of the signatories to King Charles' death warrant and after the Restoration he was put on trial as a regicide. After being found guilty he was sentenced to death, though this was later commuted to life imprisonment, possibly on account of his age and infirmity. He died in Jersey in 1666.

✴ **Edward Whalley** was a wealthy wool merchant from Screveton and was related to Oliver Cromwell. At the outbreak of the Civil War he joined the Parliamentary army and quickly rose through the ranks. He fought at the battles of Gainsborough and Marston Moor, by which time he had risen to the rank of Lieutenant Colonel. When Cromwell formed the New Model Army in 1645 Whalley was given command of one of its two sections. In November 1647 he was sent to Hampton Court to guard the King. Fearing an assassination attempt, however, he allowed him to escape. Following the second Civil War he was appointed as one of the judges to try the King. Present throughout the trial, his was the fourth signatory on the royal death warrant. When Cromwell dissolved the Long Parliament it fell to Whalley to remove the Parliamentary mace. During the rule of the Major Generals he governed the counties of Nottinghamshire, Derbyshire, Leicestershire, Lincolnshire and Warwickshire. Following the Restoration he fled the country with a price on his head. He sailed to America and sought refuge among the Puritan descendents of the Pilgrim Fathers. At first he was welcomed, but as his enemies pursued him he was forced to go into hiding. It is thought that he died, a hunted man, around 1675.

Luddites

The Luddites were groups of men who attacked mills and destroyed framework knitting machinery in the early years of the 19th century. They believed, with some justification, that the introduction of new machinery would result in lower wages or unemployment. The first attacks on the frame-working districts in Nottinghamshire were accompanied by warning letters signed 'Ned Ludd', 'Captain Ludd' or 'General Ludd' and as a consequence these machine breakers became known as Luddites. Luddite activity in Nottinghamshire was at its height between 1811 and 1817. In an attempt to quell these attacks Nottingham Corporation imposed a curfew. Anyone seen out of his house after 10 o'clock at night was to be apprehended by the constables and held in custody until they could be taken before a magistrate. Alehouse keepers were also required to close their premises at the same time or risk losing their licenses. Rewards were offered for information leading to the conviction of those involved in rioting or machine breaking and the Corporation established at least two secret committees to combat the activities of the luddites. In January 1812 according to a contemporary account a great number of men armed with pistols hammers and clubs entered the dwelling house of George Ball, framework knitter of Lenton near Nottingham, disguised with masks and handkerchiefs over their faces and in other ways, and after striking and abusing the said George Ball they wantonly and feloniously broke and destroyed five stocking frames standing in the workshop; four of which belonged to George Ball, and one frame, 40 gauge, belonging to Francis Braithwaite, hosier, Nottingham. Similar attacks took place in the surrounding areas and a report in the *Nottingham Journal* recorded that: 'A party of armed men, to the number of about 20 entered the house of Mr Shepherd in the parish of Stapleford and demolished four frames... and not contented with this atrocity they carried off a flitch of bacon, and stole and took away the children's clothes, two pairs of shoes and other articles'.

By this time the government feared the spread of Luddite activity and regarded the luddites as dangerous revolutionaries. A new law was passed which imposed the death penalty on those found guilty of machine breaking. This bill was opposed by Lord Byron. In his maiden speech in the House of Lords he spoke of men meagre with famine and sullen with despair and asked the question; 'Will you erect a gibbet in every field and hang up men like scarecrows?'. In response to this harsh and repressive legislation Luddite activity became more violent. In 1816 a group of Nottinghamshire luddites attacked Heathcoat's Mill in Loughborough burning the lace and destroying most of the 55 machines housed there. Six of those involved including James Towle, one of the chief organisers of the luddites in Nottinghamshire, were hanged at Leicester in the following year. In Nottingham earlier in the same year Daniel Diggle was hanged for the shooting of George Kerry in a bungled Luddite raid in Radford in December 1816. These executions marked the end of serious Luddite activity in Nottinghamshire. Eventually Luddism declined; to be replaced by the growth of trade unions, friendly societies and the chartist movement, although a number of those who took part in the Pentrich revolution had previously been engaged in Luddite activity.

Suffragettes in Nottinghamshire

There had been a steady growth in democracy in Britain over a number of centuries, but at the start of the 20th century women were still regarded as second class citizens. They were not able to exercise many of the rights enjoyed by men and in particular did not have the right to vote in parliamentary elections. Large numbers of women were determined to fight for equal rights and began to campaign, organising public meetings and petitions. One of these campaigners was Mrs Emmeline Pankhurst. Along with her daughter, Christabel, she formed the Women's Social and Political Union (WSPU) in 1903. Because they campaigned for the women's suffrage (the vote) the *Daily Mail* dubbed them the suffragettes. The Nottingham branch of the WSPU was founded early in 1908. Later in the same year, on 7 May Mrs Pankhurst addressed an audience of over 1,000 supporters at the Mechanics Hall, where the chair was taken by Revd Lloyd Thomas, a staunch local supporter of women's suffrage. By this time membership of the Nottingham branch had grown to around 200, representing all classes of women and including teachers, doctors, nurses, dressmakers, clerks, shop assistants lace workers and domestic servants. A mass demonstration in favour of votes for women was held in Nottingham on 18 July 1908 and was addressed by several leading members of the WSPU including Mrs Pankhurst, Mrs Pethic-Lawrence and Flora Drummond. Over 20,000 people attended and by November 1910 the Nottingham WSPU had opened an office in the city in Carlton Street. One of the most active suffragettes in Nottingham was Helen Watts. The daughter of the vicar of Lenton, she joined the WSPU in December 1907 after hearing a speech by Christabel Pankhurst in Nottingham. She was not a very active member at first but she was arrested during a demonstration outside the House of Commons on 24 February 1909 and subsequently imprisoned. On her release on the 24 March she enjoyed a welcome supper organised by members of the WSPU at Morley's Café in Nottingham. On 29 April at a huge rally in the Albert Hall she was presented with an illuminated scroll commemorating her imprisonment for the cause. In September 1909 she was again arrested after taking part in a demonstration at Leicester outside a meeting being held by Winston Churchill. She went on hunger strike for 90 hours in Leicester Gaol and was released. She later wrote that women's suffrage 'will not be won by drawing room chatter…it has got to be fought for in the market places, and if we don't fight for it, no-one else will'. Although she continued to speak at public meetings she was not arrested again until January 1910 when she took part in a demonstration outside a meeting held in Nottingham by Herbert Samuel. On this occasion she was released without charge. Another leading local suffragette who was arrested several times was Anna Hutchinson, a nurse and church worker in the parish of St Mary the Virgin, Egmanton and a member of the Church League for Women's Suffrage. Other prominent Nottingham WSPU members included Mrs Leonora Shaw and Muriel Wallis, daughter of the director and curator of Nottingham Art Gallery. Both these women took part in the Black Friday demonstration in Parliament Square in November 1910. By 1913 the suffragette campaign had become more violent. In Nottingham there were a number of arson attacks. In May 1913 a boathouse was destroyed and a pavilion set on fire. In the following month there were attacks on a mansion and a number of business premises. During the same period Papplewick Hall was also slightly damaged by fire. Not all suffragettes agreed with these methods. Helen Watts was one of those who resigned from the WSPU and joined the Women's Freedom League. During World War One Helen worked as a nurse at the Mineral Water Hospital in Bath. Later she worked in both the War Office and the Ministry of Labour. Between 1914 and 1918 many women served as nurses or worked in jobs previously done by men. As a reward for their contribution to the war effort, women over the age of 30 were given the vote in 1918. Ten years later women were granted the right to vote on the same basis as men.

Robin Hood and Sherwood Forest

Robin Hood is well known throughout the world as the outlaw who robbed the rich to give to the poor. The stories of his exploits date back to at least the middle of the 14th century in the form of ballads sung by minstrels and other local entertainers. In 1340 the Scottish historian Fordum wrote of the Robin Hood stories; 'the foolish and vulgar are delighted to hear the jesters and minstrels sing them above all others. Robin Hood is also mentioned in an early poem by Robert Langland. In The Visions of Piers Ploughman one of his characters declares; 'I can rhymes of Robin Hode' The first written account of Robins adventures come in a manuscript dating from around 1510 and is entitled 'The Little Geste of Robin Hood'. The first printing press in England was set up by William Caxton in 1476 and by the early 16th century the tales of Robin Hood were being told in simple chap books which were sold at fairs by itinerant pedlars and chap men. These early stories were embellished and added to in the Tudor period, and Maid Marion first appears in this time in a play written by the Elizabethan playwright, Anthony Munday. This same playwright was also the first to proclaim the outlaw to be the Earl of Huntingdon. Later still in the 19th century Sir Walter Scott introduced a character called Robin of Loxley in his novel Ivanhoe. Since this time, many historian have tried to authentic the legend and person of Robin Hood. Several theories have been suggested to identify the real Robin Hood. Whatever the truth, Robin Hood is timeless; he lives on in stories and comic books, in pantomime and video game and in film and television. The latest film about Robin Hood starred Russell Crowe and was released in 2010. He is also a citizen of the world. Stories, books, films and TV series have been produced in many languages throughout the world. Robin Hood has lived in our imagination for over 700 years. He is our oldest and longest surviving hero.

✣ A certain Robin Hood is mentioned in the Pipe Rolls of 1225, 1228, 1230 and 1231. He appears to be a fugitive from the justice administered by the Sheriff of Yorkshire.

✣ Another Robin Hood was recorded as having slain Ralph or Cirencester around 1213–16. But this individual was a servant of the Abbot of Cirencester, a long way from the traditional haunts of the legendary Robin Hood

✣ A different Robin Hood was imprisoned in 1354 for offences against the laws of the forest of Rockingham.

✣ During the reign of Henry III (1216–72) Robert Hod, with Richard de Riperia and others were accused of a raid on a monastic grange in Yorkshire.

✳ Some historians have attempted to link Robin Hood with King Edward II, who may be the King Edward mention in the little Geste of Robin Hood. After his royal progress to the North someone called Robin Hood was found in his service.

✳ The Scottish historian John Major, writing in 1521, maintained that Robin Hood was active in 1193–94 at the time of Prince John's rebellion against King Richard.

✳ Historians and others have found numerous and sometimes rather dubious references to Robin Hood over the years but Hod, Hood or Hode were all common surnames in England during the mediaeval period, and Robert and Robin were equally popular Christian names.

Ballads

There are 38 traditional ballads which tell of the exploits of Robin Hood. They all appeared in chap books or broadsides from the 17th century onwards. In modern English they are entitled:

The Bold Pedlar and Robin Hood
Jolly Pinder of Wakefield
King's Disguise and friendship with Robin Hood
Little John and the Four Beggars
The Noble Fisherman or Robin Hood's Preferment
Robin Hood and Alan a 'Dale
Robin Hood and Guy of Gisborne
Robin Hood and Little John
Robin Hood and Queen Katherine
Renowned Robin Hood
Robin Hood, Scarlet and John
Robin Hood and the Beggar
Robin Hood and the Bishop
Robin Hood and the Bishop of Hereford
Robin Hood and the Butcher
Robin Hood and the Curtal Friar
Robin Hood and the Golden Arrow
Robin Hood and the Monk
Robin Hood and the Peddlers
Robin Hood and the Potter
Robin Hood and the Ranger
Robin Hood and the Scotchman
Robin Hood and the Shepherd
Robin Hood and the Tanner
Robin Hood and the Tinker
Robin Hood and the Valiant Knight
Robin Hood Newly Revived; or His Meeting and his Fighting with his Cousin Scarlet

Robin Hood rescuing the Widow's three sons from the Sheriff
Robin Hood rescuing three squires from Nottingham gallows
Robin Hood rescuing Will Stutly
Robin Hood and the Prince of Aragon
Robin Hood's Birth, Breeding, Valour and Marriage
Robin Hood's Chase
Robin Hood's Death and Burial
Robin Hood's Delight
Robin Hood's Golden Prize
Robin Hood's Progress to Nottingham
A True Tale of Robin Hood

The Merry Men and other Characters in the tales of Robin Hood

✳ Maid Marion was Robin's sweetheart. She did not appear in the stories until the 16th century and has been linked to the character of the Queen of the May. According to the legends she was originally a lady of noble birth who abandoned a life of privilege to fight for the right of the poor alongside Robin. According to some accounts she married Robin in Edwinstowe Church.

✳ Little John was Robin Hood's principal lieutenant and most trusted companion. The two became friends after a quarterstaff fight on a log bridge. He is reputed to have been a giant of a man. His real name was John Little but was changed by Robin in a humorous reference to his size. According to some accounts he was with Robin at his death and helped him to draw his last bow. According to legend he is buried in Hathersage churchyard where his burial marker can still be seen.

✳ Friar Tuck had a close association with Lenton Priory in Nottingham. In the story of Robin Hood and the Curtail Friar he appears as living like a hermit at Fountaindale. Friars were more popular with the ordinary people as they lived among the poor and lived simple lives. It seems likely that Friar Tuck ministered to the spiritual needs of the outlaw band.

✳ Alan a Dale was the minstrel who chronicled the adventures of Robin Hood and turned them into ballads. According to one legend he joined the band of outlaws after Robin Hood had rescued his sweetheart from the threat of marriage to an elderly knight.

✳ Will Scarlet appears in several versions of the tales of Robin Hood. He was related to Robin and may have been his cousin or his nephew. Some have suggested that his name is derived from the word Scathelocke or Scarlock, meaning red hair. According to some accounts Will came from Mansfield. A local legend tells the story of a cap and clothing of Lincoln green being discovered in a secret room of an ancient house just before it was demolished.

✤ Much the Millers Son was another member of the band of outlaws. Not much is known about him and in some rhymes he is described as Midge the Millers son. Some scholars have suggested that Much was derived from the Old English, Muchel, which had various spellings and meant 'great'.

✤ Sir Richard of Lee was not a member of the outlaw band but appears in the first printed account of Robin's adventures. In this story Robin pays off a debt owed by Sir Richard who later provides refuge for the outlaws at his castle, believed to be Annesley Castle, which stood about eight miles north of Nottingham.

✤ The Sheriff of Nottingham was the traditional enemy of Robin and his men. Robin frequently outwits the Sherriff who is seen as the representative of bad King John.

Places Associated with Robin Hood

✤ St Mary's Church in Nottingham is where Robin Hood came to pray in the ballad of Robin Hood and the Monk. St Mary's Church was recorded in the *Domesday Book* and the present church dates largely from 1474.

✤ Fountain Dale, is said to be where Friar Tuck first met Robin Hood.

✤ Blidworth is said to be the birthplace of Maid Marion as well as the final resting place of Will Scarlet.

✤ Robin Hood's Stables is a cave near Papplewick. It is on private land and difficult to find. Legend has it that Robin Hood and his men kept their horses safely hidden here.

✤ St Mary's Church, Edwinstowe, is where Robin Hood and Maid Marion were married.

✤ Robin Hood's Cave is at Cresswell Crags on the Derbyshire-Nottinghamshire border.

✤ Robin Hood's Larder was a tree in Sherwood Forest where Robin was supposed to have hung his venison. Photographs of the tree still exist but it was blown down by strong winds in 1960.

✤ Robin Hood's Race was a turf maze near the then village of Deinton. It is mentioned in Deering's History of Nottingham in 1751 but was ploughed up in 1797.

✤ St Peter's Church, Headon, contains the tomb slab of Simon de Heaton, the Sheriff of Nottingham in 1259. It is believed that he was the very Sheriff who was Robin Hood's arch enemy.

- Alan a Dale is said to have been married at St James' Church at Papplewick. Robin Hood is also said to have cut his bows from yew trees in the churchyard.

Images of Robin Hood

Statues and painting of Robin Hood can be found throughout Nottinghamshire. The most famous is probably the statue of Robin outside the walls of Nottingham Castle. This was sculptured by James Woodward and presented to the city by Phillip Clay, a local businessman, to commemorate the visit of Princess Elizabeth and the Duke of Edinburgh on 28 June 1949 during the city's Quincentenary celebrations. Cast in bronze it stands 7ft high and weighs over half a ton. Close by you will also find statues of other members of the outlaw band.

- Throughout Nottinghamshire you will also find statues, carvings and paintings depicting Robin Hood and his merry men.

- In the centre of Edwinstowe is statue showing Robin Hood proposing to Maid Marion.

- In the library at Thoresby Hall there is a chimney piece depicting a scene from Sherwood Forest with statue supports of Robin Hood and Little John.

- Robin Hood appears on a number of Pub signs in Nottinghamshire and elsewhere throughout the country.

- Archway House, a folly built in 1842, is decorated with statues of Robin Hood, Maid Marion and Little John. On the north side are statues of Friar Tuck, King Richard I and Allan a Dale.

- Wooden statues of Robin Hood and Maid Marion can be found supporting the entrance canopy of Ma Hibbard's pub and Restaurant at Edwinstowe.

Statue of Robin Hood.

✳ The interior of the dome in the Exchange Arcade, Nottingham, is decorated with frescos by two local artists, Noel Denham Davies and Hammersley Ball. The scenes which show important events in Nottingham's history include one depicting Robin Hood and his outlaw band.

✳ The Severn Building has a number of reliefs showing Robin Hood with Maid Marion and Friar Tuck; King Richard joining Marion's hand with that of Robin, Robin and Little John engaged on a quarterstaff fight, and Robin shooting his last arrow.

✳ Bestwood Lodge Hotel is noted for its statues of Robin Hood characters.

✳ A statue of a young Robin Hood stands in the courtyard of the Stable Gallery at Thoresby. It was made in 1948 by Tissaud-Bird, a grandson of Madam Tissaud of waxwork fame.

✳ The Worksop coat of arms shows a depiction of Robin Hood and a mediaeval crusader knight standing beside a shield with a lion, bird, mining tools and an oak tree. Squirrels rampant are on top of a castellated helm. Some people have suggested that the depiction of Robin Hood bares a strong resemblance to Errol Flynn.

Robin Hood in Books and Comics

Collections of Robin Hood ballads in printed form were published from the 17th century. Known as garlands they could contain as many as a hundred pages. The earliest known of these publications was called *Robin Hood's Garland* and was published in 1663.

✳ Robin Hood appears in the novel *Ivanhoe* by Sir Walter Scott.

✳ Enid Blyton wrote *Tales of Robin Hood*, stories for children in 1930.

✳ Geoffrey Treece wrote *Bows against the Barons* in 1934. This was the author's first novel and is notable for reinterpreting the Robin Hood story from a left wing perspective. It also did a great deal to revitalise children's fiction at the time.

✳ Rosemary Sutcliffe wrote *Chronicles of Robin Hood* in 1950, one of a number of very successful works of historical fiction aimed at children.

✳ Ladybird Books published two titles in their Robin Hood series: *The Silver Arrow* (1954) and *The Ambush* (1955). Both were written by Max Kester and illustrated by John Kenny, the artists for many Ladybird books.

✳ The American author Nancy Springer has written a series of books about Rowan Hood, Outlaw Girl of Sherwood Forest. They include *Lionclaw* (2002), *Outlaw Princess of Sherwood* (2003) and *Rowan Hood Returns* (2005).

✳ The King Raven trilogy, *Hood*, *Scarlet* and *Tuck*, written by Stephen R. Lawhead between 2006 and 2009 relocates the Robin Hood legend to Wales.

✳ *Robin the Hoodie* by Hans Christian Asbosen (2009) re-imagines Robin Hood as a young trouble maker in modern day Nottingham.

Robin Hood on Film and Television

The earliest film about the adventures of Robin Hood was probably shown in the early years of the 20th century. Since then he has appeared on the silver screen and the small screen on numerous occasions. Some of the best known include:

1908 – *Robin Hood and His Merry Men* (unknown lead actor)

1912 – *Robin Hood Outlawed* (Starring A. Brian Plant)

1922 – *Robin Hood* (Starring Douglas Fairbanks and Enid Bennett)

1938 – *The Adventures of Robin Hood* (Starring Errol Flynn and Olivia de Havilland)

1952 – *The Story of Robin Hood* (Starring Richard Todd and Joan Price)

1955 – *Robin of Sherwood* (A TV series which ran until 1960, starring Richard Greene as Robin Hood)

1961 – *The Sword of Sherwood Forest* (Starring Richard Greene)

1973 – *Robin Hood* (A full length Walt Disney cartoon version)

1975 – *Robin and Marian* (Starring Sean Connery and Audrey Hepburn)

1984 – *Robin of Sherwood* (A TV series which ran until 1986, starring Jason Connery with theme music by Clanaad)

1991 – *Robin Hood* (Starring Patrick Bergen)

1991 – *Robin Hood Prince of Thieves* (Starring Kevin Costner)

2010 – *Robin Hood* (Starring Russell Crowe)

Proverbs and sayings associated with Robin Hood

Robin Hood robbed the rich to give to the poor.

Many talk of Robin Hood that never bent his bow (many people talk of things of which they have no experience).

Robin Hood's mile (a distance far longer than a normal mile).

Robin Hood's pennyworths (goods sold for much less than their real value).

To go round Robin Hood's barn (to take the long way to anywhere).

To overshoot Robin Hood (to make an exaggerated claim).

As crooked as Robin Hood's bow (believed to refer to physical appearance).

Tales of Robin Hood are good enough for fools (suggesting that myths and legends should not be taken seriously).

Come stay and drink with Robin Hood (once in common usage because of its appearance on inn signs or above the doors of public houses).

The Robin Hood 'brand'

✳ Home Ales Brewery used the trademark of Robin Hood shooting his arrow on their beer mats. When the brewery was taken over by Scottish and Newcastle new Home Bitter pump clips appeared, linking the beer to Robin Hood. At the same time Home Mild was linked to Will Scarlet.

�֍ Robin Hood Engineering was a British kit car manufacturer based in Mansfield Woodhouse. Founded in 1984 it operated successfully for many years before its assets were sold to Great British Sports Cars Ltd in 2006.

✷ The Robin Hood Foundation is a charitable organisation which attempts to alleviate poverty in New York City.

✷ Robin Hood Travel is a coach company based in Hucknall which provides both minibus and coach services to both public and corporate customers.

✷ Nottinghamshire marketed itself as 'Robin Hood County' for a period.

✷ Robin Hood Cabs is based in Grangewood Road Nottingham.

✷ The Robin Hood Theatre is in Averham.

✷ The Robin Hood Fish Bar in Nottingham is one of a number named after Robin Hood or one of his men. Other fish and chip shops named after Robin Hood or Friar Tuck can be found throughout the country.

✷ The Robin Hood steam locomotive was one of a number of Britannia Class locomotives which became the flagship express locos of the newly formed British Railways in the 1950s.

✷ Robin Hood Boats is a narrow boat hire company based at Sawley Marina on the borders of Nottinghamshire, Derbyshire and Leicestershire.

✷ Robin Hood Archery is based in California, USA. The company provides lessons and coaching as well as selling a wide range of bows and other equipment for the sport of archery.

✷ Robin Hood Industries is one of the leading manufacturers and suppliers of kitchen and laundry equipment in Australia.

✷ Robin Hood flour and baking mixes are produced by Smucker Foods of Canada. Other Robin Hood branded foods include a grilled chicken wrap and a tuna sandwich.

Robin Hood Factoids
✷ In 2007 the University of Nottingham offered an MA course on the subject of Robin Hood.

✽ Lego had a theme based on Robin Hood and his merry men called Forest men. The series was launched in 1987 and discontinued after 1990.

✽ Robin Hood Airport is in the outskirts of Doncaster, less than a mile from the border with Nottinghamshire. It opened officially on 28 April 2005 on the site of the former RAF Finningley.

✽ Robin Hood appears in some versions of the pantomime, *Babes in the Wood* in which he saves the children.

✽ Street names associated with Robin Hood include Maid Marion Way in the centre of the city and Robin Hood Street in Sneinton.

✽ *The Lytle Geste of Robyn Hode* is generally accepted as being the first printed story about Robin Hood.

✽ Bracken is known in some areas as Robin Hood's Sheep.

✽ The red campion flower is sometimes known as 'Robin Hood'.

✽ Lincoln Green is the colour of the clothing generally thought to have been worn by Robin and his Merry Men. The colour was applied to the cloth by first dying it blue with woad and then over-dying it with yellow, obtained from weld or dyers green-weed.

✽ Locksley, or Loxley, is the place often associated with Robin Hood and in some accounts he is known as Earl of Loxley or Robin of Loxley. According to an early ballad it lay in Nottingham but other accounts place it in Staffordshire or Yorkshire.

✽ When the statue of Robin Hood was unveiled in Nottingham in 1952 the archers of Nottingham acted as a guard of honour and were afterwards entertained to lunch at the Council House by the Lord Mayor. Venison and mead were on the menu.

✽ Melvyn Bragg made Robin Hood the subject of one of his *In our Times* series on BBC Radio 4.

✽ Billy Hardcastle is the name of a character in the long running TV series, *Last of the Summer Wine*. Played by Keith Cliff he believes himself to be a descendant of Robin Hood. The character first appears in 1999 when he tries to persuade his companions to join his band of Merry Men.

✽ Around 1401 a short poem beginning 'Robyn hod in Scherewood stood' was scribbled into a Lincoln Cathedral manuscript.

✵ About 1405 a Franciscan friar complained that people would rather hear 'a tale or song of Robyn Hode' than hear mass or matins.

✵ Robin Hood featured in the TV series, *In Search of British Heroes* broadcast on Channel 4 in 2003. Presented by Tony Robinson the series also included the lives of *Boudicca, King Harold of England* and *Macbeth.*

✵ A Google search for 'Robin Hood' will turn up 10,500,000 hits in under a second.

✵ The Great British Teddy Bear Company produces a Robin Hood bear. Standing 34cm tall he is dressed in a green tunic with a lime green collar. He holds a bow in his hand and strapped to his back is a quiver complete with a wooden arrow.

✵ The first postage stamp to feature Robin Hood was issued in Grenada in 1972 to commemorate UNICEF.

✵ Disney has produced a Winnie the Pooh, Robin Hood set of soft toys. They comprise Winnie the Pooh as Robin Hood, Piglet John, Friar Eeyore and Tigger A'Dale.

✵ In a recent survey in Nottingham 32 per cent of visitors and 28 per cent of locals named Robin Hood in response to the question; 'If I say Nottingham to you what immediately comes to mind?'

Sherwood Forest

✵ Robin Hood has been linked to Sherwood Forest for centuries in myth and legend as well as ballads, stories, films and even electronic games. In the Middle Ages Sherwood Forest covered around 100,000 acres of land. Of these around 25 square miles was under tree cover, divided into coppices. Elsewhere it comprised large areas of sandy heath and rough grassland. It stretched from Nottingham in the South to the River Meden in the North. The River Leen formed part of its western boundary. The town of Mansfield lay within its boundaries as well as villages such as Edwinstowe, Thorsby and Gleadthorpe. Sherwood was first recorded in AD958 when it was called Sciryuda which meant the forest of the shire. It became a royal forest after the Norman Conquest and was popular with many Norman Kings, particularly King John and Edward I. Rufford Abbey was established within the bounds of the forest and several other monasteries. The Forest had considerable economic value. The woodland was carefully managed using coppicing and pollarding to produce poles and lathes for building and under-wood was collected and sold for domestic fuel. Charcoal burning was carried out within the forest and oak bark was used in the tanning of leather. Pigs were fed on acorns during the autumn and other animals were grazed on the woodland pasture. Monastic orders established religious houses in the area during the 12th and 13th centuries, the most important of which was Rufford Abbey. They continued the economic development of Sherwood and a number of new settlements were established during this period. After the dissolution of the monasteries in 1536 former monastic land was granted or sold into private ownership (sometimes at 'knock-down' prices). By the 18th century large areas of Crown land in Sherwood had been sold off to members of the nobility. These private landlords created the fine country estates of Thorsby, Rufford, Welbeck and Newstead. Ducal palaces were created either by constructing new houses or converting monastic buildings. Because of the titled aristocrats who owned them, these estates became known collectively as the Dukeries, a term which is still commonly used today. These landowners gained substantial profits from their estates as well as using them for hunting, shooting and entertaining their friends. Livestock and arable farming were important aspects of this rural economy and woodland was carefully managed to provide timber for buildings, furniture, pit props and the ships of the Royal Navy. During Victorian times Sherwood began to attract large numbers of tourists whose interest in the area was encouraged by the growth of an interest in the Middle Ages and in particular the popularity of romantic novels such as Ivanhoe by Sir Walter Scott. Guidebooks were published and local people began to provide refreshments and accommodation for visitors. Tourism continued to expand, encouraged in the second half of the 20th century by increased private car ownership. Part of the Forest was made a Site of Special Scientific Interest in 1954 and in 1969, 87 acres of the ancient oak woodland was leased from the Thorsby estate and made into a country park by Nottinghamshire County Council. A visitor centre was opened in 1976 and today Sherwood Forest Country Park attracts almost a million visitors a year. The come to enjoy the wildlife and the countryside but many are still attracted by the magic of Robin Hood!

✤ Pollen records show that there has been an unbroken cover of woodland here since the end of the last Ice Age, around 10,000 years ago.

✤ Sherwood Forest was once one of the largest of about 90 royal forests which, at their greatest extent in the 13th century, covered around one third of England.

✤ Sir Ralph Plumpton held land at Mansfield Woodhouse in mediaeval times that was called 'wolf hunt land' as it was reputedly given to him for his services in driving wolves out of Sherwood.

✤ In mediaeval times a forest was a legal term meaning an area which was subject to special laws designed to protect the animals such as red deer and roe deer.

✤ The royal forest was divided into separate wards each of which was supposed to hold a court every 42 days at Linby Calverton, Mansfield and Edwinstowe.

✳ Those who were accused of breaking the forest laws were brought before Woodmote courts. Fines were imposed for minor infringements of the forest laws.

✳ Hawking in the forest was a popular pastime for royalty and the privileged lord and ladies of his entourage.

✳ In mediaeval times there were three royal deer parks within Sherwood Forest. These were at Nottingham (now the Park Estate), Bestwood Park and Clipstone. The ruins of King John's Hinting Lodge can still be seen at Clipstone.

✳ Royal use of the forest is commemorated at 'King's Stand' on the edge of Mansfield.

✳ During World War Two a major ammunition sub depot was established in Sherwood Forest. Although this was closed in 1954 the Ministry of Defence continued to own and use areas of Sherwood.

✳ Among the mammals to be found within Sherwood Forest today are fallow deer, occasional red deer and grey squirrels.

✳ The Major Oak is a huge oak tree thought to be around 800 years old. It is located close to the Sherwood Forest Visitor Centre and can be visited at any time the Centre is open to the public. Originally known as the Cockpen Tree (on account of its use as a site for cock fighting), it later became known as the Queen Oak. In 1790 Major Haymen Rooke included the tree in his popular book about the ancient oaks in Sherwood. As a consequence it became known as The Major's Oak and later simply the Major Oak. The Major Oak's vital statistics are impressive. It weighs around three tons, has a circumference of 10m and a spread of 28m, making the largest oak tree in Britain. The tree still has a good acorn crop every three to four years when it can produce as many as 150,000 acorns. Although reputed to be the hiding place of Robin Hood the tree itself would only have been an acorn during that period. The Major Oak was featured in the 2005 BBC TV programme, *Seven Natural Wonders*, as one of the natural wonders of the midlands.

The Officials of the Forest during the Middle Ages

Agister	– An officer responsible for collecting money for grazing rights
Collectors	– These were responsible for collecting the fines and taxes levied in accordance with the laws of the forest
Foresters	– They were sworn to preserve the vert and venison of the forest. It was their duty to attach those who they caught offending against the forest laws and present them to the forest courts
Ranger	– An officer responsible for a certain area of the forest

Woodward   – An official responsible for timber

In addition to these formal appointments local people were employed from time to time in a range of duties which included repairing and maintaining fences, cutting timber and assisting with royal hunts.

Forest Terminology

Assart   – The act of clearing trees and enclosing land for cultivation
Herbage   – Dues collected for grazing cattle and horses in forest pasture
Pannage   – The right to graze pigs
Vert   – Any trees or plants with green leaves
Bloody hand   – Caught in the act of killing the King's deer
Agistment   – Grazing rights in the forest
Back Bear   – Found carrying a dead deer on the shoulders

Forest Place Names

Bilsthorpe   – Old Danish meaning Bild's village
Birklands   – Old Danish meaning birch woods
Edwinstowe   – Old English meaning the chapel of St Edwin, King and Martyr
Farnsfield   – Old English meaning open land covered in ferns
Gleadthorpe   – Old English possibly meaning village of the kites (birds)
Mansfield   – Old English meaning open land by a hill
Sutton-in-Ashfield   – Old English meaning village south of open land with ash trees
Thoresby   – Norse (Viking) meaning Thori's village
Walesby   – Norse meaning Val's village

The Forest Code

Guide against all risk of fire including barbeques
Protect all trees and wildlife
Leave all things as you find them, take nothing away
Keep dogs under proper control and clear up after them
Avoid damaging buildings, fences, hedges, walls and signs
Leave no litter – use the bins or take it home
But most of all, enjoy your visit

Quote – Unquote

Albert Ball VC
World War One flying ace who was born in Nottingham

I love flying, and as they are very short of pilots, I may do a little good...I think I shall make a good pilot.

I only scrap because it is my duty but I do not think anything bad about the Hun.

Oh. Won't it be nice when all the beastly killing is over, and we can enjoy ourselves and not hurt anyone.

Jesse Boot
Philanthropist and founder of the Pharmaceutical Company which bears his name

Our mutual interests are by no means restricted to business in any limited sense. Fellowship in recreation, fellowship in ideals, common sympathies and common humanity bind us together and whatever fosters this happy union is valuable.

We declare:

For Pure Drugs

For Qualified Assistants

For First class Shops

For Reasonable Prices

For your Good Health

For our Moderate Profits

We minister to the comfort of the community in a hundred ways

When we build factories in which it is a joy to work, when we establish pension funds which relieve our workers of fears for their old age, when we reduce the number of working days in the week, or give long holidays with pay to our retail assistants we are setting a standard which Governments in due time will be able to make universal.

William Booth
Founder of the Salvation Army, who was born in Sneinton

But what is the use of preaching the Gospel to men whose whole attention is concentrated upon a mad, desperate struggle to keep themselves alive.

The profession of a prostitute is the only career in which the maximum income is paid to the newest apprentice.

Why should the devil have all the best tunes.

Many a man takes to beer, not from love of beer, but from a natural craving for the light, warmth, company and comfort which is thrown in along with the beer and which he cannot get except by buying beer.

The tap room is in many cases the poor man's parlour.

William Bradford
One of the Pilgrim Fathers, who came from Nottinghamshire
> The loss of...honest and industrious men's lives cannot be valued at any price.
> Behold now, another providence of God. A ship comes into harbour.
> Cold comfort to fill their hungry bellies.

Jeremiah Brandreth
The Nottingham Captain, leader of the Pentrich Revolution composed the following verse to encourage his followers:
> Every man his skill must try,
> He must turn out and not deny;
> No bloody soldier must he dread,
> He must turn out and fight for bread;
> The time has come you plainly see,
> The government opposed must be

Lord Byron
The famous poet who lived briefly at Newstead Abbey and is buried in Hucknall Church
> A pretty woman is a welcome guest.
> Always laugh when you can. It is a cheap medicine.
> What men call gallantry and gods adultery is much more common where the climate's sultry.
> Opinions are made to be changed – or how is truth to be got at.
> What a strange thing a man is; and what a stranger thing woman.
> I have great hope that we shall love each other as much as if we had never married at all.
> Man, being reasonable must get drunk; the best of life is but intoxication.
> A woman should never be seen eating or drinking unless it be lobster salad and champagne, the only true feminine and becoming viands.

Brian Clough
Football manager
> I wouldn't say I was the best manager in the business. But I was in the top one.
> I like my women to be feminine, not sliding into tackles and covered in mud.
> The River Trent is lovely, I know this because I have walked on it for 18 years.
> They say Rome wasn't built in a day, but I wasn't on that particular job.
> Don't send me flowers when I'm dead. If you like me send them while I'm alive.

William Ewart Gladstone
Nineteenth-century Prime Minister who began his political career at Newark-on-Trent
> All the world over I will back the masses against the classes.
> You cannot fight against the future. Time is on our side.
> No man ever became great or good except through many and great mistakes.
> Justice delayed is justice denied.

Be happy with what you have and are, be generous with both and you won't have to hunt for happiness.

Good laws make it easier to do right and harder to do wrong.

Robert Harris
Author

To say she was my girlfriend was absurd; no one the wrong side of 30 has a girlfriend.

Power brings a man many luxuries but a clean pair of hands is seldom among them.

The art of life is to deal with one's problems as they arise; rather than destroy your spirits by worrying about them too far in advance.

John Harvey
Created the Nottingham detective, Inspector Charlie Resnick. His descriptions of Nottingham are vivid, sometimes stark and occasionally humorous.

When it had been announced that London had won the bid for the 2012 Olympics, the joke had been that with several of the events being outsourced, the rowing would be at Henley, the horse riding at Badminton and the shooting would be at Nottingham (a reference to the city's gun crime).

Early evening at the A & E at the Queen's Medical Centre housed the usual miscellany: elderly ladies who had lost their footing on slippery, uneven pavements; men of uncertain years with voices like rusted industrial saws, whose clothes stank of stale urine and hostel disinfectant; a trainee chef with the first two joints of his middle finger safe in a plastic bag of slowly melting ice; a young Muslim girl who had just started her first period; a charmless 14-year-old boy, alarmed and obese who had been taunted into swallowing the dregs of a bottle of toilet cleaner: each and everyone waiting.

Harold Larwood
Cricketer

Cricket was my reason for living.

Down the mine I dreamed of cricket; I bowled imaginary balls in the dark; I sent stumps spinning and heard them rattling in the tunnels.

A cricket tour in Australia would be the most delightful period in one's life, if one was deaf.

D.H. Lawrence
Novelist

Hitch your wagon to a star or you will just stay where you are.

How beautiful maleness is, if it finds the right expression.

I never saw a wild thing sorry for itself. A bird will fall frozen dead from a bough without ever feeling sorry for itself.

Robert Lowe
Victorian Politician, born in Bingham

Let us begin by assuming that we are all damn fools – and now to business (on opening a committee).

The Chancellor of the Exchequer is a man whose duties make him more or less a taxing machine. He is entrusted with a certain amount of misery which is his duty to distribute as fairly as he can.

Stella Rimington
First female Head of MI5 who was born in Nottingham

James Bond has about as much to do with the intelligence profession as Billy Bunter has to do with public schools.

It would be better that the government recognised that there are risks, rather than frightening people in order to be able to pass laws which restrict civil liberties, precisely one of the objects of terrorism – that we live in fear and under a police state.

Alan Sillitoe
The author of *Saturday Night and Sunday Morning* drew heavily on his experience of growing up in post war Nottingham. His characters make the following observations about the city:

Once out of doors they were more aware of the factory rumbling a hundred yards away over the high wall. Generators whined all night, and during the day giant milling machines working away on cranks and pedals in then turnery gave to the terrace a sensation of living within breathing distance of some monstrous being that suffered from a disease of the stomach. Disinfectant-suds, grease, and newly cut steel permeated the air over the suburb of four roomed houses built around the factory, streets and terraces hanging onto its belly and flanks like calves sucking the udders of some great mother.

I hate the castle ... more than I've ever hated owt in my time before, and I'd like to plant a thousand tons of TNT in the tunnel called Mortimer's Hole and send it to Kingdom Cum, so nob'dy 'ud ever see it again.

If you stood between the lions in front of the Council House for an hour a week everybody who lived in the town would sooner or later pass by.

It was a long, straight and cobble-stoned with lamp-posts and intersections at regular intervals, terraces branching off here and there. You stepped out of the front door and found yourself on the pavement. Red ochre had been blackened by soot, paint was faded and cracked, everything was a hundred years old except the furniture.

Paul Smith
Fashion Designer

The Japanese are hard to understand, but once you do the world is your oyster.

Donald Woolfit
Nottingham-born actor

Dying is easy. Comedy is hard (on his deathbed).

Spare us the mischief unleashed by instructions of good speech.

Principal Towns

✳ **Beeston** is a small town located about three miles south-west of Nottingham. It has a population of around 21,000. The Humber factory manufactured bicycles and later motorcycles and cars until 1907. In the 20th century Boots and Plessey were major employers in the area but they have both relocated, and the majority of the population are now engaged in the retail and service sectors of the economy although some commute daily to Nottingham. Beeston's main shopping area is situated along the High Road, much of which has been pedestrianised. There are some chain stores in Beeston but the town is best known for its selection of high quality independent stores including

Statue of a Beekeeper in Beeston.

specialist South East Asian and Mediterranean food shops. The town is well served with two supermarkets and at the time of writing a large Tesco store was being built. The town has a number of historic buildings including a manor house and the parish church of St John the Baptist. Both are included in a conservation area which extends to some interesting older houses in West End. A number of older industrial buildings also remain, including the Anglo-Scotian Mills which have recently been converted into apartments. The town has a railway station and frequent bus services operate to Nottingham, Derby, Loughborough and the East Midlands Airport. The bee features in the coat of arms of the town and an interesting sculpture of a man sitting next to a beehive can be found on the pedestrianised area of High Road.

✳ **Bingham** is a market town with a population of around 9,000 people. It lies about nine miles east of Nottingham and a similar distance to the south west of Newark-on-Trent. It can trace its history back to the Roman settlement of Margidunum and was later settled by the Saxons. It is mentioned in the *Domesday Book* when it was a substantial settlement with a population of around 250. Today most people travel to Nottingham to work although a number of industrial units in the town provide work for a small number of residents. Secondary education is provided by Toothill Comprehensive School and South Nottinghamshire College also has a campus in the town. A market is held every Thursday in the town centre and the town also provides shopping, medical, and leisure facilities for those living in the surrounding villages. Transport links are good. The local railway station provides services to Nottingham, Grantham and beyond, and Trent Barton provides a frequent and well used bus service to Nottingham for commuters, shoppers and nightlife. Bingham is twinned with the town of Wallenfels in Bavaria and regular exchange visits have taken place in the past

✴ **Bulwell** is a market town which has become a suburb of Nottingham. It lies about 4.5 miles north west from the city centre and has a population of 30,000, which accounts for about 10 per cent of the population of the city. The town grew up on a crossing place over the River Leen and a market developed here. The town still hosts a bustling market on Tuesdays, Fridays and Saturdays. Limestone was quarried here from the Middle Ages and coal mines in the area were among the first to be operated on a commercial basis in the late 16th century. The town grew rapidly in the 20th century and a number of large housing estates were built here. The town has good transport links. There are three stops serving Bulwell on the Nottingham Express Transit tram system: Bulwell, Bulwell Forest and Moor Bridge. These provide access to Nottingham city centre and Hucknall. The town's railway station is situated on the Robin Hood Line which links Nottingham to Worksop. A large bus station provides a frequent services to the city centre and elsewhere. People travel to the centre of Nottingham for some of the shopping and entertainment needs but Bulwell does have a library, swimming pool and several fast food restaurants. A variety of shops provide for most regular purchases and national chain stores such as Argos, Boots and Wilkinsons are represented in the town.

✴ **Eastwood** is a former coal mining town which lies about eight miles northwest of Nottingham on the border between Derbyshire and Nottinghamshire. It has a population of around 19,000 people and is well known as the birthplace of D.H. Lawrence. Eastwood may have originated as a Viking age clearing in Sherwood Forest but in the Domesday Survey it was recorded as waste. By the end of the 17th century the population was still less than 200 and it remained a small village until 1770 when the opening of the Erewash Canal led to the rapid expansion of the coal mining industry. The last mine closed in 1985 and tourism has become more important to the local economy. The town has a good range of shops and a modern library but the Giltbrook Retail Park, just outside the town, attracts shoppers from much further afield. The huge IKEA store dominates the site but a number of other major retails are located there including Comet, British Home Stores, Boots and Next. Secondary education is provided by Eastwood Comprehensive School which is a Specialist Arts College. Castle College in Nottingham also has a centre in the town and the Eastwood Skills Shop offers a range of courses including arts and crafts, and information technology. Eastwood Community Sports Centre has a four-court sports hall and two junior and two full size football pitches. The town supports

Eastwood Library and Millennium Clock.

a number of sports clubs including Eastwood Town FC, known as the Badgers, who play in Conference North. Eastwood Hall, previously the regional headquarters of the NCB is now a hotel and conference centre. The local newspaper is the *Eastwood and Kimberley Advertiser*.

✻ **Hucknall** is situated to the north of Nottingham and has a population of around 30,000. The town dates back to the Saxon period and is mentioned in the *Domesday Book* as Hochenhale. The town's prosperity was based on textiles and coal mining. Hucknall was a mining town from 1861 to 1986 and a bronze statue commemorating the 'lost' mining industry was recently placed in the town. The main figure stands on top of a Davy lamp whist another collier is depicted hewing coal 'inside' the lamp 'glass'. The Rolls-Royce Test Flight Centre operated at Hucknall from 1927 until 1971 and engines were tested here until 2008. Hucknall has a number of old buildings including framework knitters cottages, 19th-century miners' houses, the oldest board school in Nottinghamshire and the Chequers Inn, the former Watson Fothergill Coffee House. The market place is dominated by the St Mary Magdalen Church which contains the remains of Lord Byron, the famous poet. Hucknall has a good variety of shops, a library, a community centre and theatre, and a modern leisure centre. The town is the northern terminus of the Nottingham Express Transit tram system as well as sharing a station on the Robin Hood line. Regular bus services link the town with Nottingham, Mansfield, Bullwell, Eastwood and Heanor. Titchfield Park, donated to the town in 1914 by the Duke of Portland, provides peaceful walks, sports pitches and a children's play area.

* **Kirkby in Ashfield** is a market town with a population of around 25,000. It is part of the Mansfield Urban Area and the headquarters of Ashfield District Council are located here. The town is mentioned in the *Domesday Book* when it had a population of around 75. A priest and a church are also mentioned as well as two water mills. The town still has two main churches, St Wilfred's, a Norman church which was gutted by fire in 1907 but quickly restored to its former glory, and St Thomas's which was built in the early 20th century in the neo-gothic style. Kirkby-in-Ashfield was once an important centre of coal mining and railways in west Nottinghamshire, with three active coal mines and a central junction where both the London Midland and Scottish Railway and the Great Central Railway met. The town expanded rapidly during the 19th century but the closure of local coal mines in the 1980s and early 1990s led to an increase in unemployment. Kirkby town centre features an open market on Friday and Saturday with a few stalls on most days of the week. The centre also offers many quaint and specialist shops with a railway station in the middle of the town. This is on the Robin Hood line and provides a link to Nottingham and Mansfield. The area around St Wilfred's Church is a designated conservation area which includes a number of former farm buildings built from local stone and the remains of a 13th-century village cross. The Kirkby and District Conservation Society run a heritage centre and shop on Kingsway where they are happy to discuss aspects of the town's heritage with visitors. Portland Park, Kingsway Park and Kirkby cross Conservation area provide open spaces where local people can enjoy the countryside.

* **Mansfield** is the largest town in Nottinghamshire and has a population of 67,885. It is situated in the east of the county and lies on the River Maun, from which the name of the town is derived. Celia Feinnes who visited the town in the 17th century wrote, 'There is nothing remarkable here'. This was perhaps unfair as the town retains some interesting features even today. The tower of the church is Norman with a top stage added around 1300. Its spire was erected in the late 17th century. Elsewhere in the town a number of old and interesting buildings can still be seen including the Moot Hall, the Bentinck Memorial and the impressive railway viaduct built in 1875 for the Midland Railway Company. A more recent landmark is the 'Tribute to the British Miner', a three metre high sculpture of a miner by Nikolaos Kiotiamanis, which celebrates Mansfield's coal mining heritage and the contribution that miners made to the economy of Great Britain and the local area. Mansfield was also the home of

Tribute to the British Miner in Mansfield.

Mansfield Brewery, once the largest independent brewery in the UK. Following its takeover by Wolverhampton & Dudley Breweries in 1999 production moved elsewhere. With the decline of the mining, brewing and textile industries unemployment in Mansfield is above the national average but it remains a lively and vibrant place. In addition to a thriving market Mansfield also boasts two indoor shopping centres and wide range of national retailers including Debenhams, Primark, HMV, WHSmith and Marks and Spencer, are represented in the town. Entertainment facilities include the Palace Theatre, a multi-screen cinema, and a number of pubs, clubs and music venues. A museum traces the history of the town and features displays relating to local industries, transport and social history. The local newspaper is the *Chad* (formerly *Chronicle Advertiser*) and Mansfield also has its own local radio station; Mansfield 103.2. A number of bus companies operate services to surrounding areas. The railway station is served by the Robin Hood line, a relatively new rail link connecting the town with Nottingham and Worksop.

* **Mansfield Woodhouse** is a small town located in the Meden Valley about 2km North of Mansfield itself. The history of the town dates back to the Romans who established a fortlet and a civilian settlement in the area. The village itself probably grew up in the early 12th century with the clearance of people living in nearby Sherwood Forest. In 1304 the village and church burnt down, with the church being rebuilt shortly afterwards. For the next 500 years Mansfield Woodhouse remained a relatively small settlement populated mainly by farmers, foresters and quarrymen although the town also prospered with the growth of the textile and hosiery trades in the 19th century. Sherwood Colliery was opened in 1903 and Mansfield Woodhouse grew rapidly into a small mining town as large numbers of houses were built to accommodate the expanding workforce. Today the town has a population of around 18,000 and is well provided with a wide range of shops and services. A variety of locally owned shops in the town centre are complemented by a large supermarket and a small shopping precinct. Sports are well catered for. A wide range of amateur sporting clubs exist in the town and in 2002 a £1.9 million indoor sports centre was opened. The town is served by a number of primary schools and at the age of 11 pupils transfer to The Manor School, a specialist sports college. Transport links are good and the town has a station on the Robin Hood Line, the local train line linking Nottingham with Worksop. The town also has a quarterly newsletter, the *Mansfield Warbler*, which is distributed free over a wide area. Mansfield Woodhouse is still developing. A new police station was opened in 2007 and new houses are being built near the railway station to replace the older terraced houses which stood there previously.

* **Newark-on-Trent** is a historic market town about 15 miles north-east of Nottingham and 15 miles from Lincoln. It was described by Arthur Mee as 'a busy little Trent town still wearing its mediaeval dress'. Originally a Saxon settlement, Newark-on-Trent was laid out by Alexander the Magnificent,

Bishop of Lincoln in the 12th century. Mediaeval kings visited the town on a number of occasions and King John died in the Castle gatehouse in 1216, During the Civil War it was a royalist stronghold which withstood a number of sieges. The town owed its prosperity to the major transport links of the Trent, the Fosse Way, and the Great North Road, and was a centre of agriculture, particularly wool in the middle ages. Later malting and brewing became important to the economy of the town. By 1801 Newark had a population of 6,730 and was the county's second town. By the end of the 19th century its principal industries included malting, brewing, flour milling, textiles and the manufacture of agricultural machinery. The town's slow decline as a commercial and manufacturing centre has resulted in many of its historic buildings surviving. In 1964 the Council for British Archaeology included Newark in its list of 51 towns of historic quality. The town has a number of mediaeval timber framed buildings as well as several elegant 18th-century town houses. Other buildings of significance include the parish church, the 18th-century town hall and the Osington Coffee Palace. The castle ruins and the recently refurbished Victorian gardens also attract large numbers of visitors. The town centre has plenty of shops, banks and supermarkets, and the historic butter market provides accommodation for a number of interesting local retail outlets. Markets are held in the town on Mondays, Wednesdays, Fridays and Saturdays with antique and craft markets on a Wednesday and Thursday. The town has a local newspaper, the *Newark Advertiser* and a community radio station called Boundary radio. In addition to local services a number of bus companies also provide services to Southwell, Lincoln and Grantham. Newark has two railway stations linked to the national network. The East Coast Main Line runs through North Gate railway station. The Newark Castle railway station lies on the Leicester-Nottingham-Lincoln line providing cross-country regional links.

✳ **Nottingham**, known as the Queen of the Midlands is a major city and an important regional centre. It achieved city status in 1897 and is now a unitary authority with a population of almost 300,000 people. The wider Nottingham Urban area has a population of around 667,000 and is the seventh-largest urban areas in the UK, ranking between those of Liverpool and Sheffield. Founded by the Saxons it was for a period part of the Kingdom of Mercia. It was captured by the Danes in 867 and later became one of the five burghs of the Danelaw. William the Conqueror ordered the building of a castle here and by the time of the Domesday survey the population was at least a thousand. A church and a priest, as well as a mint are recorded at this time. Both town and castle continued to grow throughout the middle ages and the town was visited by a number of mediaeval Kings including Henry I, Richard I and John. The wool industry was important at this time and pottery was also manufactured in the town. There were also the same craftsmen that you would find in any town. These included carpenters, blacksmiths, tanners. The town continued to grow but in 1348–49 almost half the population was wiped out by the Black Death. By the 15th century the town had established itself as the centre of a thriving export trade in religious sculpture made from alabaster. Henry VII visited the town in 1511 and two years later a grammar school was established. Charles I raised his standard here at the start of the Civil War but the response to his call to arms was only 300 men and the town became a Parliamentarian stronghold when the King departed. In the 18th and 19th centuries hosiery and then lace became important industries, and the Lace Market remains a distinctive part of the city even today. By the early years of the 20th century the economy and employment was dominated by Boots, Players and Raleigh. There is little manufacturing in the city today although a number of major companies have their head offices in the city. Nottingham is also the home of H M Revenue and Customs, and the Driving Standards Agency. The creative industries are increasingly important to the economy of the city. Nottingham is a major shopping centre and was recently positioned fifth in the retail shopping league in England. There are two main shopping centres; the Broadmarsh Centre and the Victoria Centre. There are smaller and more specialist shopping centres elsewhere in the city including the Exchange Arcade within the Council House. The city has two football clubs, Notts County FC and Nottingham Forest FC, and Trent Bridge, the home of Nottinghamshire Cricket Club, is a major international cricket venue with a capacity of 17,000. The National Ice Centre is also located in Nottingham and is the home venue for the Nottingham Panthers ice hockey club. Nottingham Tennis Centre regularly hosts major tournaments. Nottingham is also a city of culture with two large capacity theatres, several art galleries and a number of museums. Nottingham Castle Museum and Art Gallery is home to the city's decorative Art and Fine Art collections, along with the story of Nottingham galleries and the Sherwood Foresters Regimental Museum. Classical music is also well catered for with long established groups such as the city's Symphony Orchestra, Philharmonic Orchestra, Nottingham Harmonic Society, Bach Choir and others, giving regular performances in the city. Nottingham also attracts over 300,000 overseas visitor each year. Many are attracted by the legend of Robin Hood but popular tourist attractions include Nottingham Castle, the City of Caves, The Galleries of Justice, Goose Fair and the City's ancient pubs. It is also home to two universities. Nottingham University is a member of the Russell Group and one of the top universities in the UK while Nottingham Trent University is one of the most successful post-1992 universities. Students now make up a significant proportion of the population of the city. The city's newspaper, the *Nottingham Evening Post*, is owned by the Northcliffe Group and is published daily from Monday to Saturday. BBC Radio Nottingham provides a number of local interest programmes and the city is also home to a number of commercial radio stations. Transport links are good. In addition to national and local bus services the city is also served by the Nottingham Express Transit tramway system. There is a frequent rail service between Nottingham and London St Pancras with over 30 direct trains each day. The journey time is around 1hr 50mins. Paris is now less than five hours away via Eurostar from St Pancras International. By almost every definition Nottingham is a thriving 21st-century city.

✳ **Ollerton** was the only new town to emerge in Nottinghamshire in the 20th century, growing from only 690 inhabitants to a population of over 7,000 by the 1980s. Ollerton was originally known as Alreton or Allerton, meaning 'farm among the alders'. It is mentioned in the *Domesday Book* when it had a population of around 75 and two watermills. Situated at the crossroads of York to London, Worksop to Newark, and Lincoln to Mansfield roads, Ollerton became a meeting place for forest officials, commissioners and Justices of the Peace, leading to the establishment of two coaching inns, the White Hart and the Hop Pole. For many years the main occupation in Ollerton was hop growing and from the late 17th century a weekly hop market was held here on a Friday. The opening of Ollerton Colliery in the 1920s led to the building of New Ollerton. The mine closed in 1994 but the site was cleared and replaced with the Sherwood Energy Village. The area is well served with shops, banks and libraries and Ollerton even has its own tourist information centre. Ollerton Railway station closed in 1964 but locally based bus companies provide services to Mansfield, Newark, Worksop and Nottingham.

✳ **Retford** is a market town in the North East of the county about 31 miles from Nottingham. In 1887 John Bartholomew's Gazetteer of the British Isles stated; 'Retford as a well built town with a spacious market space in the centre, a handsome town hall, a corn exchange and a grammar school. It carries a considerable trade in horses, cattle, cheese and hops. The industrial establishments include iron foundries and paper mills'. The Town Hall, a French-inspired Victorian building, still stands and a market is held in the town every Thursday and Saturday. Just across from the Marker Square is Cannon Square where you will find a canon captured from the Russians during the Crimean War. With a population of only 21,000 people, the town is remarkably well provided with facilities and services including a museum, leisure centre and two theatres. Retford also has its own newspaper, the *Retford Times*. Sports are well catered for and the town's football team. Retford United Football Club, known as the Badgers, currently play in the Northern Premier League, Premier Division. A new bus station was opened in 2007 at a cost of £1.4 million. In addition to providing a base for local bus companies it is also the terminus of the National Express coach service between Victoria Coach Station in London and Retford. A regular bus service also connects the town with the nearby Robin Hood Airport. The town's railway station is served by both the East Coast Mainline and the Sheffield to Lincoln Line.

✳ **Southwell** is a small but prosperous town situated about 14 miles northeast of Nottingham and a similar distance from Newark. It lies on the River Geet and has a population of around 7,000. Settlement in the area dates from Roman times and the remains of a substantial villa have been discovered here. It was an important place at the time of the Domesday survey with a population of around 500 people, two mills, a fishpond and a ferry. Three clerics are mentioned here as well as six men at arms. The town is dominated by Southwell Minster which was

The Saracen's Head, Southwell.

built in the 12th century. The chapter house, completed in the late 13th century, contains some of the finest examples of naturalistic carvings in the country. Southwell boasts more than 150 listed buildings including the bishops palace, several prebendal houses, the Saracens Head public house and Burgage House, where Lord Byron lived from 1804 to 1807. Southwell Workhouse, on the edge of the town, was built in 1824 and is the most complete workhouse in the country. It is owned by the National trust and attracts thousands of visitors each year. The Minster School is a state secondary school which supplies the Minster choir and until recently there was a boarding section for choir boys in the town. The main shopping area in the town is King Street where you will find a range of shops including boutiques, banks and bistros. Some of these shops are exclusive and expensive and the *Nottingham Evening Post* recently described the town as the millionaire capital of Nottinghamshire. The town has also been described as 'visibly affluent'. Commuters from Southwell use the railway station at the nearby village of Fiskerton which is on the Nottingham-Lincoln line. Local bus services provide links to Nottingham, Mansfield and Newark. Southwell is twinned with Sees, a small town in France. Like Southwell it has an impressive cathedral with twin spires.

* **Stapleford** is a small town with a population of around 17,000. It lies in the Erewash valley close to the Derbyshire-Nottinghamshire border. The town dates from Saxon times and the name Stapleford is believed to derive from 'the

The Arthur Mee Centre at Stapleford.

post by the ford'. There is an 11th-century Saxon Cross in the churchyard, one of the best examples in the county. Stapleford remained a farming community for hundreds of years but during the 19th century a number of lace manufacturers built factories in the town. In the 20th century many of these were taken over and used by other companies including Carr Fastener, Chambers pencils, and Johnson & Barnes. Sandicliffe Garages are today the largest employer in the area. In the centre of the town there are two small supermarkets. Most of the other shops are small independent retailers or charity shops. The town does have a library and a Health Centre and secondary school pupils attend the George Spencer Foundation School and Technology College. Regular bus services link the town with Nottingham, Derby, Loughborough, Long Eaton, Ilkeston and Beeston. Most residents travel to Nottingham for employment, shopping and entertainment.

✳ **Sutton in Ashfield** is situated four miles west of Mansfield close to the Derbyshire border. The town has a population of around 43,000 and dates from Saxon times. In the past most people were employed in the hosiery and coal mining industries. Today Sutton in Ashfield has a lively and vibrant town centre with an indoor market based inside the Idlewells shopping centre and a bustling outdoor market on Tuesday, Friday and Saturday. The East Midlands Designer Outlet village also sits on the edge of the town adjacent to Junction 28 of the M1. The main tourist attraction in the town is the largest sundial in

Europe, which is located in the town centre on Portland Square, it reaches 10m skyward. The town is also well served with a wide range of leisure facilities. The Lammas Leisure Centre contains a fully equipped 100 station fitness suite, sports hall, two swimming pools, six rink indoor bowls hall, three multi-use rooms, two squash courts, a purpose built crèche and an ice rink. There are a number of parks and open spaces including Sutton Lawn and Brierly Forest Park. The Ashfield Show, held on Sutton Lawn is the largest free community show in the East Midlands. It celebrated its 32nd year in 2010 and regularly includes attractions such as fairground rides displays from local businesses, live music, classic cars and steam engines. Secondary education is provided by the Sutton Centre Community College. The town is served by Sutton Parkway railway station, two miles south of the town centre. This is served by the Robin Hood Line. Regular bus servicers also link the town with Mansfield, Nottingham and Derby.

✳ **Worksop** is the largest town in the Bassetlaw district of Nottinghamshire and has a population of around 40,000 people. It is situated close to Sherwood forest and only 19 miles from Sheffield. The town promotes itself as 'The Gateway to the Dukeries'. It is mentioned in the *Domesday Book* when it was known as Werchesope and had a population of around 150. Early in the 12th century William de Lovetot established a castle and an Augustinian Priory here and subsequently Worksop grew into a market town. Markets are still held here on Wednesdays, Fridays and Saturdays. In the 17th century the town was known for the cultivation of liquorice and later for its malting industry. The construction of the Chesterfield Canal and later the Manchester, Sheffield and Lincolnshire Railway stimulated the growth of the town and by the time Manton Colliery was opened in 1898 Worksop had become more of an industrial centre than a country market town. Today major employers in the area include Premier Foods, Wilkinson and B&Q. The railway station is the Northern terminus of the Robin Hood line from Nottingham and Mansfield. It is also an intermediate stop on the regional service from Lincoln to Sheffield operated by Northern Trains. The town also has its own newspaper, the *Worksop Guardian*. The town has a number of interesting and historic buildings including the Priory Church of St Mary and St Cuthbert, the town hall and the 16th-century Old Ship Inn. Perhaps the most fascinating place in the town is Mr Straws house. This ordinary semi-detached house with original interior decoration from 1923 was the home of the Straw family. For over 60 years the family threw little away and chose to live without many of the modern comforts which we take for granted. Photographs, letters, Victorian furniture, and household documents can still be seen exactly where their owners left them.

Notable Buildings

✳ There are over 5,000 listed buildings in Nottinghamshire. These include great houses such as Wollaton Hall, impressive churches such as Southwell Minster and a number of mills, factories and railway stations. Add to these a variety of mediaeval merchant's houses, ancient inns and humble terraces and you begin to get a flavour of the county's amazing architectural and historic heritage. The county also has a good number of innovative 21st-century buildings, many of which have been listed or received awards for their design. The following, therefore, represents only a tiny proportion of the buildings which are worth a visit.

✳ The orangery at Rufford Abbey started life as bath house and summer pavilion. It was built in 1729 by Sir George Saville to a design by John Hallam. The building was converted into an orangery or hothouse for exotic plants by Sir John Saville in 1889. After years of neglect Nottinghamshire County Council restored the Orangery in 1995.

✳ The former Boots store on High Street Nottingham, a major work by Albert Nelson Bromley has recently been restored by fashion chain, Zara.

✳ The Woolpack public house on Stodman Street Newark was built around 1452 as a rich merchant's house. Originally the building had three bays, with the upper floors jettied forward.

✳ The former Great Northern (Low Level) station was designed by Thomas Hine and opened in 1857. It closed to passenger traffic and lay derelict and in need of a new use for several years. The building was successfully refurbished between 1998 and 2001 as a health club with a complete internal and external restoration.

✳ The Church of the Good Shepherd in Woodthorpe has been described as one of the outstanding 1960s buildings in Nottingham. The architect was Gerald Goalen and it won an award from the Royal Institute of British Architects in 1966. A light and spacious building with attractive contemporary stained glass it was recognised by English Heritage with the award of a Grade II listing in 1998.

✳ The former High Pavement Chapel (designed by Stuart Coleman in 1876) is now the Pitcher and Piano, a highly popular bar. It retains the magnificent stained glass by William Morris and Edward Burne-Jones.

✳ The Boots D10 building in Beeston, described as a 'crystal palace of industry', opened in July 1933. Widely regarded as a milestone in modern British architecture it underwent a major refurbishment between 1991 and 1994.

✳ The Inland Revenue Headquarters designed by Michael Hipkins is regarded as one of the key late 20th-century landmarks in Nottingham. Constructed between 1992 and 1995 the project brought 2000 new jobs to the city and launched the regeneration of the then neglected canal corridor.

✳ The Anglo-Scotian lace mills at Beeston are architecturally one of the most interesting factories in the region. They were built in the Gothic style in the 19th century with turrets and crenulations.

✳ Brewhouse Yard in Nottingham is a collection of 17th-century houses which have been converted into a museum which explore social life in Nottingham from the Victorian period to the 1920s. A number of period rooms have been recreated as well a variety of shops, from chemists to cobblers.

✳ The Corn Exchange in Newark was opened in 1848 and it was here that farmers and merchants conducted their business at a time when Newark was known as the 'Granary of England'. This impressive building is decorated with shells which have ears of corn springing out of them.

✳ The Residence and Vicars Court in Southwell occupies the site of the mediaeval College of Vicars. The Residence, built in 1689, is the home of the Dean of Southwell.

✳ The Governors House in Newark is a fine timber-framed building which was built in 1474. It takes its name from the fact that it was used by the Governor of Newark during the Civil War. It was also here that Charles I quarrelled with his nephew, Prince Rupert, after his defeat at the Battle of Bristol. Today the building is a bake house and tearoom.

✳ The Nottingham Building Society building in the Market Place at Newark was once the Old White Hart Inn. It was described by Pevsner in 1979 as 'one of the paramount examples of 15th-century timber framed architecture in England' but recent research has found that the rear range dates from the early 14th century. The building was saved from collapse and restored in the 1970s. The small plaster figures on the front of the building depict Saint Anthony of Padua and Saint Barbara, repeated over and over. The walls of the building society display mediaeval wall painting (vines with grapes) referring to the room's original function.

✳ Teversall Manor is an 18th-century manor house in the village of Teversall near Sutton in Ashfield. It is believed to be the inspiration for D.H. Lawrence's Wragby Hall in the controversial novel, *Lady Chatterley's Lover* and was once owned by the fifth Earl of Carnarvon who financed the expedition to unearth the tomb of Tutankhamen.

✳ The Old White Hart is the oldest surviving Inn in Newark and dates from the early 14th century. The ornate façade of the front section, created in 1459, was extensively restored in the 1980s but is authentic in style and colour as sufficient original material remained for copies to be made.

✢ The National Ice Centre is a stunning contemporary building which was opened in 2000 by Jayne Torville. The centre provides top class facilities and training for a wide range of ice sports as well as skating sessions for people of all ages and standards. The building is also home to the Trent FM Arena (formerly Nottingham Arena) a concert venue with capacity for up to 10,000.

✢ Newark Town Hall is one of the finest in the country. It was designed in the Palladian style by the eminent architect, John Carr of York. It is a Grade 1 listed building and is still used as a working town hall. The building houses part of the museum as well as an art gallery.

✢ The Moot Hall in Mansfield was built in 1752 and was paid for by Henrietta Cavendish Hollis who lived at nearby Welbeck Abbey. The ground floor was used as a trading and meeting place while the first floor, originally one large assembly room, was used for music, dancing and card playing. It was also venue for scientific lectures.

✢ Papplewick Pumping Station near Ravenshead has been described as the finest Victorian water pumping station in Britain. The ornate brickwork and carved stone of the exterior is matched by richly decorated pillars and stained glass on the inside of the building. Built to provide a clean water supply to Nottingham it is powered by two single-cylinder rotating engines. These were built by James Watt & Co. in 1884 and are fired by six Lancashire boilers. The building is open on Sundays from April to October and steaming days are held from time to time. A similar Pumping Station exists at Bestwood. This was built in 1873 in the Italian Gothic style.

✢ The Jubilee Campus of the University of Nottingham was built between 1996 and 2004 on a site that was formerly occupied by the low rise sheds of the Raleigh Cycle Factory. Designed by Hopkins Architects, the most exciting feature of the site is the iconic circular library. The whole campus was designed with an emphasis on energy efficiency and their green credentials are impeccable. The extension to the Jubilee Campus built between 2006 and 2008 are even more stunning and have been designed to an aesthetic of strong form and vivid colour – they really do need to be seen to be appreciated!

✢ The Corner House in Nottingham is a stunning entertainment complex close to the Theatre Royal and Royal Concert Hall. Completed in 2001 at a cost of over £40 million it makes good use of glass and light weight construction materials. A recent study of new buildings in the city described the interior as glitzy with a significant wow factor and declared; 'In terms of the city

The Corner House, Nottingham.

centre's renaissance...the Cornerhouse has made a significant contribution and works well as a decent piece of urban fabric'.

✳ The Bentinck Memorial in the Market Place, Mansfield, was erected in 1849 by public subscription to honour the memory of Lord George Bentinck of Welbeck Abbey. Bentinck was a well known politician whose family owned much of the land in and around Mansfield.

✳ Ossington Coffee Palace in Newark was built in 1882 by Viscountess Ossington as a temperance hotel. Designed by fashionable London architects Ernest, George and Harold Peto, it is a lavish combination of 16th and 17th-century styles. Today it is a popular bar and restaurant.

✳ Papplewick Pumping Station was built in 1885 to supply Nottingham with water. It is a magnificent monument to Victorian municipal engineering and architecture with lavishly ornamented pillars, delicate metalwork and stained glass windows featuring water motifs. Two rotating beam engines built by James Watt are regularly steamed by volunteers. The building is now in the hands of a preservation trust.

✳ The Palace of the Archbishops of York at Southwell dates from the 14th and 15th centuries. It was a favourite residence and retreat of many archbishops and it is known that Cardinal Woolsey stayed here for a few weeks in 1530 attempting to avoid the wrath of King Henry VIII. Much of the building is now in ruins but part of the Palace is still in use including a parlour or state room which is now known as the Great Hall.

✳ The Adams Building in the Lace Market area of Nottingham was designed by T.C. Hine and opened in 1855. It is probably the largest and finest example of a Victorian lace warehouse in the country and is a Grade II listed building of architectural and historical significance. The building now forms part of the City Campus of New College, Nottingham.

The Adams Building.

- Upton Hall is a magnificent Grade II listed building which is now the home of the British Horological Institute. It contains a fascinating collection of clocks and watches including the actual watch worn by Captain Scott on his ill-fated Antarctic Expedition and the first self-winding wristwatch.

- Nottingham Magistrates Court was completed in 1995. With a stunning glass atrium the building comprises 24 courts and an office building. Opening out into a public space the building overlooks an attractive section of the Nottingham Canal close to the railway station and centre of the city.

- Nottingham Contemporary at Weekday Cross is one of the largest contemporary art centres in the Britain. Designed by Caruso St John, it opened in November 2009 with an exhibition of early works by David Hockney and current works by the Los Angeles based artist Frances Stark. It comprises four galleries, an auditorium, educational facilities, a café bar and a shop. It stages a number of major exhibitions each year and was chosen to launch the British Art Show 7 in October 2010.

- The Shire Hall in Nottingham's Lace Market district was built in 1770 and comprised two court rooms, a gaol and a site for executions. It ceased to be a court in the 1980s. Today the building houses the Galleries of Justice, a museum dedicated to the history of the justice system.

- Nottingham Playhouse has been described as the most important twentieth century building in Nottingham's city centre and the most imaginative post-war theatre in the

The new magistrates court building in Nottingham.

Southwell Workhouse.

country. Built between 1961–63 by Peter Moro its most distinctive feature is a round auditorium. Today the Playhouse stages a wide variety of productions ranging from traditional drama and musicals to comedy, dance and a very popular annual pantomime.

✳ Bromley House is the home of Nottingham's Subscription Library which was founded in 1816. The house itself was built in 1752 by George Smith and is regarded as one of the city's finest 18th-century houses.

✳ The workhouse at Southwell, built in 1824, is one of the best preserved remaining examples of hundreds of workhouses built across the country. It is now owned by the National Trust and is open Wednesday to Sunday from April to October.

✳ The Holocaust Centre in the north of the county was established in 1995. The exhibition here provides a human and personal perspective on the Holocaust, focusing on Jewish life in Europe before World War Two, the rise of National Socialism, the Holocaust, survival and post-war justice. The centre attracts over 20,000 visitors each year.

✳ Annersley Hall, a Grade II listed building, was once the home of William Chaworth who was fatally wounded in a dual with Lord Byron's great uncle. It is now reputed to be one of the most haunted buildings in the country.

✳ Nottinghamshire has around 20 windmills but most of these are in a ruinous state. Three still exist in working order at North Leverton, Tuxford and Sneinton (Green's Mill).

✳ The Bell Inn in Angel Row, Nottingham was first recorded in 1638 although some of its timbers date from much earlier. It is built over a number of caves. These contain the so-called Monks Well which was found to be full of early 15th-century rubbish when it was excavated in 1998.

Nottingham Theatre Royal.

* The Severn's Building is a 14th-century timber-framed building which previously stood in the Middle Pavement. It was originally the front range of a mediaeval merchants house comprising a three bay hall over a ground-floor shop and workroom. It was moved to Castle Gate in 1969–70 when the area was redeveloped to create the Broadmarsh Centre. For many years it housed the Lace Centre, an important tourist attraction, but this closed in 2009.

* The Theatre Royal in Nottingham opened in 1865. It's Classical façade and Corinthian columns, designed by Charles J. Phipps, remain a well-known and popular feature of the urban landscape. In 1978 the 1,186 auditorium was carefully restored in Victorian style green and guilt decor and with fully comprehensive and technically upgraded backstage facilities. The Theatre Royal is now regarded as one of the best touring venues for drama, ballet, opera and West End musicals as well as a very popular annual pantomime.

Twin Towns

Town twinning began in the years following World War Two as way of developing international understanding. A number of places in Nottinghamshire are twinned with towns in Europe and elsewhere. These are often formal arrangements endorsed by the respective councils but in other cases the links may be informal, inactive or dormant. Some are links are more active than others. The following may not be a definitive list.

✳ Bassetlaw District is twinned with Garbsen in Germany, Pfungset in Germany, Aurillac in France and Framers Branch in the USA.

✳ Garbsen, which is in lower Saxony lies just west of the city of Hannover. It has a population of over 60,000. The present town was created in 1974 by the amalgamation of several districts including Old Garbsen, Barenbostel, Havelse and Auf der Horst. As a result, Garbsen suffered for many years from the lack of an identifiable centre. This problem was overcome in 1998 with the opening of a new town hall. The opening ceremony was attended by representatives of Bassetlaw District Council and its twinning association. Employment in Garbsen is similar to Worksop. Many of its people are engaged in light industry and others commute to the nearby city of Hannover.

✳ Pfungset is the largest town in the district of Darmstadt-Dieburg in the state of Hesse. The cities of Frankfurt and Heidelberg are both within 30 minutes drive. Originally a village with several corn mills, Pfungstadt has grown into a substantial provincial town and an important industrial centre. The town in also famous for its beer, Pfungstaedter, which can be found all over Germany.

✳ Aurillac is a historic town in the Auvergne region of Central France. The capital of Cantal, it has a population of around 30,000 and is well known for the manufacture of umbrellas. More recently the creation of a business park has led to the growth of employment opportunities in the field of information technology. Aurillac is also an important cultural centre with a municipal theatre, a conservatory of music and dance and a museum of art and archaeology housed in a 17th-century convent building.

✳ Farmers Branch is a city in Dallas County, Texas with a population of around 32,000 people. It is close to Dallas and only 10 minutes drive from Dallas/Fort Worth International Airport. Founded in the 1840s as Mustang Branch it was incorporated as a city in 1946 and grew rapidly in the 1950s and 1960s. The city is now home to around 2,500 companies and 70 corporate headquarters and as a result its population swells to around 100,000 during normal working hours. The heritage of the city is commemorated in a Historical Park where some of the original buildings of the 1840s are gathered together in the form of a village. Each year in December the city holds a 'Dickens in the Park' festival and 'English Yuletide Teas' are served each Saturday.

✳ Bingham is twinned with Wallenfells in Germany. Wallenfells is a town in the district of Kronach in the Frankenwald (Franconian Forest) Bavaria. With a population of 7,500 it has been twinned with Bingham since 1984. This area is popular with tourists, particularly walkers and cyclists.

✳ Broxtowe has been twinned with Gutersloh in Germany since 1988. Guttdersloh is a town in North Rhine-Westphalia. It has a population of around 96,000 and is the administrative centre for a district of the same name. It is an industrial town whose major employers include Meile who manufacture domestic appliances, and Bertelsmann, a media corporation. The town has a wide range of recreational amenities including parks, adventure playgrounds, swimming pools and an amphitheatre. Gutersloh is also home to a British army base.

✳ Collingham is twinned with Villeneuve in the Burgundy region of France. A small town with a population of less than 6,000, it lies on the River Yonne between the cities of Sens and Joigny. The main sights include the church of Our Lady of the Assumption and the gates and towers of the mediaeval town walls.

✳ Gedling is twinned with Rotenburg au der Fulda in Germany, Messolonghi in Greece and Vandoevre les Nancy in France.

✳ Rotenburg au de Fulda is a picturesque holiday town located about 80 miles east of Frankfurt in the state of Hesse. The old town has a number of historic buildings including a castle, a 16th-century town hall and several churches. It has a population of around 14,000. Some are employed in textiles and light industry but the majority work in the service sector. Especially important to the town is the HZK Cardiovascular Centre. A Christmas Market is held in the town each year which boasts Germany's tallest Christmas Pyramid.

✳ Missolonghi is the capital of Aetolia-Acarnania and its second largest town with a population of around 18,000. It is located between the Acheloos and Evenos rivers and has a port on the Gulf of Patras. It trades in fish, wine and tobacco. The connection between Messolonghi and the Gedling area stretches back as far as 1824 when Lord Byron of Newstead Abbey was welcomed as a benefactor and citizen of the town. A hero of the Greek war of independence it is said that his heart was buried in Messolonghi.

✳ Vandoevre les Nancy has been twinned with Gedling since 1996. With a population of around 35,000 it is the second largest commune in the Meuthe-Moselle department after the capital Nancy, of which it is a suburb. It is the home of the National School of Agronomy and Food Industries. Nancy itself is a university city, the seat of the Diocese of Nancy and the home of the Opera National de Lorraine. The Place Stanislas is a World Heritage Site.

✳ Keyworth is twinned with Feignes in France. Feignes is in the Nord-Pas-de-Calais and is only five miles from the Belgian border. A small town with a population of around 7,000 people it became twinned with Keyworth in 1977.

✳ Kimberley is twinned with Echiroles in France and Grugliasco in Italy.

✳ Echiroles is a commune in the Isere Department in South Eastern France. A suburb of Grenoble it has a population of 33,000. A former industrial village, the majority of inhabitants worked in the viscose factories, a fabric which was invented in Echiroles in 1884.

✳ Grugliasco is a commune in the Province of Turin in the Piedmont region of Italy. Situated about five miles west of Turin it has a population of about 40,000. Grugliasco is an attractive tow with a number of historic buildings including a late mediaeval bell tower, a number of 17th and 18th-century villas and a number of churches and chapels. Today most people are employed in engineering and technology. In recent years a number of faculties of the University of Turin have relocated to Grugliasco.

✳ Mansfield is twinned with Heiligenhaus in Germany and has links with other towns called Mansfield through a 'Sister Cities' organisation. It was also visited by a delegation from Mansfield, Massachusetts. In the past it has had informal links with Reutov in Russia and Stryj in the Ukraine.

✳ Heiligenhaus is a town in the district of Mettmann in North Rhine-Westphalia, Germany. It lies in a semi-rural area between Dusseldorf and Essen. A number of medium sized companies are based in the town but it also serves as a dormitory for those who work in Dusseldorf and other industrial areas.

✳ Reutov is a town within the Moscow Oblast in Russia. Situated to the west of Moscow it has a population of around 80,000. It has the status of a science city and many of its inhabitants work in the textile and aerospace industries including involvement in the Russian space programme.

✳ Stryj is a city in the Lviv province of Western Ukraine. Previously part of Poland it has a population of around 58,000. During the Cold War it was home to a Soviet air base. Today the people of Stryj are employed in the engineering, woodworking and food industries.

✳ Mansfield, Massachusetts was founded in 1775 as part of the Commonwealth of Massachusetts. It received its name in 1770 in honour of William Murray,

Earl of Mansfield in Nottinghamshire. Mansfield lies about 28 miles south of Boston and has a population of about 23,000. Employment in the town is mainly in the areas of construction, finance, public administration and the service industries.

✳ Newark on Trent is twinned with Emmendingen in Germany, Saint-Cyr-Sur-Loire in France and Sandomierze in Poland.

✳ Emmendingen is a town in Baden-Worttemberg with a population of about 25,000. Located midway between Strasbourg and Basel in the Black Forest area Emmendingen is a mixture of old and modern with a historic town hall and its modern replacement, museums, picturesque 18th-century houses and a water wheel that generates enough electricity for 60 households. The surrounding area is popular with skiers inn Winter and walkers inn Summer and the hillsides are covered in vines producing god quality white wines.

✳ Saint-Cyr-Sur-Loire is a commune in the Indre-et-Loire in Central France. It has a population of 17,000 and is situated on the opposite side of the River Loire from Tours. The industrial development of the town began after World War Two and it is now the third biggest town in the department of Indre-et-Loire, after Tours and Joue-les-Tours.

✳ Sandomierze was twinned with Newark in 2007. It is situated on the River Vistula in South Eastern Poland and has a population of 26,000. Sandomierze is well known for its old town and is a popular tourist destination. The tourist season lasts from April to October. The town retains its original mediaeval street plan and features 120 different historic sites. The most popular ones include the Opatowska Gate, Castle, Cathedral and the 400-year-old Collegium Gostomanum, one of the oldest schools in Poland.

✳ Newark also has strong friendship links with Newark in California dating back to 1985 when the Newark Sister Cities was formed. There are many other Newarks throughout the world, mainly in the USA, with Newark, New Jersey being probably the best known. Newark has links with these other towns and cities through the 'Newarks of the World' organisation, which organises bi-annual reunions. In 1995 the reunion was held outside the USA for the first time when delegates gathered at Newark-on-Trent in Nottinghamshire.

✳ In the USA there are towns or cities named Newark in the following states: Arkansas, California, Delaware, Georgia, Illinois, Indiana, Iowa, Kansas, Maryland, Michigan, Nebraska, Nevada, New Jersey, New York, Ohio, South Dakota, Texas, Vermont, West Virginia and Wisconsin.

✳ Elsewhere in the world there are towns called Newark in Australia, New Zealand and South Africa.

✤ Nottingham is twinned with Ghent in Belgium, Harare in Zimbabwe, Karlsruhe in Germany, Lublijana in Slovenia, Minsk in Belaraus, Ningbo in China and Timisoara in Romania.

✤ Ghent is the capital and largest city in East Flanders and has a population of around 237,000. Situated on the confluence of the Scheldt and the Leie. It is a busy industrial and commercial city with a port and a university. The presence of large numbers of students and young people has turned the city into an important cultural centre. It has a historic centre with a wealth of beautiful buildings and tourism is becoming increasingly important to the local economy. Every year a 10 day long street festival is held in the city attracting around two million visitors. Ghent is also the flower city of Belgium. Flower growers from the region around Ghent sell their begonias and azaleas all over the world.

✤ Harare is the capital of Zimbabwe and has a population of 1,600,000. Until 1982 it was known as Salisbury. Manufactures include textiles, and steel and chemicals, and the city is a trade centre for tobacco, maize, cotton and citrus fruits. The country currently suffers from grave political and economic problems and in 2009 Harare was voted to be the toughest city to live in according to the Economist Intelligence Unit's liveability poll. Harare is the site of the University of Zimbabwe. It has an international airport and two cathedrals (Roman Catholic and Anglican). It is also home to the National Gallery of Zimbabwe and the Queen Victoria Museum.

✤ Karlsruhe is a city in the South West of Germany with a population of 290,000. The city was planned with the palace in the centre and 32 streets radiating from it. Much of the centre was destroyed by allied bombing but was rebuilt after World War Two. It is an industrial and commercial centre and Germany's largest oil refinery is located at the western edge of the city on the banks of the River Rhine. The University of Karlsruhe is the oldest technical university in Germany and 20 per cent of the regions jobs are in research and development. Local attractions include museums and art galleries, a zoo, two botanical gardens and numerous historic buildings and churches. Each year, in July, the city hosts a free open air festival lasting three days.

✤ Lublijana is the Capital of Slovenia. With a population of 270,000 it is also the largest city in Slovenia and its most important economic centre. It has a university and is home to numerous theatres, galleries and museums. It also boasts one of the world's oldest philharmonic orchestras in the world; the Academia Philharmonicorum. In 2010 the city held the title of UNESCO World Book Capital. The city has many attractive buildings and is becoming increasingly popular as a tourist destination.

✤ Minsk was twinned with Nottingham in 1966. It is the capital city of Belarus and has a population of 1,700,000. It is located in the centre of the country on the banks of the rivers Svislach and Niamiha. About 40 per cent of the population are employed in manufacturing; particularly tractors, motor vehicles and domestic electrical goods. Minsk is the major cultural centre of the country with 11 theatres and six museums. It is also home to a number of universities. Minsk International Airport is situated 26 miles to the east of the city.

* Ningbo was twinned with Nottingham in 2005 and is situated in the Zhejiang Province of China. Its deepwater harbour is capable of handling 300,000 ton vessels and is also the headquarters of the East Sea Fleet of the Chinese Navy. Ningbo is an important modern commercial and industrial city which produces a wide range of consumer goods, electrical products, textiles and industrial tools. It has three universities.

* Radcliffe has been twinned with Bussy-St-Georges in France since 1999. Bussy-St-George is a commune in the Seine-et-Marne department in the Ile-de-France region of north-central France, and only 17 miles from Paris. With a population of about 20,000 it is a city of parks and gardens with a wide range of sporting and cultural facilities. An annual carnival is held in March.

* Southwell is twinned with Sees in Normandy, France. Sees is a historic city with a magnificent cathedral, which was built in the Gothic style in the 13th and 14th-centuries. The film producer Luc Besson shot part of his film, Joan of Arc here.

* Nottinghamshire is twinned with the province of Weilkopolska in Poland and with its capital city, Poznan. Weilkopolska is the second largest region in Poland and the third most densely populated. It covers an area of 11,516 square miles and is divided into two distinct geographical areas: a lake district in the North and a flat plain in the South. It has a population of 3.4 million of whom 58 per cent live in towns and cities. The region plays a dominant part in the national production of food and its industries include food and beverage production and cigarette manufacture. Poznan is the capital of the Weilkopolska region. It is one of the oldest cities in Poland and has a population of over 500,000. It is an important centre for trade and industry as well as being a university city. Like Nottingham it has a modern tramway system.

Nottinghamshire and the Arts

Actors and Comedians with a Nottinghamshire Link

- **Richard Bacon** was born at Mansfield in 1947 and studied at Worksop College. His began his TV career as a reporter on LIVE TV and went on to achieve fame as one of the presenters of the BBC television programme, *Blue Peter*. Since leaving the show he has presented *The Big Breakfast*, *Top of the Pops*, *Back to Reality* and ITV's *This Morning*. More recently he has worked as a radio presenter on a number of local and national radio stations.

- **Richard Beckinsale** was born in Carlton and studied acting at Clarendon College. This led to a place at RADA. He made his TV debut in 1969 as a police constable in *Coronation Street* before winning his first starring role as Geoffrey in the sitcom *The Lovers*. He is best known for his starring roles in *Porridge* and *Rising Damp*. He died in 1979 at the early age of 31.

- **John Bird** the well known comedian and satirist grew up in Nottingham and attended the city's High Pavement Grammar School. He is best known for his appearances in *Bremner, Bird and Fortune*. He was awarded an honorary degree from the University of Nottingham in 2002.

- **Leslie Crowther** Born in West Bridgford in 1993, Leslie Crowther achieved fame as a comedian, actor and game-show host. He was the presenter of several popular TV shows including *The Black and White Minstrel Show* and *Crackerjack*. He is best known as the host of the popular game show *The Price is Right* and his catchphrase, 'Come on Down' entered into TV folklore. In 1990 he was chosen to host *Stars in Their Eyes*. He was awarded the CBE in 1993 for his charitable work. He died of a heart attack in 1996.

- **Barry Foster** was born at Beeston in 1931 and is best known for his role as the Dutch detective Van de Valk in the TV series of the same name.

- **Chris Gascoine** Born in Huthwaite, Sutton in Ashfield, Chris Gascoine has played the role of Peter Barlow in *Coronation Street* since December 2002. His other TV credits include *The Secret life of Adrian Mole Aged 13 ¾* (BBC1) as Barry Kent and *Soldier, Soldier* (Central TV) as Toni Rossi.

- **Sherrie Hewson** Born in Burton Joyce as Sherie Louise Hutchinson, she worked as an usherette at the Nottingham playhouse before winning a place at RADA.

Best known for her role as Maureen Naylor, the dizzy accident-prone supermarket assistant in *Coronation Street* from 1993–71, she later appeared in *Emmerdale*. More recently she has made a number of non-acting TV appearances in shows such as *Loose Women* and *Celebrity Masterchef*.

✳ **Phillip Jackson** is a Retford born actor, singer and TV presenter, best known for his role as Inspector Japp in the TV series *Poirot*. Other TV appearances have included *Robin of Sherwood*, *A Touch of Frost*, *Foyle's War* and *Last of the Summer Wine*. He has also appeared in films such as *Scum* and *Give My Regards to Broad Street*.

✳ **Norman Pace** is an actor and comedian who grew up in Newark. He is best known as one half of the comic partnership, Hale and Pace. More recently theatre work has included starring roles in *Chicago* at the Adelphi Theatre and *Breakfast with Jonny Wilkinson* and *Our Man in Havana* at the Nottingham Playhouse.

✳ **June Spencer**, who plays Peggy Woolley in the long running Radio 4 series *The Archers*, was born in Nottingham in 1920. She has also appeared in other radio programmes including *Mrs Dale's Diary*, *Dick Barton* and *Children's Hour*. In 1991 she was awarded an OBE.

Nottinghamshire Musicians
✳ **Eric Coates** was born in Hucknall in 1886 and studied at the Royal Academy of Music in London. He worked as a viola player with the Queen's Hall Orchestra under Henry Wood. He wrote light orchestral music and is best known for the *Dambusters March* and *Sleepy Lagoon*, the theme to *Desert Island Discs*. He died in 1957.

✳ **John Crocker** was born at West Bridgford in 1940. He was the leading clarinet and saxophone player in the Chris Barber Jazz band for over 30 years, retiring in 2003. Since then he has guested with several bands including Kenny Ball and a Ken Colyer tribute band.

✳ **Bruce Dickinson** was born Paul Dickinson at Worksop in 1958. After working with a number of bands he became vocalist with Iron Maiden from 1981 to 1993. After pursuing a solo career he rejoined Iron Maiden in 1999 for the Brave New World album and tour. He presented Bruce Dickinson's *Friday Rock Show* on BBC 6 Music from 2002–10 and has made guest appearances on a number of radio and TV programmes. In addition to his music career he is a qualified pilot and an accomplished fencer. He is also a successful novelist and scriptwriter.

✳ **Christopher Hogwood** was born in Nottingham in 1941. He is a harpsichordist and musicologist, and founder of the Academy of Ancient Music. He has worked with most leading symphony orchestras and opera houses around the world and has won a number of prestigious awards. At the 2010 Beijing Music Festival he was named as Artist of the Year in recognition of his contribution to Baroque music.

✳ **Iain Paice** was born at Nottingham in 1948 and is well known as the drummer of the rock band Deep Purple, of which he was a founding member in 1968. He is the only founding member still performing with the band and the only member to appear on every album the band has released.

✳ **Alvin Stardust** is a pop star and actor who grew up in Mansfield and attended Southwell Minster School. Born Bernard Jewry, he first achieved fame as Shane Fenton with the Fentones in the 1960s. And then, more successfully as Alvin Stardust having hits with *Jealous Mind*, *My Coo Cachoo*, *Red Dress* and *Good Love*. Moving into musical theatre he starred in the UK tour of *Godspell* and played Uriah Heep in *David Copperfield – The Musical* and Sir Billy Butlin in *The Butlin Story* at the London Palladium. In 2005 he starred as the Child Catcher in *Chitty Chitty Bang Bang* also at the London Palladium. He has numerous television appearances to his credit and continues to tour as a performer and singer.

Writers and poets

✳ **Helen Cresswell** was born at Kirkby-in-Ashfield in 1934 and was educated at Nottingham High School for Girls. She was the author of over a hundred children's books including the very popular Lizzie Dripping series and the Bagthorpe saga. She also adapted a number of stories for television including *Moondial, The Famous Five* and *The Demon Headmaster*. She lived in Nottinghamshire for most of her life and died at Eakring in 2005.

✳ **Elizabeth Baguley** is a Nottinghamshire children's author whose work includes *A Long Way from Home*, *The Little Lost Robin* and *Meggie Moon*. As well as writing she is also a storyteller and organises the children's workshop at the annual Lowdham Book Festival.

✳ **Lord Byron** is one of England's most famous poets. He was brought up in Southwell and later inherited the family home of Newstead Abbey. His most famous work is *Childe Harold's Pilgrimage*, which was written over several years. He played an important role in the struggle for Greek independence and died at Missolonghi in 1824 (See also Nottinghamshire Notables).

✳ **Elizabeth Chadwick** is one of Nottinghamshire's best known and best-selling authors. Specialising in historical fiction she is well known for the quality of her research. She is the author of around 20 novels and is published internationally. Her most recent works include *A Place Beyond Courage*, and *To Defy a King*.

✳ **Raymond Flynn** spent 26 years with Nottinghamshire Constabulary. Starting as a uniformed constable, he later moved to CID, serving for 12 years as the

Detective Inspector in charge of the Fraud Squad. After retiring from the force he turned his hand to writing and was a finalist in the 1992 Ian St James Short Story Competition. In 1994 he won the Gooding Prize for short stories. He later went on to write a series of novels featuring Detective Superintendant Robert Graham, set in the fictional seaside town of Eddathorpe.

✲ **Robert Harris** was born in Sherwood, Nottingham in 1957. He attended Belvoir High School, Bottesford and King Edward VII High School, Melton Mowbray. After studying for a degree in English literature at Cambridge University he joined the BBC and worked on a number of news and current affairs programmes. In 1987 he became Political Editor of the *Observer* and a columnist with the *Sunday Times* and the *Daily Telegraph*. He became a successful non-fiction author but his first novel, *Fatherland*, published in 1992 became an international best seller which was turned into a film. Other novels have included *Enigma*, *Archangel* and *Pompeii*. His most recent novel, *Ghost*, has also been turned into a film which received its first screening in 2010.

✲ **John Harvey** is the author of the famous detective novels featuring Inspector Charlie Resnick which are set in Nottingham. A number of these novels have been televised. More recently he has created the character of the detective, Frank Elder.

✲ **Henry Kirke White** was born at Nottingham in 1785. The villages of Wilford and Clifton provided the inspiration for his collection of poems, entitled *Clifton Grove* which was published in 1803. He went on to study at St John's College, Cambridge but overwork and a weak constitution led to his death in 1805 at the early age of 21. He was buried in the church of All Saints, Cambridge.

✲ **Arthur Mee** was born at Stapleford in 1875, later moving with his family to Nottingham. After leaving school he became a reporter on the *Nottingham Daily Express*. In 1895 he became editor of the *Nottingham Evening Post*, later moving to London where he joined the *Daily Mail*. He was a prolific writer, particularly of children's books. In addition to *The Children's Encyclopaedia* he also wrote a number of biographies, the *Children's Bible*, *Children's Shakespeare* and several of books of travels around England and Europe. He was the founder and editor of the *Children's Newspaper* and was lauded as 'Journalist in Chief to British Youth'. He also devised and edited the King's England series of books, a survey of 10,000 towns and villages which ran to 41 volumes but remained unfinished at his death in 1943.

✲ **Stanley Middleton** was born at Bulwell in 1919 and educated at High Pavement Grammar School. His first book, *A Short Answer* was published in 1958 and in 1974 he won the Booker prize for his novel *Holiday*. A prolific author he had written over 40 books by the time of his death in 2009.

- **Julie Myerson** was born in Nottingham in 1960. As a well as writing fiction and on-fiction books she became well known for a long running column in *The Guardian* entitled 'Living with Teenagers', based on her own family experiences. Many of her novels have been regarded as dark and sometimes controversial but her work has been translated into several languages and she has been nominated for a number of literary awards.

- **Cecil Roberts** is a little known writer and editor. He was born in Nottingham in 1892 and he worked for the *Liverpool Post* during World War One and shortly afterwards became editor of the *Nottingham Journal*. His first novel, *Scissors*, was published in 1923. Much of his later life was spent in Italy, although he regularly returned to Nottingham. In 1965 he was made a freeman of the city of Nottingham. He died in Italy in 1976.

- **Alan Silitoe** is the author of many acclaimed novels including *Saturday Night and Sunday Morning* and *The Loneliness of the Long Distance Runner*, both of which were turned into films. Born in the Radford area of Nottingham in 1928 he left school at 14 and worked in a bicycle factory before joining the Royal Air Force in 1946. His first published work, a short story entitled *A Shot in the Dark* appeared in the *Nottinghamshire Guardian* in August 1950. He received honorary degrees from both Nottingham Trent and Nottingham University and was made an honorary freeman of the City of Nottingham. He died in 2010.

- **Geoffrey Treece** was a best-selling children's author. Born in 1909, he won a scholarship to Nottingham High School. After studying for a year at Oxford University he did literary work in London for two years before becoming a teacher at a private school. He struggled at first as a writer but achieved success in 1934 with the publication of *Bows against the Barons*, a Robin Hood story. Later novels included the Black Banner series, *Aunt Augusta's Elephant* and *Mission to Marathon*. In addition to children's books he also wrote a number of adult novels as well as biographies of D.H. Lawrence and Lord Byron. He wrote over a hundred books in total and his work was translated in to 20 different languages. He was the first chairman of the Society of Children's Writers and in 1975 he became a fellow of the Royal Society of Literature. He died in 1998.

Artists and Illustrators

- **Richard Parkes Bonington** was an English Romantic landscape painter and one of the most influential British artists of his time. Born in Arnold in 1802, he was taught to paint by his father and first exhibited his paintings at the age of 11. His family moved to Calais, and then to Paris in 1818. It was here that Bonington met Eugene Delacroix and the two became friends. After working for a while producing copies of Dutch and Flemish landscapes in the Louvre, he went on to study under Antoine-Jean Gos. His skill as a watercolour painter attracted many imitators but he went on to paint many fine works in both oil and watercolour. He exhibited at both the Paris Salon and the Royal Academy. In 1824 he won a gold medal at the Paris Salon along with John Constable and Anthony Copley Fielding. He returned to England in 1826 and died two year later at the age of 25 after a long period of illness. Nottingham Castle Art Gallery holds several examples of his work.

✳ **Thomas William Hammond** was born in Philadelphia in the United States, the son of Nottingham émigrés. He returned to England at the age of four and lived for a while with his grandparents in Mount Street, Nottingham. In 1868 at the age of 14 he enrolled at the Government School of Art and later became a designer of a lace curtains. He won several prizes for his designs and soon began to use his skills as a draughtsman to record aspects of the changing face of Nottingham. From 1882 he began showing his work at local venues and in 1890 exhibited for the first time at the Royal Academy. He enjoyed black and white sketching in charcoal and during his lifetime he produced over 300 illustrations, mainly scenes of Nottingham which have now largely disappeared.

✳ **Nick Hedderley** is a Nottingham based artist. He studied at West Notts College at Mansfield in 1980 before graduating from Birmingham School of Art in 1984. He showed considerable early promise and was awarded first prize from the Holbrook Trust, Nottingham Castle Museum. Beginning as an abstract artist he has since moved to more representational work and from the late 1990s he took his inspiration from the buildings he saw around him in Nottingham, and later London; often painting these buildings as they appeared at night or in the early morning. In 2002 he won First Prize in the Derby Open Competition and in the same year he was awarded a one man show at Nottingham Castle Museum. Since 2006 he has been represented in the permanent collection there and in 2008 one of his paintings was presented to Ningbo Museum, China on behalf of Nottinghamshire Museums and Galleries. In recent years his subject matter has included other locations such as Derby and Dublin and also subject matter seen at different times of the day.

✳ **Laura Knight** was born in Long Eaton, just over the Nottinghamshire border in 1877. She was educated at Brincliffe School and went on to study at the Nottingham School of Art. She first exhibited at the Royal Academy in 1903. At the 1928 Summer Olympics in Amsterdam she won the Silver Medal in Painting and a year later was made a Dame Commander of the Order of the British Empire. In 1936 she became the first woman to be elected to the Royal Academy. She became well known for her paintings of circus performers and ballet dancers but during World War Two she received various commissions via the War Artists Advisory Committee. These included *In For Repair*, *Balloon Site*, *Ruby Loftus* and *Take Off*. In 1945 she was one of a number of artists commissioned to document the Nuremburg War Trials. She found this a daunting ordeal but it resulted in *The Dock, Nuremburg* which was completed in 1946. With the war over she returned to London where she resumed her paintings of ballet, the circus and gypsies. She carried on painting until almost the end of her life. Her last exhibition was held in Nottingham in 1970. Sadly she never lived to see it as she died the day before it opened at the age of 93. The Castle Art Gallery holds over 20 examples of her work, many of which are shown as part of their permanent display.

✤ **Andrew McCallum** was a Victorian landscape painter. Born in Nottingham in 1821 he later became a student at the newly opened Nottingham School of Design. He exhibited his first painting at the Royal Academy in 1850 and four years later was provided with a scholarship to travel throughout Italy in order to make copies of mural decorations for use in government art schools. After returning to England McCallum was commissioned to decorate the interior of the first lecture theatre at the South Kensington Museum (now the Victoria and Albert Museum). A little later he decorated the western exterior of the museum's Sheepshanks Gallery with portraits of famous artists. He spent much of the 1860s touring Europe but continued to contribute to exhibitions in Britain. His painting of *A Glade in Sherwood Forest* helped to establish his reputation as a painter of trees. McCallum's work was popular with the public. He was awarded a silver medal by the Society of Arts and continued to show his work at a number of prestigious exhibitions. His favourite subjects included Windsor Forest, Sherwood Forest and Burnham Beeches in Buckinghamshire. He completed a number of commissions for Queen Victoria and following the death of his wife she granted him the upper storey of a tower in Windsor Great Park to use as a studio. He died in 1902.

✤ **Paul Sandby** who was born in Nottingham in 1731 was a cartographer, turned landscape painter, who along with his older brother was one of the founding members of the Royal Academy in 1768. From 1751 to 1771 he travelled throughout the kingdom, painting country houses and picturesque landscapes, mainly in watercolour. He was also a caricaturist and a rival of the famous William Hogarth. He was widely admired during his own lifetime and has been described as the father of landscape painting and watercolour.

✤ **Joseph Southall** was born at Nottingham in 1861 but moved with his family to Edgbaston, Birmingham following the death of his father. While training to be an architect he studied part time at the Birmingham School of Art. His work was very much influenced by William Morris and the Arts and Crafts movement. He painted a variety of subjects including mythological, romantic and religious subjects as well as portraits and landscapes. He achieved considerable recognition during his lifetime and was elected a member of the Royal Watercolour Society and the New English Art Club in 1925. In 1939 he was elected President of the Birmingham Royal Society of Artists, a post which he held until his death in 1944.

D.H. Lawrence and the
Country of My Heart

David Herbert (Bert) Lawrence was born at Eastwood on 11 September 1885, the fourth child of Arthur John Lawrence, a miner, and Lydia (née Beardsall) a former school teacher. He attended Beauvale Board School from 1891 until 1898, becoming the first local pupil to win a scholarship to Nottingham High School. He spent three, rather undistinguished, years there before obtaining employment as a clerk at Haywood's surgical appliance factory in Nottingham. The work did not suit him and he found the factory girls rather intimidating. A severe bought of pneumonia forced him to leave and he returned home. While convalescing he started to visit the Chambers family at Hagg Farm and began a friendship with Jessie Chambers (Miriam in *The Rainbow*) who encouraged him in his writing. From 1902 he worked as a pupil teacher (later assistant teacher) at the British School Eastwood and at the same time became a part-time student at the Ilkeston Pupil Teacher Centre. In 1906 he took up a teacher-training scholarship at University College. Here he acquired a new circle of friends, among them Louie Burrows, who he had first met at the Ilkeston Centre.

In September 1908 he left home to take up his first teaching post at Davidson Road School, Croydon. He continued to write and his first novel, *The White Peacock* was published in 1911 just a few months after the death of his mother. A teaching colleague, Helen Corke, gave him access to her intimate diaries of an unhappy love affair and this formed the basis of *The Trespasser* his second novel. His love life remained complex and confused during this period and although he became engaged to Louie Burrows in 1910 this was broken off only two years later.

It was also in 1912, after another period of serious illness, that Lawrence left his teaching post in Croydon to return to Nottinghamshire. Shortly afterwards he eloped with Frieda Weekley (née Von Richthofen) the wife of Lawrence's former modern languages professor from Nottingham University. The couple spent some time in Germany before visiting Italy. It was here in 1913 that Lawrence completed the final version of *Sons and Lovers*. After a short visit to England they returned to Italy where Lawrence began work on the first draft of a work which was to be transformed into two of his best known novels *The Rainbow* and *Women in Love*.

The couple returned to England just prior to the outbreak of World War One and were married at Kensington Register Office on 14 July 1914. Confined to England during the war years the couple came to the attention of the authorities and were suspected of being spies. It was during this time that Lawrence completed one of his greatest novels, *Women in Love*.

By the end of the war Lawrence had become disillusioned with this country. In 1919 he and his wife left England to embark upon an extensive period of travel throughout Europe and eventually further afield to Ceylon, Australia, Mexico and

Bust of D.H. Lawrence.

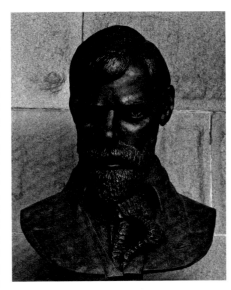

New Mexico. While in the USA he completed a number of new fictional works including *The Boy in the Bush*, *The Plumed Serpent*, *St Mawr*, *The Woman who Rode Away* and *The Princess*. He also found time to produce a number of short stories and a collection of travel writing. A further deterioration in his health forced the Lawrences to move to Italy. They settled near Florence where Lawrence wrote *The Virgin and the Gypsy* as well as various versions of *Lady Chatterley's Lover*. Despite deteriorating health Lawrence continued to write and during the last few months of his life he wrote a number of poems, essays and reviews as well as a defence of his last novel. He died on 2 March 1930 at Vence in the south of France.

His works are heavily autobiographical and the experiences of his life in Eastwood, which Lawrence described as 'the country of my heart' exerted a powerful influence on many of his most important novels.

The Novels of D.H. Lawrence

The White Peacock (1911)
The Trespasser (1912)
Sons and Lovers (1913)
The Rainbow (1915)
Women in Love (1920)
The Lost Girl (1920)
Aarons Rod (1922)
Kangaroo (1923)
The Boy in the Bush (1924)
The Plumed Serpent (1926)
Lady Chatterley's Lover (1928)
The Escaped Cock (1929). This was later republished as *The Man who Died*
The Virgin and the Gypsy (1930)

Lawrence in Film and TV

Lawrence's novels and short stories have been adapted for film and television in several countries on a number of occasions. Some of the more successful adaptations include the following:

✳ *Lady Chatterley* (2007) – Directed by Pascale Ferran and starring Marina Hands as Constance Chatterley, this film won awards for Best Cinematography and Best Actress from the French Academy of Cinema.

✳ Sons and Lovers (2003) – Adapted by filmmaker Stephen Whittaker, it starred Sarah Lancashire and Rupert Evans.

✳ *The Widowing of Mrs Holroyd* (2003) – Starring Colin Firth, Zoe Wannamaker and Stephen Dillane. This film is based on an early play of the same title about a married woman who wishes her husband dead after falling in love with another man.

✳ *Lady Chatterley* (1992) – This BBC1 TV mini-series was written and directed by Ken Russell and featured Sean Bean, Joeley Richardson, James Wilby and Shirley Ann Field. It is an amalgam of three versions of the story written by Lawrence. The music is by Karl Davis.

✳ *The Rainbow* (1988) – Another BBC TV mini-series in three parts. This version starred Imogen Stubbs as Ursula Brangwen, the beautiful naive daughter of a wealthy country squire.

✳ *Kangaroo* (1987) – Tim Burstall directed this adaptation of Lawrence's semi-autobiographical novel recalling his experiences in Australia in the early 1920s. It starred Colin Friels as writer Richard Somers and Judy Davis as his German born wife.

✳ *Trespasser* (1985) – Based on one of Lawrence's lesser known novels, it was directed by Colin Gregg and starred Alan Bates, Pauline Moran, Dinah Stubbs and Margaret Whiting.

✳ *The Horse Dealers Daughter* (1983) Based on a short story and featuring Katherine Canon and Philip Anglim. The film-writer was Robert Burgos.

✳ *Lady Chatterley's Lover* (1981) – Starring Sylvia Kristel, this rather raunchy version was popular at the box office and later as a video and DVD.

✳ *Sons and Lovers* (1981) – Based on Lawrence's semi-autobiographical novel, this seven part adaptation by Trevor Griffiths was a collaboration between the BBC and Twentieth Century Fox. Broadcast in January and February 1981, it featured Karl Johnson as Paul Morel and Leonie Mellinger as Miriam Leivers.

✳ *The Virgin and the Gypsy* (1970) – Directed by Christopher Miles and released by London Screenplays. Joanna Shimkis stars at Yvette and Harriette Harper as her sister Lucille. The gypsy is played by Franco Nero and the firm also features Honor Blackman and Maurice Denham.

✳ *Women in Love* (1969) – Starring Alan Bates, Glenda Jackson, Oliver Reed, Jennie Linden and Eleanor Bron, many of the scenes were filmed locally in Derbyshire and Nottinghamshire. The famous naked wrestling scene was shot in the Gothic Hall at Elvaston Castle near Derby. Glenda Jackson won an Oscar for her portrayal as the free-spirited artist, Gudrun, and received three further nominations for Academy Awards. Ken Russell won a BAFTA for Best Picture.

✳ *The Fox* (1967) – Based on a novella written in 1917 it tells the story of Jill (Sandy Dennis) and Ellie (Ann Heywood), a lesbian couple who live in a remote snowbound cabin. *The Fox* won a Golden Globe Award as the Best English Language Film of 1968 (it was made in Canada) and was nominated for an Oscar for Best Original Score.

✳ Six productions of Lawrence stories, all by Granada were broadcast on the ITV network in 1967. These were: *Strike Pay, Blue Moccasins, Mother and Daughter, The Prussian Officer, Then Thorn in the Flesh* and *None of That*.

✳ *Sons and Lovers* (1960) – Starring Trevor Howard as Walter Morel and Wendy Hillier as Gertrude Morel, it received an Academy Award for Best Black and White Cinematography and Trevor Howard received a nomination as Best Actor.

✳ *Lady Chatterley's Lover* (1956) – The first film adaptation of this novel was updated to the 1950s. Released by Columbia it starred Danielle Darrieux as Lady Constance Chatterley. The dialogue was toned down somewhat when it was translated into English.

✳ *The Rockinghorse Winner* (1949) – Based on a short story of a young boy with a gift of picking racetrack winners and directed by Anthony Pelissier. Starring John Mills, Valerie Hobson and John Howard Davies it was released by Two Cities Films and received great critical acclaim.

Lawrence's Eastwood

✳ Many miners from Eastwood were employed at Brinsley Colliery owned by the Barber Walker Company. Others travelled further afield to collieries at Selston, Alfreton, Cinderhill and Heanor.

✳ The Barker Walker Company erected several hundred houses in Eastwood in the 1870s and 1880s, most notably The Buildings or Squares and The Breach. One resident described them as substantial, roomy and decent, with neat front gardens filled with flowers. To the rear, back gardens led to 'Ash pit Alley' between the blocks. Some of the better houses enjoyed gas illumination from the Eastwood gas works erected by the Barber Walker Company but even these houses relied for water on a single standpipe shared between three or four homes, and earth closets and ash-pits for the disposal of excrement and rubbish.

✳ Illness and injury were a constant presence in the local community. Accidents underground were commonplace and many older or retired miners died from respiratory diseases. Epidemics of measles, diphtheria, diarrhoea and particularly scarlet fever and whooping cough accounted for a number of deaths in Eastwood in the early years of the 20th century.

✳ According to White's History and Gazetteer of Nottingham for 1894 the following types of retail outlet were trading in the Eastwood area.

General Store (Langley Mill Co-operative Society)	1
Clothing and footwear	28
Groceries and provisions	16
Publicans and beer sellers	14
Bakers and confectioners	9
Furniture and household goods	6
Hardware	2

Butchers	8
Chemists and druggists	5
Printers and stationers	4
Hairdressers and tobacconists	5
Other shopkeepers	10

✳ There were a large number of pubs and beer houses in Eastwood in Lawrence's day. These included the Sun Inn, the Three Tuns and the Ram Inn.

✳ There were a number of churches and other places of worship in Eastwood in 1894 including St Mary's Church (C of E), Congregational Church, Wesleyan Methodist Chapel, Baptist Church, Primitive Methodist Chapel and a Roman Catholic Chapel.

✳ There were four schools in Eastwood in 1900: the National which opened in 1863, the British, housed in two buildings opened in 1868 and 1876 respectively, the Undenominational, which had just opened, and Beauvale Board school which was opened in the late 1870s.

✳ The Mechanics Institute was the social centre of Eastwood. Built in 1863–64 for about £1,000 it contained, in the 1890s, a library of over 3,000 volumes, and newspaper, billiard and recreation rooms and a lecture hall capable of holding over 300 people.

✳ An important leisure pursuit of some Eastwood miners was the cultivation of gardens and allotments on which every type of vegetable was grown and where the real enthusiasts kept pigs and poultry.

✳ Other outdoor pursuits included family walks at the weekends into the surrounding countryside and further afield after the Nottingham to Ripley Tramway was opened in 1913. The annual Eastwood Statute Fair or 'statis' as it was known was eagerly anticipated and attracted large numbers of people to its rock and gingerbread stalls, sideshows and roundabouts at a penny a time.

The Country of My Heart

Lawrence described the area around Eastwood as 'the country of my heart'. He used many of these places in his novels, particularly *The Rainbow* and *Sons and Lovers*. Among the places associated with Lawrence or his novels are:

✳ **Eastwood** – Where Lawrence was born and grew to adulthood. It became Bestwood in *Sons and Lovers* and Beldover in *Women in Love*.

✳ **Eastwood Hall** – Now a hotel and conference centre. This was, for many years, the home of the Walker family who together with the Barber family owned many of the collieries in the district. It was used as a location in *Sons and Lovers*.

The D.H. Lawrence Birthplace Museum.

✻ **Beauvale Board School** – D.H. Lawrence attended this school from 1893 to 1898. It was recently renamed.

✻ **Brinsley Colliery** – Lawrence's father worked at this pit. Nothing remains of the colliery buildings although the original headstocks have recently been relocated on the site.

✻ **Birthplace Museum** – Situated at 8A Walker Street, Eastwood, D.H. Lawrence was born here on 11 September 1885. Today it is displayed as it would have been in Lawrences time.

✻ **British School, Eastwood** – Lawrence worked here as a pupil teacher between 1905 and 1906. He wrote of his experience; 'When you've done the day's teaching all your brightness has gone. By the time I get back to the writing I'm another man'.

✻ **Haggs Farm** – This was Willey Farm in *Sons and Lovers*. It was also the home of the Chambers family. Lawrence was a regular visitor here between 1901 and 1908.

✻ **Lamb Close House, Moorgreen** – This was the home of the Barber family, owners of Eastwood Collieries. It was used by Lawrence in his novels as Highclose in *The White Peacock*, Shortlands in *Women in Love* and also in *Sons and Lovers* and *Lady Chatterley's Lover*.

Durban House, Eastwood.

* **Greasley Church** – This features as Greymede Church in *The White Peacock* and Minton Church in *Sons and Lovers*.

* **The Sun Inn, Eastwood** – This Inn was patronised by Lawrence's father. The original market place stood in front of the Inn. In *Sons and Lovers* Lawrence wrote; 'Morel loved her marketing. In the tiny market-place on the top of the hill, where four roads from Nottingham and Derby, Ilkeston and Mansfield meet, many stalls were erected.'

* **Durban House** – Built in 1896 for the Barber Walker Mining Company, and was once the wages office for Brinsley Colliery where D.H. Lawrence's father worked. This was where the young Bert Lawrence would call to collect his father's pay. After lying derelict for some time the building has been renovated and now houses exhibitions relating to the life and times of Lawrence.

* **Cossal** – This features as Cossethay in *The Rainbow*. Church Cottage in Cossal was the house of the Burrows family. Lawrence was briefly engaged to Louie Burrows. In the novel it becomes the home of Will and Ann Brangwen.

* The ruins of **Beauvale Priory** provided the inspiration for *A fragment of stained glass* one of Lawrence's earliest short stories. Two fragments of glass from the Priory are incorporated into one of the windows in Greasley Church.

* **Moorgreen Reservoir** was built to supply water to the local canal system. It became Willey Water in *Women in Love* and Nethermere in *The White Peacock* and *Sons and Lovers*. The drowning scene in *Women in Love* is based on a real accident which took place here.

* **Felley Mill** features as Strelley Mill in *The White Peacock*.

* **Walker Street, Eastwood** – D.H. Lawrence and his family lived in Walker Street between 1891 and 1902. The settings for nearly all his local stories, with the exception of *The Rainbow*, can be seen from here.

* Dialect words were used by D.H. Lawrence in many of his novels and poetry. They are the words and phrases he would have heard growing up in Eastwood. Many of the words were peculiar to the Erewash Valley area though others were in more general usage in mining communities in other parts of Nottinghamshire. Some of the following words and phrases can still be heard today particularly among older members of the community.

Addle	Earn
Argy-bargin	Arguing
Axin	Asking
Bacca	Tobacco
Bantle	The number of men who ride in a pit cage together
Batchy	Silly, stupid
Battle-twig	Earwig
Bertie-Willie	A dandy, a smartly dressed man
Besom	A woman of lose or slovenly habits
Bezzle	Drink immoderately
Bletherin	Talkative
Blort	Talk nonsense
Boss eyed	Cross eyed
Brakes	Railway carriages
Chelp	Impudent talk
Childers	Children
Chomp	Chew, eat noisily
Chunter	Grumble or mutter
Clammed	Hungry, starving
Clat-fart	Gossip
Cod	Penis
Colleyfogle	Cheat, deceive
Crowflower	Buttercup
Crozzled	Shrivelled up with heat
Dool-owl	Spectre or hobgoblin
Frit	Frightened
Frowsty	Rough, untidy or dirty

Gammy	Deformed
Gassin	Talking idly
Gleg	Look
Gorp	Stare at
Guttle	Eat or drink greedily
Hurtle	Crouch
Hutch-up	Move nearer
Ikey	proud or conceited
Knivey	Miserly or mean
May-blobs	Marsh marigolds
Moudiwarp	Mole
Nesh	Weak, tender or sensitive
Noggin	Small portion
Otchel	Hump back person
Pap	Baby food
Scroddy	Puny or meagre
Sharp-shins	An intelligent child
Slutherers	Wastrels or slipshod people
Smarmy	Ingratiating
Snap	Food, a miner's lunch
Spink	Chaffinch
Tabs	Ears
Stool-arsed	Having an office job, a sedentary occupation
Strap	Credit
Strapping	Strong, well-built
Tip callin	Gossip
Tilts	Encounters, fights
Wake	Celebration or fair

Universities in Nottinghamshire

Nottingham University

History
The origins of the University of Nottingham can be traced back to an Adult School established in 1798 and the University Extension Lectures, inaugurated by the University of Cambridge in 1873, the first of their kind in the country. In 1879 an anonymous benefactor provided £10,000 to secure this work on a permanent basis, and Nottingham Corporation agreed to erect and maintain a building for this purpose and to supply funds to employ the lecturers. The foundation stone of the original University College building in Shakespeare Street was laid on 27 September 1877 and the building was formally opened in 1881 by Prince Leopold, the Duke of Albany, although the Charter incorporating the University College of Nottingham was not granted until 1903.

Initially there were four professors; of Literature, Physics, Chemistry and Natural Science. New departments and chairs quickly followed. Engineering in 1884, Classics combined with Philosophy in 1893 and French in 1897. A Department of Education was founded in 1905 and in the same year the combined Department of Physics and Mathematics became two separate entities. Over the next few years other departments and chairs were created including English, Mining, Economics, Geology combined with Geography, History and Pharmacy.

After World War One the College outgrew its premises in the city centre. A generous gift by Sir Jesse Boot of 35 acres of land at Highfields enabled the College to move to what is now its main campus at University Park in 1928. Initially the College was accommodated within one major building named the Trent Building. Designed by Morley Horder, the Trent Building's construction was one of the largest building projects in the city during the 1920s. The College continued to grow and to broaden the range of subjects which it offered. In 1933–34 the Departments of Electrical Engineering, Zoology and Geography, which had been combined with other subjects, were made independent; and in 1938 a supplemental charter provided for much wider representation on the college council.

In 1948 University College Nottingham received its Royal Charter and the power to confer degrees. The name changed to The University of Nottingham. This change of status encouraged a growth in students numbers which rose to over 2,000 in 1949. During the second half of the 20th century the university expanded considerably. New buildings were erected including in, 1956, the Portland Building, which included dining facilities, an art gallery and concourse lounges. New halls of residence were built and government backing for new science and technology projects led to the creation of Basil Spence's 'Technopolis' with its science library and Tower Block. The 1970s and 1980s also saw an increase both in the range of subjects taught and total student numbers which had risen to around 7,500 by the late 1980s. A new medical school was added in 1970, the first to be established in the UK since 1893. Other developments on the main campus included a Student Health Centre, a Sports Hall a new Computer Centre and the central University Library for the Arts and Social Sciences. In 1999 a new Jubilee Campus was opened on the former site of the Raleigh Cycle Works, about a mile from the main University Park Campus. This houses the Schools of Education and Computer Science as well as The Nottingham University Business School. The site is also home to the National College of School Leadership. In 1999 the University became a truly international university when it opened a campus in Singapore. The University has continued to grow and expand in the 21st century. In 2001 another overseas campus was opened, this time in China, and in 2005 the Kings Meadow Campus was created on the site of the former Carlton TV Studios. In the 21st century the University of Nottingham is one of the world's best universities, distinguished for its commitment to learning and internationally renowned world class research

Chancellors
Lord Trent (1949–54)
The Duke of Portland (1954–71)
Sir Francis Hill (1971–78)
Sir Gordon Hobday (1978–93)
Lord Dearing of Kingston-upon-Hull (1993–2000)
Professor Fujia Yang (2000–date)

Vice-Chancellors
Bertrand Hallwood (1948–65)
Lord Dainton of Hallam Moors (1965–70)
Lord Butterfield of Stechford (1971–75)
Professor Basil Weedon (1976–88)
Sir Colin Campbell (1988–2008)
Professor David Greenaway (2008–date)

Notable Alumni
Stewart Adams – Inventor of Ibuprofen
George Carey – Archbishop of Canterbury 1991–2002
Chris Choi – ITV News journalist
Sir Clive Grainger – 2003 Nobel Leureate, Economics
Sir Michael Lyons – Chairman, BBC Trust
Tim Martin – Chairman of Wetherspoons
Jeff Randall – *Daily Telegraph* editor-at-large and Sky television presenter
Professor Ian Wilmut – Embryologist who managed the team who cloned Dolly the sheep
Ruth Wilson – Actress

Factoids

✽ It has been awarded University of the Year (2006) and Entrepreneurial University of the Year (2008).

✽ The University is ranked in the UK's Top 10 and the World's Top 100 universities.

✽ Academics from the University have been awarded two Nobel Prizes since 2003.

✽ Twelve libraries provide access to more than one million books and journals, more than 3 million manuscripts, over 12,000 e-journals and 650,000 e-book items.

✽ The Students' Union has more than 190 societies and 75 sports clubs and runs a magazine, cinema and radio station.

✽ It has one of the lowest drop-out rates in the country at 3.5 per cent.

✽ It has a student population of around 30,000 students from more than 140 countries.

✽ The undergraduate gender ratio is 49 per cent female to 51 per cent male.

✽ With over 40,000 applications every year, the University is one of the top five most popular universities in the UK.

✽ The motto of the University is 'A City is Built on Wisdom'.

Nottingham Trent University
History

Nottingham Trent University, created from Nottingham Polytechnic, evolved and morphed from a number of institutions including the School of Art and Design, Nottingham College of Education and Nottingham Technical College. The University can trace its history back to the creation of the Nottingham Government School of Design in 1843. This evolved and developed into the School of Art and Design, which was managed by a committee of Nottingham Corporation. It provided both fine-art instruction, including painting and sculpture for middle class students, as well as more practical courses in drawing and draughtsmanship, aimed at those students who were hoping to find employment in one of principal industries of the town. In 1934 it became the College of Arts and Crafts and soon became recognised as the centre for architectural training in the East Midlands. It also developed courses in advertising, commercial art and photography. By the 1970s it was offering diploma and degree courses although these were taught under the auspices of Trent Polytechnic.

The development of Trent Polytechnic began with the creation of the Nottingham District Technical College in Shakespeare Street in August 1945. Almost 2,000 full and part-time students were enrolled during its first year of operation and it soon developed a reputation for the quality of its teaching. By the 1950s it was offering a range of higher level courses including London University external degrees. In 1958 it became a regional college supported by Nottingham City Council and Nottinghamshire and Derbyshire County Councils. At this time it offered a range of courses including textiles, mining, building and civil engineering, mathematics, physics, pure science, commerce, printing, bread making and confectionary. It was also around this time (1959) that the Nottingham College of Education was opened at Clifton. In June 1970 the regional College of Technology became Trent Polytechnic with government funding supplementing that provided by local councils. New degree courses, validated by the Council for National Academic Awards, were soon introduced across all departments. In 1975 it was a amalgamated with Nottingham College of Education. The 1980s were a period of rapid growth and in 1988 its official name was changed to Nottingham Polytechnic. In the following year it was removed from local authority control and gained full autonomy. In 1991 the government decided to end the distinction between universities and polytechnics and in November 1992 Nottingham Trent University was created. Since then changes and improvements have been made to all aspects of the university. In 2004 the university was restructured with the existing faculties being amalgamated into four

The Nottingham Trent City Centre Campus.

The Boots Library, Nottingham Trent University.

colleges: links have also been established with a number of national and multinational companies including Microsoft, Toyota, Boots and Rolls Royce. Research facilities have been developed in a number of areas including cancer research. To support these changes a substantial building programme has taken place. The Boots Library opened on the city campus in 1988 providing one of the most up to date university libraries in the country. More recently a new £8 million Computing and Informatics Centre was opened on the Clifton Campus and in 2008 the Earl of Wessex opened a new Veterinary Nursing Centre and Animal unit at the Brackenhurst Campus. The University has gained a reputation both for the quality of its teaching and research, and the employability of its graduates. In 1998 Nottingham Trent University was named as the top post-1992 university. The University's motto, 'Shaping Futures' seems to be particularly appropriate.

Chancellor
Sir Michael Parkinson (2008–date)

Vice Chancellors
Professor Ray Cowell (1992–2003)
Professor Neil T Gorman (2003–date)

Well Known Alumni
Hazel Blears MP – Secretary of State for Communities and Local Government from 2007 to 2009
Steve Hogarth – Lead singer with Marillion
Paul Kay – Actor and comedian
Ana Boulter – Actress and television presenter
Nick Waplington – Artist and photographer
Simon Starling – Turner Prize winner, 2005
Alan Simpson – MP for Nottingham South from 1992 to 2010

Factoids
✷ Voted the top post-1992 university in 2008 by *The Complete University Guide* (in association with *The Independent*).

✳ 24,000 students from a wealth of backgrounds and cultures include students and staff from over 80 countries.

✳ It has one of the best employability records of any university in England and Wales with 97 per cent of students in full-time employment or study within six months of graduation.

✳ The University's £13 million Boots library boasts 531,000 books, 2,800 journals and 9,000 e-journals.

✳ The Students' Union supports over 50 cultural, faith, academic political and social societies.

✳ The University co-hosts 'Gamecity', a five day video game festival which takes gaming into the streets, shops and cinemas in Nottingham. It takes place in October each year.

✳ In February 2010 the University launched a historic lace archive of more than 75,000 intricate lace samples, considered to be of international importance.

✳ The University came top out of 126 universities graded by People and Planet for their 'Green League 2009', an assessment of environmental performance.

✳ Its partner universities are the Ching Yun University, Taiwan and the Espeme-EDHEC Business School, Lille-Nice, France.

✳ FlyFM, the students' union radio station, broadcasts online five days a week and has won a number of gold Student Radio awards.

Sport in Nottinghamshire

✳ **Rebecca Adlington** is the Mansfield swimmer who won two gold medals in the 2008 Olympics Games, winning the women's 400m and 800m and breaking the 19-year-old record of Janet Evans in the 800m Final. Adlington became Britain's first Olympic Swimming Champion since 1988, the first British swimmer to win two Olympic gold medals since 1908 and Great Britain's most successful swimmer for 100 years. In 2008 she was named as the Sports Journalists' Association of Great Britain, Sportsman of the Year. She was awarded an OBE in the 2009 New Year's Honours. In 2010 the Mansfield Leisure Centre was renamed the Rebecca Adlington Centre in her honour.

✳ **Viv Anderson** is a former Nottingham Forest defender who became the first black player to represent England. Born in Clifton in 1956 he joined Nottingham forest in 1974 and became a regular player after the arrival of Brian Clough as manager. He was part of the side which won promotion to the First Division in 1977, winning the title along with the League Cup a year later. He continued to play for Nottingham Forest for a further six years and was an important part of the club's success during this period. He made his England debut against Czechoslovakia at Wembley on 27 November. He went on to win 30 international caps and two European Cup winners' medals After leaving Nottingham Forest in 1984 he went on to play for Arsenal, Manchester United and Sheffield Wednesday. He is still remembered with great affection by Forest fans and was voted their best ever right-back by a 96 per cent majority in a 1997 poll. He was awarded an MBE in January 2000 and was inducted into the English Football Hall of Fame in 2004.

✳ **Bendigo**, the famous Victorian prize fighter came from Nottingham. Born in 1811, he was the youngest of 21 children and was himself one of triplets. The family was poor and after a period in the workhouse he found work selling oysters in the streets of the town. Later he became an iron turner which helped him to develop his muscular physique. During his boxing career he was engaged in 21 matched fights and was never defeated. Later in life he became a celebrated preacher, attracting large crowds. He died on 23 August 1880 after falling down the stairs of his home in Beeston. His funeral procession was a mile long. There is a tombstone to his memory, in the shape of a lion, in St Mary's Cemetery, Bath Street, Sneinton.

✳ **Tom Blower** was a famous long-distance swimmer who became known as 'Torpedo' after making a series of record breaking long-distance swims in the 1930s and 1940s. Born in Nottingham in 1913, he broke the cross-channel swimming record in 1937 by completing the crossing from France to England in only 13 hours 24 minutes. He later won fame as the first person to swim the North Channel between Northern Ireland and Scotland. He died in 1955 at the early age of 42 and is buried in Bulwell Cemetery, Nottingham.

✴ **Tim Brabants** is a sprint kayaker who has competed in three Summer Olympics. In 2000 at Sydney he won a bronze medal in the Men's K1 1,000m. The 2004 games were a disappointment. He completed the fasted time in the heats but was placed only fifth in the Final of the 1,000m race. At Beijing in 2010, however, he struck gold by coming first in the Men's K1 1,000m. At the same games he added to Britain's tally of medals by winning bronze in the Men's K1 1,500m. He was awarded an MBE in the 2009 New Year's Honours for his services to kayaking. Although born in Walton-on-Thames, he completed his medical training at Nottingham University and worked for a period as a doctor at the Queens Medical Centre. He is a member of Nottingham Kayak Club and undertakes some of his training at Holme Pierrepont.

✴ **Brian Clough** OBE is regarded by many commentators as one of the most successful English football managers of all time. He achieved particular fame as manager of Nottingham Forest Football Club. Born in Middlesbrough in 1939, he joined his local club at the age of 16. He made his first-team debut for Middlesbrough in a League match against Barnsley in September 1955 and over the next six seasons he scored 917 goals in 213 League appearances. It was also during this period that he earned two England caps, against Wales and Sweden, both in 1959. He transferred to Sunderland in 1961 where he continued to score goals at a prolific rate. A football accident at the age of 30 brought an end to his playing career. His career in football management started at Hartlepool in 1965 when he became the youngest manager in the Football League. Two years later he moved to Derby County which he led to the League Championship in 1972 and the European Cup semi-finals a year later. He resigned from Derby County in 1973 and after brief periods with Brighton and Leeds he became manager of Nottingham Forest. When Clough took over they were an undistinguished Second Division side but under his leadership they quickly won promotion to the First Division. In the first season after promotion (1977–78) they won the League Cup and the Championship. In the following year they retained the League Cup and rounded off the season with victory in the European Cup. A year later Clough guided the club to a second successive European Cup and a third successive League Cup Final, though this time they were defeated. The club won the

Statue of Brian Clough in the centre of Nottingham.

League Cup again in 1989 and 1990. The following year Forest reached the FA Cup Final but lost 2–1 to Tottenham Hotspur. In 1992 they reached the Cup Final again but were again defeated, this time by Manchester United. In 1993, after 16 years in the top flight, Nottingham Forest were relegated from the newly created Premier Division and Brian Clough announced his retirement as manager. He was awarded an OBE in the 1991 Queen's Birthday Honours for services to association football. He died on 20 September 2004 of stomach cancer. In August 2005 a stretch of the A52 linking Nottingham and Derby was renamed Brian Clough Way. On 6 November 2008 a statue of Brian Clough was unveiled by his widow, Barbara, at the junction of King Street and Queen Street in the centre of Nottingham.

✳ **William Gunn** was born in Nottingham in 1858 and has been described as one of the greatest and most graceful batsmen of his day. He was also a great football player. He played both cricket and football for England and was the founder of a successful business of sports outfitters and cricket bar makers trading under the name of Gunn & Moore.

✳ **Sam Hynd** is a swimmer who won two medals at the Beijing Paralympics in 2008. Sam has a neuromuscular myopathy, weakening his legs, which mean that he relies entirely on upper-body strength when in the water. Sam, who trains regularly at the Water Meadows Swimming and Fitness Complex, won Gold in the 400m Freestyle and Bronze in the 200m Individual Medley. In November 2008 he was awarded the freedom of the District of Mansfield.

✳ **Harold Larwood** was the famous cricketer who played a major role in the famous bodyline series against Australia in 1933. He was born at Nuncar in Nottinghamshire in 1904 and from an early age played for his local village cricket team. At 18 he was invited to trial for Nottinghamshire and was offered a professional contract. He soon won a reputation as an extremely fast bowler. Larwood played in his first test match against Australia in 1926 but did not secure a permanent place in the team until 1928. He played in a number of tests but is best remembered for his part in the infamous bodyline test against Australia in 1933. Following the instructions of his captain, the amateur Douglas Jardine, he adopted an aggressive bodyline technique in his bowling. This involved aiming directly at the line of the body and at a height which threatened the head and chest of the batsmen. This proved extremely effective but resulted in injuries to a number of Australian players. This led to a serious deterioration in relations between the two countries. On his return to England Larwood was reprimanded by the MCC and instructed to sign a letter of apology to the Australians. This he refused to do and as a consequence never again played for England, although he continued to play for Nottinghamshire until the outbreak of World War Two. In 1950 he emigrated to Australia where he was amazed by the warm welcome which he received. In 1993 he was belatedly awarded the MBE by the cricket-loving Prime Minister, John Major. He died aged 90, on 22 July 1995 at

Randwick, New South Wales, Australia. A statue of Harold Larwood stands in the centre of Kirby-in-Ashfield.

✳ **Mansfield Town Football Club**, nicknamed the Stags, play in the Blue Square Premier League. Founded in 1897 under the name of Mansfield Wesleyans, they adopted their present name in 1910. After several attempts they won election to the Football League in 1931. The most successful period in the club's history came in the 1970s under the management of Dave Smith becoming Division Four champions in 1975 and Division Three champions in 1977. They won promotion to the Second Division but were relegated after only one season. The club won the Freight Rover Trophy in 1987 but suffered mixed fortunes in the years which followed. Mansfield Town's 77-year stay in the Football League finally ended in 2008.

✳ **The National Ice Centre** in Nottingham was opened by Olympic Ice Skating Champion Jane Torville in 2000. Built at a cost of £43 million, it provides two Olympic sized ice rinks offering everything from public ice skating to a top class training facility for elite athletes. The NIC is also home to the GMB Nottingham Panthers Ice Hockey Team and home of the Trent FM Arena Nottingham inside its wider complex.

✳ **The National Watersports Centre** at Holme Pierrepont was opened in 1999. It is set in 270 acres of parkland and has a regatta lake, multi-purpose white water canoe slalom course and a water ski lagoon with course, jump and ski capability. Activities available at the centre include white water rafting, water skiing, power boating, kayaking, canoeing and sailing.

✳ Nottingham's three rowing clubs; **Nottingham and Union Rowing Club, Nottingham Boat Club** and **Britannia Rowing Club** compete against each other at the National Watersports Centre and, weather permitting, a traditional Head of the Trent Race still takes place, starting at Clifton.

✳ **Nottingham Forest Football Club** was founded in 1865 by a group of shinty players, as Nottingham Forest Football and Bandy Club. They joined the Football Alliance in 1888 and won the competition in 1892 after which they became part of the Football League. Their first major success came in 1898 when they won the FA Cup, beating Derby County 3–1 at Crystal Palace. The club suffered mixed fortunes in the first half of the 20th century, spending most of their time in the second and third divisions. A brief period of glory followed towards the end of the 1950s with promotion to first division in 1957 and an FA Cup win in 1959. The club's most successful period came in the 1970s and 1980s under the management team of Brian Clough and Peter Taylor. After winning promotion the first division in 1977 the team went on to win the First Division Championship in 1978 and 1979 as well as the Football League Cup in 1978 and 1979. Victories in the European Cup came in 1979 and 1980. Peter Taylor retired in 1982 but Clough went on to win more trophies including the Football League Cup in 1989 and 1990. Brian Clough's reign as manager ended in May 1993 when the club was relegated from then inaugural Premier League after 16 successive years in top-flight football. Nottingham Forest continued to do well under a succession of managers, but the early years of this century brought mixed fortunes for the club. The club was relegated in 2005 but managed to climb back into the Championship league in 2008. The club has continued to make progress and narrowly missed promotion to the Premiership at the end of the 2009–10 season.

✳ **Nottingham Panthers** are a professional ice hockey club based in Nottingham and are known officially as the GMB Nottingham Panthers due to a sponsorship agreement with the GMB union. Their home arena is the National Ice Centre. Founded in 1946 they disbanded on the demise of the British National League in 1960. In 1980 players and officials from the Sheffield Lancers relocated to Nottingham and reformed the Panthers. The club currently plays in the Elite Ice Hockey League in which they have achieved considerable success.

✳ **Nottinghamshire Cricket Club** was formally created in 1841, although a Nottinghamshire county team had played against Sussex at Brighton in August 1835. The club achieved considerable success in the 19th century due in part to the contribution of such outstanding players as Alfred Shaw and Arthur Shrewsbury. This success continued into the 20th century and the team won the County Championship in 1907. Between the wars Nottinghamshire enjoyed the services of the famous bowlers Harold Larwood and Bill Voce. This, together with strong batting from Arthur Carr, George Gunn and William (Dodger) Whysall, saw them emerge as champions again in 1929. Further Championship wins came in 1981, 1987 and 2005. In 2008 they came close to winning both the County Championship and the NatWest pro40 outright, losing to Hampshire on the final day and Sussex in the final ball respectively. Today the club is regarded as one of the most consistent and most successful sides in the country.

✳ **Notts County Football Club** is the oldest Football League club in the country. Founded in 1862, it was one of the 12 founder members of the Football League and achieved considerable success in its early years. In 1894 the club achieved its first and only victory in the FA Cup when they beat Bolton Wanderers 4–1. The first half of the 20th century saw mixed fortunes for the club. League football was suspended during World War Two but the arrival of Tommy Lawton in 1947 brought increased support for the club and in 1950 promotion to Division Two. By 1968, however, the club was languishing at the bottom of the Fourth Division. The clubs most successful period came in the 1970s with Jimmy Sirrel as manager. He guided the Magpies to the First Division where they spent three consecutive seasons. Financial problems contributed to a decline in the fortunes of the club in the 21st century and in 2004 it was relegated to Division Two. The club continued to struggle both financially and on the field, but in 2010 they were promoted to Division One of the Football League.

✱ **Nova Centurion Swimming Club** is the competitive outlet of the Nottinghamshire County Council Swimming Squad. The county swim squad was one of the first squads to operate in the country and formed a model for many similar types of squads across Britain. There are three main sites; at Nottingham, Mansfield and Bassetlaw, all with a full time coach so that no swimmer has too far to travel to receive top quality training. With the support of the city council the squad has become one of the most successful in the country, having won the Great Britain Club Team Championship and been the top team at both the National Senior and the area group championships on numerous occasions.

✱ **Tim Reddish** is a swimmer and para-olympian. In 1988 he was diagnosed with retinitis pigmentosa which affected his sight. A year later he took part in the European Championships, winning two gold, five silver and 10 bronze medals. A 13 year international sporting career he attended three para-olympic games, three World Championships and five European Championships winning a total of 22 gold, 11 silver and 10 bronze medals. Retiring from competitive swimming he helped to encourage and develop Paralympics swimming in other parts of the world. In December 2006 as Director of British Disability Swimming he led the British team in the World Championships where they won 24 gold, 14 silver and 14 bronze medals. He became a Freeman of the City of Nottingham in 2005 and was awarded an MBE in 2009.

✱ **Doug Scott** is the Nottingham born mountaineer who, along with the late Dougal Haston, was the first to make an ascent of the South-West face of Mount Everest on 24 September 1975. In recognition of this achievement he was made a Freeman of the City of Nottingham in 1976. He went on to achieve further success in 1979 when, with Peter Boardman and Joe Tasker, he made the first ascent of Kangchenjunga's North ridge in the lightweight style without oxygen. Kangchenjunga is the third largest mountain in the world but is a much more technically demanding mountain than Everest. During his climbing career he has made 45 expeditions to the high mountains of Asia. He has reached the summit of 40 peaks of which half were climbed by new routes or for the first time in Alpine Style. In 1994 he was presented with a CBE for services to mountaineering. In 1999 he was awarded the Royal Geographical Society Patron's Gold Medal.

✱ **Southwell Race Course** is one of only two racecourses in the whole of Britain staging all weather flat, turf flat and national hunt races. Racing at Southwell dates back to the 17th century. At that time local farmers had to gather for the payment of rents to their landlord, the Diocese of Southwell. As many of them had to remain overnight, for entertainment they started racing their horses. Contemporary accounts indicate that the races were held over a circular course which started and finished at the Burgage. The modern racecourse opened in 1897 and a new all weather race track was opened in 1989. Most of the fixtures at Southall are all weather flat race meetings although a few national hunt meetings are held each year.

✱ **Trent Bridge Cricket Ground** is the home of Nottinghamshire County Cricket Club and the world's third oldest test ground. The founder, William Clarke, married the landlady of the Trent bridge Inn and then proceeded to lay out a cricket field at the rear of the Inn. When Clarke died in 1856 the ground was administered by the County Cricket Club, who purchased the ground in December 1919. Trent Bridge held its first international cricket match between England and Australia in 1899. Trent Bridge Cricket Ground has developed steadily ever since. Following the construction of new stands in recent years it can now accommodate 17,500 spectators on match days. It continues to attract important international fixtures and in 2009 it co-hosted the Twenty20 World Cup Cricket Tournament.

✱ **Jane Torville** and **Christopher Dean** are widely regarded as the most successful and most famous British ice skaters of all time. They are most famous for winning the 1984 Figure Skating Championships in the Winter Olympics at Sarajevo. It was here that they received 12 perfect 6.0 scores for their passionate routine set to Ravel's *Bolero*. Following their success the pair turned professional but regained their amateur status in order to compete in the 1994 Winter Olympics at Lillehammer. Here they achieved only a bronze medal and quickly returned to their professional career. They continued to tour with their highly successful *Face the Music* show which was followed by numerous other projects. The pair officially retired in 1998 but continued to coach and choreograph separately. Since 2006 they have acted as coaches, choreographers and presenters of ITV's popular *Dancing on Ice* show.

✱ **Lee Westwood** was born in Nottingham in 1973. He started playing golf at the age of 13 and became Junior Champion of Nottinghamshire less than two years later. He became a professional golfer in 1993 and won his first professional tournament, the Volvo Scandinavian Masters in 1996. He is one of the few golfers who have won tournaments in every major continent as well as victories on the European Tour and the PGA Tour. For much of his career he has been in the top 10 of the Official World Golf Rankings. He was named player of the year for the 1998, 2000 and 2009 seasons and in 2010 he won a career-best second place in the Masters Tournament. On 31 October 2010 he became world number one golfer, ending the reign of Tiger Woods.

✱ **John Whetton** was a successful middle distance runner in the 1960s. Born at Sutton-in-Ashfield in 1941 he won six consecutive AAA indoor mile/1,500m titles between 1963 and 1968 as well as reaching the Olympic finals in 1963 and 1968. In 1969, when almost at the end of his career, he surprised everyone by winning the gold medal for the 1,500m in the World Championships held in Athens.

Wildlife and Countryside

✳ As part of its countryside appraisal Nottinghamshire County Council has identified 10 regional character areas. These are:

Nottinghamshire Coalfield – A densely settled, heavily industrialised region, characterised by closely spaced mining settlements, pit heaps and small pastoral farms.

Magnesium Limestone Ridge – A gently rolling, and in places urbanised, agricultural landscape with a regular pattern of large fields and distinctive stone villages.

Sherwood – A well wooded, and in places industrialised, region characterised by semi-natural woodlands and heaths, historic country estates, large pine plantations, mining settlements and a planned layout of roads and fields.

Idle Lowlands – A varied low-lying region characterised by sparsely settled carrlands, levels and rolling sand lands with village settlements.

Mid-Nottinghamshire Farmlands – A rural agricultural region characterised by small nucleated red brick villages, narrow country lanes, ancient woodlands, wooded 'dumble' streams and a variable pattern of fields.

Trent Washlands – A low-lying agricultural region associated with the broad valleys of the Trent and Soar, characterised by productive arable farming, meadowlands, small nucleated villages, market towns and cities, power stations and quarries.

East Nottinghamshire – A remote low-lying agricultural region characterised by a well-ordered layout of fields and roads, small red brick villages, a varied pattern of woodland cover and pockets of healthy vegetation.

South Nottinghamshire Farmlands – A prosperous lowland agricultural region with a simple rural character of large arable fields, village settlements and broad alluvial levels.

Nottinghamshire Wolds – A sparsely settled and remote rural region characterised by rolling clay wolds, mixed farming, small red brick villages and narrow country lanes.

Vale of Belvoir – A low-lying clay vale with a strong tradition of dairying characterised by large hedged fields, small rural villages and wide views to rising ground.

✳ The farmed landscape of Nottinghamshire has changed dramatically over the last hundred years or so, particularly during World War Two. More intensive farming and increased mechanisation have led to the removal of hedgerows and the creation of large fields.

✳ Nottinghamshire Wildlife Trust is the leading conservation charity working to protect and enhance the wildlife and habitats of Nottinghamshire. They care for over 60 nature reserves covering more than 2,000 acres of valuable wildlife habitat ranging from wildflower meadows to ancient woodland.

✳ Some hedgerows in Nottinghamshire are over 1000 years old and contain several species of wildwood tree as well as some of the more recently introduced species including sycamore and horse chestnut.

✳ Stoke Wood was originally planted to provide fuel for river steamers, It is now managed for the benefit of wildlife and visitors.

✳ A farmer in Nottinghamshire produces more than 2,000 tonnes of spinach each year for supermarkets such as Tesco and Waitrose.

✳ 90 per cent of Nottinghamshire heath-land has been lost since 1922, mostly due to agriculture, conifer plantation and urban development.

✳ Clumber Park on the edge of Sherwood Forest covers an area of around 3,800 acres. The extensive woodland, together with heath-land and grassland are remnants from a time when vegetation like this covered much of the area. The area is a haven for insects which live in the wood of ancient oak and beech trees. The park's breeding birds include the nightingale, hawfinch, woodcock, lesser spotted woodpecker, redstart and long eared owl.

✳ Bestwood Park is situated on the Northern edge of Nottingham between Arnold and Bestwood Village. This 650 acre park was once part of the Mediaeval Sherwood Forest which covered large areas of Nottinghamshire. The Park was enclosed in 1341 and was used by a number of monarchs for hunting. In 1681 Charles I leased Bestwood Lodge to Nell Gwyn, one of his mistresses, later arranging for the mortgage to be redeemed and for the hereditary title of Duke of St Albans on her son. In 1858 the 10th Duke of St Albans demolished the old lodge house and replaced it with a larger and more ornate building (now a privately owned hotel). Alexandra Lodge, currently used by the Park Ranger Service was built as a park gatehouse in 1877. During the 19th century the area was used for coal mining and iron smelting. Coal production only ceased in 1971 with the closure of Bestwood Colliery. In 1985 Gedling Borough Council and Nottinghamshire County Council pooled their land holdings in the area to create Bestwood Country Park. The park now contains a number of different wildlife habitats including a large area of mixed secondary woodland on an ancient woodland site, 200 acres of grassland and scrub, and 150 acres of lakes and meadows. The Park is claimed to be one of the Midland's most important sites for bird watching with over 150 species listed. A wide range of woodland and grassland birds are attracted here including all three species of woodpecker and six species of tit. In summer breeding birds include hawfinch, reed warbler, turtle dove and lesser spotted woodpecker. Birds of prey observed here include the merlin in the winter and the hobby in summer. A large number of butterflies and dragonflies are attracted here and most of the species associated with woodland and grassland sites are to be found. Over 200 different types of fungi are to be found within the park and the site's woods and grassland shelter a rich variety of flora. The Park also contains the Winding Engine House of the old Bestwood Colliery which is currently undergoing restoration. Bestwood Park attracts over 400,000 visitors each year.

✳ The Lime Tree Avenue at Clumber Park is the longest tree avenue of its kind in Europe. Planted in 1840 it is over 3km long and consists of 1,296 common limes planted in a double row on each side of a drive. In 2007 two species of fungi new to Britain were discovered here.

✳ Sherwood Forest contains some of the best examples of old oak/birch woodlands in Britain.

✳ Rare insects such as the wolf, zebra and telegraph spiders, and green tiger, longhorn and both soldier and sailor beetles are all found in Nottinghamshire.

✳ Twenty-one species of dragonfly have been observed in Nottinghamshire including the Emperor, Brown Hawker, Southern Hawker, Migrant Hawker, Common Darter, Broad Bodied Chaser and Black Tailed Skimmer.

✳ Old trees and heath-land in parts of Sherwood Forest provide a rich habitat for a host of rare wildlife including birds such as the nightjar, restart, nuthatch and tree-creeper.

✳ The Robin Hood Way is a long distance footpath which runs for 105 miles from Nottingham Castle to Edwinstowe. It passes through Sherwood Forest taking in Clumber Park, Farnsfield, Greasley, Kimberley, Rainworth, Cresswell Crags, Kirton and Bothamsall.

✳ Nottingham catchfly is a rare plant whose fragrant drooping white flowers open at night between May and August. It was so named because it was first found on the walls of Nottingham Castle. It grows naturally on limestone rocks and banks and also on coastal shingle in south east England. Sadly it is no longer found in Nottinghamshire.

✳ The Naturescape Wildflower Farm and Visitor Centre near Langar comprises 40 acres of wildflower crops, grown for seed, wildlife hedgerows totalling a mile in length and a wildlife garden representing different habitats.

✳ There are 15 species of bat in Britain, of which seven have been found in Nottinghamshire; the pipistrelle, long eared, noctule, Daubenton's, natterers, whiskered and serotine. Bats are nocturnal creatures.

✳ The common frog is Britain's most numerous amphibian and is found in many parts of Nottinghamshire. A survey undertaken a few years ago indicated that 67.1 per cent of the frogs recorded were from gardens or allotments, while just 7.4 per cent were from field ponds.

✳ The common toad is the second in abundance to the frog in Nottinghamshire. It feeds on all sorts of small creatures including earthworms, molluscs, caterpillars and beetles and is, therefore, popular with gardeners. It is found mainly on the western side of the county.

✳ Three species of newt are native to Britain; the great crested, smooth and palmate. All are found in Nottinghamshire, though palmate are rare and at the time of writing occur at only one site within the county.

✳ The smooth newt is the third most numerous amphibian in Nottinghamshire. It is found in a wide range of habitats including gardens, woodland, and grassland and wetland sites. For breeding it prefers shallow weedy ponds. On land smooth newts enjoy a varied diet of earthworms, slugs, snails and small insects. In water they feed upon small aquatic insects, crustaceans and tadpoles.

✳ Common lizards are found mainly on the western side of Nottinghamshire. They prefer rough grassland and heath-land and can often be seen sunning themselves on the path that runs between the visitor centre and the Major Oak in Sherwood Forest Country Park. Other colonies thrive at Clumber Park, Rainworth Heath, Clipstone Forest and the Centre Parcs holiday village.

✳ There are six native species of reptile in the UK. Four of these occur in Nottinghamshire; adder, common lizard, grass snake and slow worm.

✳ The grass snake is Britain's largest snake and can reach well over 120cm in length. In common with other snakes it can dislocate its jaw in order to swallow bulky items of prey such as frogs, young birds and even small rodents. The grass snake population in Nottinghamshire has declined in recent years but they are still common in wetland areas where there are plenty of frogs, which form an important part of their diet. In recent years grass snakes have been observed in places such as the Erewash Valley, along the Chesterfield Canal and at Warsop Vale. Other grass snake sites include Newstead Abbey Park, woodland and gardens around Teversall and damp grasslands at West Burton.

✳ A few years ago a lady arrived at the Natural History Museum at Wollaton Hall. She brought with her a live grass snake which had been caught by her pet cat. In the grass snake's jaw was a crushed and half swallowed frog. In the frog's stomach staff discovered the remains of its last meal; a newt tadpole. The grass snake was released into the wild but it was too late for the frog and the newt!

✳ According to a recent publication by Nottingham Natural History Museum baby grass snakes were observed at East Retford gently licking the cobwebs on an ivy-clad wall. Whenever a spider emerged, mistaking the tugs on its web for a snared insect, it was devoured by one of the grass snakes. It is not clear whether the snakes were drinking moisture droplets from the web and fooling the spider by chance or had learned how to get a tasty meal.

✳ The adder, Britain's only venomous snake is rare in Nottinghamshire and is known to exist in only one small area in Sherwood Forest. Adders are distinctively marked with a dark zigzag running down the length of the spine and an inverted 'V' shape on the neck.

✳ Water voles are among Nottinghamshire's most threatened mammals. Numbers have dropped in recent years mainly due to the loss of habitat and being hunted by American mink. They are still found in parts of Nottinghamshire on the vegetated banks of ditchers, rivers, streams, canals, ponds and marshes with still water or little flow, and where water is present all year round. They are generally herbivorous and feed on the stems and leaves of waterside plant.

✳ Otters were extinct in Nottinghamshire from the mid-1950s until the late 1980s. They have recently returned to the River Trent and have been seen near Newark and at Attenborough. Otters make their home in the river bank in special dens known as holts. They eat mostly fish, especially eel but will also take frogs and waterside birds. Otters are a good indicator of clean water, free from pollutants.

✳ Around 1,500 species of beetle have been recorded in Sherwood Forest. These include some of the rarest in Britain, which feed on the fungi of rotting wood or which live in oak wood mould.

✳ In 2010 over 8,000 people took part in a garden bird watch in Nottinghamshire. The top 10 species observed were:
    1. House sparrow
    2. Blackbird
    3. Starling
    4. Woodpigeon
    5. Blue tit
    6. Chaffinch
    7. Goldfinch
    8. Collared dove
    9. Robin
    10. Dunnock

✳ A recent survey of wildlife in schools has revealed that woodpigeon and starlings are the most common visitors to school grounds in Nottinghamshire.

✳ The Trent valley is an important passage route for birds. Large numbers of migrant waders and wildfowl use the wet-landscapes and nature reserves.

✳ Breeding colonies of cormorants spread along the Trent during the 1990s. While welcomed by many, others consider them to be greedy predators responsible for reducing fish numbers.

✳ The Mallard is probably the most common duck in Nottinghamshire and is found from the smallest pond to the largest gravel pit.

✳ Several finches are to be found in Nottinghamshire including the Chaffinch, Brambling, Greenfinch, Goldfinch, Linnet, Lesser Redpoll, Bullfinch and Hawfinch.

✳ The Chaffinch is one of Nottinghamshire's best known and commonest birds. One of its old Nottinghamshire names is Spink, after its main call.

✳ The ash landfill site at Ratcliffe-on-Soar Power Station attracts increasing numbers of sand martins each year with a colony of more than 80 breeding pairs flying nearly 2,000 miles from South of the Sahara in Africa.

✳ All three species of woodpecker are found in Nottinghamshire. The green woodpecker is the largest. It is green-grey in colour with a bright green rump and red on the top of its head. The great spotted woodpecker is about the size of a blackbird with distinctive black and white plumage. The lesser spotted woodpecker is the smallest of the three woodpeckers resident in Britain. It is also the rarest although it can be seen regularly at Wollaton Park, among other places during the winter months.

✳ Marsh Harriers were discovered breeding in Nottinghamshire for the first time in 2010. A pair has nested at the Langford Lowfields nature reserve, just north of Newark on Trent. Marsh Harriers are rarer than the Golden Eagle and there are only around 360 breeding females remaining in the whole of Britain.

✳ The Honey Buzzard has been a regular summer visitor to sites in the Dukeries for many years. A relative of the Common Buzzard it takes its name from its habit of feeding on large insects, especially bees, hence honey.

✳ The Nightjar is a summer visitor from Africa. It nests in a few heath-land areas in Nottinghamshire such as the Sherwood Pines Forest Park.

✴ Swallows, sand martins and house martins are all common summer visitors to Nottinghamshire. They tend to depend on buildings for breeding.

✴ Nottinghamshire's first marsh harrier chicks were recently spotted at Langford Lowlands nature Reserve near Newark-on-Trent. The birds are rarer than the golden eagle and there are only 360 breeding females left in Britain.

✴ An osprey with a 5ft wingspan was shot by a keeper at Clumber in 1825.

✴ There were 16 recorded sightings of Kingfishers in Nottinghamshire during 2010. Most of the sightings were along the River Trent. Kingfishers are becoming less common in Nottinghamshire but are easily recognised by their bright blue and orange plumage. They fly rapidly, low over water and hunt fish from riverside perches, occasionally hovering above the water's surface.

✴ All three native species of deer are found in Nottinghamshire. Red deer inhabit areas of Clumber Park and Clipstone Forest as well as Wollaton Park on the edge of Nottingham. Fallow Deer and Roe Deer are more widely dispersed and have been observed in many parts of the county.

✴ Wollaton Hall is surrounded by a 500-acre historic deer park. Herds of red and fallow deer roam freely throughout the park.

✴ Muntjac deer have spread into Nottinghamshire in recent years. They are a non-native species which originate in China. Their numbers have been steadily increasing since some were released from Woburn Park in 1925.

✴ Rare black Hebridian sheep are kept in one of Bestwood Park's ancient flower meadows.

✴ The grey squirrel is common throughout Nottinghamshire in both woodland and urban areas.

✴ Rabbits were introduced into Nottinghamshire by the Normans.

✴ Badgers are to be found in various parts of Nottinghamshire. They are nocturnal animals who live in underground setts.

✴ Stoats have been observed along some of the sand-land hedgerows of West Nottinghamshire.

✴ Polecat sightings are on the increase in Nottinghamshire. Having been extinct in the county since the early years of the 20th century they are slowly moving back into the area.

✳ The mole population is on the increase in Nottinghamshire. This increase is presenting problems to gardeners and pest control officers.

✳ Nottinghamshire's largest species of spider is the Meta Bourneti, commonly known as the Cave Spider. There are believed to be only two sites where it occurs within the county.

✳ The rare stripe-winged grasshopper is found at only one place in Nottinghamshire, at Budby Common.

✳ The Harlequin ladybird first appeared in the UK in 2004. It was first recorded in Nottinghamshire in 2006 and remains rare. They have been observed at Eakring and Hare Hill Wood.

✳ Over 20 species of butterfly have been observed at Eakring Meadows. The Small Tortoise, Peacock and Comma are all common and migrants such as Red Admiral, Clouded Yellow and Painted Lady have also been seen here.

✳ One of Nottinghamshire's rarest butterflies, the White Admiral, is on the wing through June and July. The most accessible site to see the White Admiral is at Eaton Wood near Retford.

✳ The Marbled White butterfly is known at only one site in Nottinghamshire in a small section of Portland Park between Kirby-in-Ashfield and Annersley.

✳ A number of rare moths have been recorded in Sherwood Forest in recent years. These include: Yellow-legged Clearwing, Large Red Belted Clearwing, Great Oak Beauty, Grass Wave, Alder Kitten and Orange Footman.

✳ Nottingham Beekeepers Association has an apiary near Southwell where it offers help and advice to new and prospective beekeepers.

✳ There are about 35 different types of fish living in the River Trent. The main types are roach, chub, dace, bream, carp, pike and gugeon. There are also some salmon and eels.

✳ Since 1998 around 80,000 2in long salmon parr have been released into the Trent's River Dove tributary in a joint project managed by Trent Rivers Trust and Severn Trent Water plc. In 2001 the first few adults returned.

✳ A bridge at Willow Holt Nature Reserve in Farndon includes a flap to allow fish and other inhabitants of the River Trent to get into the reserve.

✳ 90 per cent of Nottinghamshire heath-land has been lost since 1922, mostly due to agriculture, conifer plantation and urban development.

✳ In April 2010 Nottinghamshire Wildlife Trust launched the Mini Meadow campaign designed to help people create wildflower meadows in their own back gardens. The project caught the imagination of thousands and within two months volunteers had handed out more than 6,000 'mini-meadow' seed packets; creating up to 6,000sq m of wildflower meadows throughout the county.

✳ A rare Winter Stalkball mushroom was found at Attenborough Nature Reserve in November 2010. The species was more common in the Victorian era and the last time the species was observed in Nottinghamshire was at Colwick Park in 1898.

✳ The poisonous Magpie Ink-Cap, a rare foot-high fungi, was discovered in Nottinghamshire (at Tresswell Wood near Retford) for only the sixth time since records began.

✳ A record number of species found on one day in one location was set on Saturday 17 January 2010. The Nottinghamshire Biodiversity Action Group, with help from members of the public, recorded 640 different species at the 'Bio-blitz' event held at Ratcliffe Country Park.

✳ The Newark and Nottinghamshire County Show takes place in May each year at the County Showground, Newark.

✳ Nottingham City Council in partnership with Nottinghamshire Wildlife Trust launched a 'Wildlife in the City' project in 2010. The three year scheme is aimed at reconnecting urban Nottingham with its local green space. The project will focus on 10 areas including Clifton, Aspley, Broxtowe, Bulwell, The Meadows, Sneinton and Bestwood. Wildlife activity sessions, family events and training will be offered at natural green spaces in these areas.

Swans may be observed on the River Trent and at several nature reserves in the county.

Nature Reserves in Nottinghamshire

❉ **Ashton's Meadow** in North Nottinghamshire was purchased by the Nottinghamshire Wildlife Trust in 1985. It has been described as the best example of a species rich neutral grassland environment in Nottinghamshire. Ancient ridge and furrow landscape can clearly be seen and because the area has not been ploughed or chemically treated in recent times this traditional meadow supports a wide variety of flowers and grasses including cowslip, green winged orchid, yellow rattle, pignut and oxeye daisy.

❉ **Annersley Woodhouse Quarry** is a grassland reserve. It's soils support a number of plants including tor-grass, cowslip, yellow wort and birdsfoot trefoil. A small area of marshland on the site supports a number of wetland plants including marsh marigold, fen bedstraw and marsh valerian. Birds such as willow warbler and redpoll breed on the site which is also home to a number of butterfly species including the fern and Howorth's pug.

❉ **Attenborough Nature Reserve** was established in 1966 and comprises around 360 acres of flooded former gravel pits and islands. The reserve is best known for its birds and since recording began in 1944 over 250 different species have been

Visitor Centre at Attenborough Nature Reserve.

seen here, from swans and starlings to the elusive kingfisher and the even rarer bittern. Today the area is best known for its waterfowl. A wide variety of different duck species have been recorded, including mallard and teal. Sawbills, sea ducks and cormorants have also been sighted. In summer the great crested grebe, shelduck, little green plover and common tern all breed here. Other wildlife includes foxes, stoats, toads and newts as well as numerous species of butterflies, moths and other invertebrates. The network of islands and paths is home to a wide range of trees, shrubs and wildflowers including water forget-me-not which thrives at the water's edge. Recently otters have been observed here. The award-winning visitor centre provides a wide range of facilities and activities.

✳ **Beacon Hill Conservation Park** was created in 2001 on a former gypsum mine to the north east of Newark town centre. The 19.4 hectare site contains a wide range of habitats of significant wildlife value including scrub, woodland, hedgerows and grassland. A large area in the centre of the reserve (previously a landfill site) has been restored as a wildflower meadow. The site is still being developed but is already home to two notable moths which are rare in Nottinghamshire. The area also attracts a number of bird and butterfly species.

✳ **Bentinck Banks** lies less than 1 km south of Kirby-in-Ashfield and comprises a series of disused railway tracks and their embankments, which are now covered with grassland and scrub habitat. In addition to varieties of grasses the site also contains several types of orchid, some of which are rare in Nottinghamshire. The scrubland along the embankment and the adjacent area of woodland provide a home for a variety of birds including thrushes and finches.

✳ **Besthorpe Nature Reserve** is a wetland site. Formerly a gravel extraction site it lies on the east bank of the River Trent close to the village of Besthorpe. Plant species found there include Yorkshire fog, great burnet, lady's bedstraw, common knapweed and meadow vetchling. Elsewhere on the site aquatic flora include spiked water milfoil and common water crowfoot. The site is also an important haven for birds, Mons Pool contains a colony of nesting cormorants and a heronry. It also attracts a variety of ducks in winter including tufted duck, pochard and goosander.

✳ **Breck's Plantation** is an area of mixed urban woodland close to the Clifton Estate. Most of the site was planted towards the end of the 19th century and comprises small stands of oak, ash, sycamore, larch and Norway spruce. A number of common woodland birds are attracted to the site including all three types of woodpecker, spotted flycatcher, tree creeper, greenfinch and fieldfare.

✳ **Bunny old Wood** (West) is an ancient coppiced woodland site which is mentioned in the *Domesday Book*. Coppiced ash, wych elm and field maple are all common on the site and oak, cherry and wild crab apple can also be found along the southern boundary of the site. Flowering plants include wood anemone, stitchwort, and barren strawberry. Around 50 different types of bird have been recorded here and summer visitors include the spotted flycatcher, blackcap and tree pipit. A wide range of butterflies are also found here and animals include the fox, grey squirrel and grass snake.

✳ **Calverton Road Nature Reserve** is a small area of woodland in the Borough of Gedling. This site is a reclaimed domestic tip and trees planted as part of the restoration process include alder, rowan, whitebeam, field maple, red oak and a small number of sycamores. The roadside hedge contains a number of species including hawthorn, ash, field maple, buckthorn and crab apple. Birds such as linnet, wood pigeon and chaffinch are common here and in summer willow warblers and whitethroat can be seen.

✳ **Chilwell Meadow** is a small wet meadow site which was formally established in 1986. In a biological survey in 1977, however, the meadow was included in the top 10 exceptional areas out of 1,500 grassland sites surveyed. A wide range of plants grow here including marsh arrow grass, adder tongue, ragged robin, marsh marigold and the common spotted orchid.

✳ **Clearborough Tunnel** is an area of grassland and scrub woodland three miles from Retford. Most of the reserve is over the railway tunnel constructed in 1849. The grassland is rich in flowering plants including cowslip, hoary plantain, yellow wort, oxeye daisy and several types of orchid. A small pond on the site was deepened in 1984 to encourage a greater variety of pond life and great crested newts were recorded here in 1985. Many different species of woodland birds have been observed here.

✳ **Daneshill Gravel** pits is a wetland reserve containing a number of habitats including open water, damp willow woodland, drier woodland and scrub. A wide range of butterflies are attracted to the site including brimstone, common blue, meadow brown, gatekeeper and ringlet. This is also a good site for dragonflies and damselflies. In common with other wetland sites within the county a range of wildfowl can be seen here outside the breeding season.

✳ **Duke's Wood** combines a woodland nature reserve with an industrial archaeological site. Duke's Wood and the surrounding area was the location of Britain's first onshore oilfield and produced 280,000 tons of oil between 1939 and 1966. Some of the original pumps, known as nodding donkeys have been restored and a bronze statue of an oil worker stands close by. The woodland is dominated by oak, ash, hazel and birch. Wild flowers abound here and include primrose, centaury, violet, bluebell, wood anemone and broad-leaved helleborine. The area attracts a wide variety of butterflies and woodland birds. Red deer, fox, stoat and badger have occasionally been seen here.

✳ **Dyscarr Wood** is situated on the Nottinghamshire/South Yorkshire border, west of Langold. The site covers an area of 17 hectares and comprises an area of woodland which is home to a number of plants including sweet woodruff, yellow archangel, enchanter's nightshade, hedge woundwort and sanicle. Around 50 species of bird have been recorded here including all three types of woodpecker, little and tawny owls, and sparrow-hawks. Winter visitors include brambling and fieldfare and in summer flycatcher and blackcap can be seen. Butterflies abound here and over a dozen different species have been observed including the small copper, brimstone, orange tip, red admiral and painted lady.

✳ **Eakring Meadows Nature Reserve** covers a series of five wet meadows close to the villages of Kersall and Mapleback. Described as one of the best remaining neutral grasslands in Nottinghamshire, it provides a good breeding habitat for a variety of birds including lapwing, reed bunting, sedge warbler, snipe and tawny owl. The meadows are also home to a number of small mammals including field vole, pygmy shrew, water vole, mole and pipestrelle bat. A wide variety of butterflies are also to be found here.

✳ **Eaton and Gamston Woods** is a nature reserve near Retford. Oak, ash and beech are the predominant trees together with silver birch, field maple and overgrown hazel coppice. The woodland floor is covered with a wide range of species including primrose, bluebell, wood anemone, sweet woodruff and several different types of orchid. Over 20 different types of butterfly have been recorded here including the white admiral which is not found anywhere else in Nottinghamshire.

✳ **Fairham Brook** is a nature reserve on Green Lane in Clifton. It covers an area of 26 acres and is made up of meadow, scrubland and lowland fen bog. The reserve is home to a variety of invertebrates including butterflies, moths and dragonflies. Kingfishers have also been seen flying over the brook.

✳ **Farndon Willow Holt** is a woodland nature reserve in the village of Farndon. It is one of the few remaining willow holts which were once a feature of many Trentside villages. The site is particularly important as it houses an internationally-known collection of willows and hybrid species created by the late Lever and Barbara Howith after World War Two. In recent years a large number of cricket bat willows have been harvested, a new working willow holt has been planted and a new collection of willow species has been established.

✳ **Foxcovert Plantation** is a wetland nature reserve which was established in 1975. Believed to have been part of the ancient Sherwood Forest it contains a wide range of deciduous trees including oak, birch, sycamore, sweet chestnut, coppiced lime and a number of other species. In winter the woodland is home to goldcrest, redpoll and long tailed tit. In summer a number of common woodland species are joined by willow warblers, chiffchaff and blackcap.

✳ **Glapton Wood** is a small area of mixed woodland in the Clifton Estate. Oak, elder, ash, Scots pine, sycamore and hazel are all found here. A number of birds can be seen in the wood including great spotted woodpecker, goldcrest, spotted flycatcher and pied wagtail. A number of dead trees provide a habitat for insects and fungi.

✳ **Harrison's Plantation** is a small woodland nature reserve dominated by sycamore with ash, wild cherry and oak. The woodland floor is covered by a number of typical plants including dog's mercury, red campion, nettle leaved bellflower and bramble. The site is home to a number of birds including green spotted woodpecker, kingfisher, nuthatch, blackcap, redpoll and spotted flycatcher. Raleigh Pond at the east end of the wood supports breeding mallard and Canada geese and provides an excellent habitat for frogs and toads.

✳ **Idle Valley Nature Reserve** is a unique wetland landscape which has developed as a consequence of 50 years of aggregates extraction. It is home to a rich assemblage of birds including nationally important numbers of black-necked grebe, garganey and wigeon. The site is recognised as being of regional significance for wildlife.

✳ **Jacksdale Nature Reserve** comprises a small area of woodland scrub, railway embankment, rough grassland and riverbank. The area attracts a number of species of butterfly which feed on the knapweed vetches and burnet which thrive there. Birds such as kestrel and skylark have been observed here and kingfishers have been seen flying along the river.

✳ **Kimberley Cutting Nature Reserve** was established in a former railway cutting. It is owned by a national brewery chain and managed by Nottinghamshire Wildlife Trust. This former railway line is regarded as an important wildlife corridor because of its geology and the rich variety of species of mosses and liverworts which are found here.

✳ **Kingsmeadow Nature Reserve** in the Lenton area was created in 1992 in order to preserve the diverse flora and fauna which had developed on the former Wilford Power Station. This largely man-made site supports a number of wildlife habitats. A number of species considered rare can be found here including the southern marsh orchid and the common spotted orchid. The site also provides a home for a number of invertebrates which are found nowhere else in the city.

✳ **Kirton Wood Nature Reserve** is situated between Kirton and Egmanton. It is a woodland area of ash and wych elm wood although many elm trees have been affected by Dutch elm disease in recent years. A rich layer of shrubs include hazel, hawthorn, field maple, dogwood and privet. The area attracts a variety of butterflies and a wide range of different birds. Sparrowhawks have been observed here and roding woodcock can occasionally be seen at dusk on Spring evenings.

✳ **Lady Lee Quarry** is a wetland reserve created in a disused flooded quarry. Various types of dragonflies and damselflies are found here as well as frogs, toads and great crested newts. The site has been surveyed on a number of occasions in recent years and is known to support 158 species of plant, 55 fungi, 83 birds and over 300 invertebrates. Kingfishers are regularly seen here and other birds recorded include blackcap, goldcrest, great crested grebe, snipe and heron.

✳ **Mansley Common** is a grassland reserve close to the village of Eakring. It is a traditional piece of common land dominated by tufted hair grass. The common attracts a variety of different woodland and farmland birds. A flock of Hebredian sheep have also been grazed here.

✳ **Meden Trail** near Mansfield is an area of woodland and scrub as well as interesting limestone crags and fissures. The area is rich in wild flowers which attract a number of common butterfly species. A wide range of woodland birds are found here including nuthatch and hawfinch. In summer the area is visited by a number of different warblers.

✳ **Misson Carr** in North Nottinghamshire contains a variety of habitats including nationally rare wet woodlands, marsh and old grazing pasture. It also has the city's largest area of fenland system that was once covered much of the local landscape. Moths abound here and include large numbers of nationally rare and scarce species.

✳ **Moorbridge Pond** in Bulwell is one of a very few wetlands remaining within the city boundary. The marshland here supports a number of attractive plants including hairy willow herb, skullcap, ladies smock, figwort and yellow flag. The area is a breeding site for reed bunting and reed warbler and is also visited by whitethroat, linnet, bullfinch, song thrush, wren, snipe, kestrel and yellow hammer.

✳ **North Muskham Lake** was created from former gravel workings. Landscaping has led to the restoration of a number of wetland habitats. Most regular duck species have been recorded here.

✳ **Osmanthorpe Nature Reserve** is unusual as it was formerly an orchard. Originally it was planted with apple, pear and plum trees although the pear trees no-longer exist. Many of the apple trees are very old and include examples of Bramley's seedling. It is thought that these could be among the first Bramley trees to be planted.

✳ **Ploughman Wood** between Lambley and Woodborough, dates back as far as the 13th century. Most of the trees here are oak and ash although hazel, holly, field maple and beech are also found. Large quantities of dead wood provide an excellent habitat for a wide range of wildlife, plants and fungi. Bats, beetles and hole nesting birds are attracted here. In addition over 280 species of invertebrates have been recorded.

✳ **Quarry Holes Plantation** is a small area of mixed woodland with areas of grassland and scrub. Situated in a disused limestone quarry, over 80 flowering plants have been recorded here. Within the woodland birds such as willow tit, wren, greenfinch, bullfinch and song thrush have all been recorded here.

✳ **Rainworth Heath Nature Reserve** is a scarce area of wet and dry heathland close to the old Rufford Colliery. The wet areas are dominated by plants such as purple moor grass, cross leaved heath. Common sedge and cotton grass. The drier heathland is home to a variety of species including heather, bell heather, wavy hair grass, bracken, sheep's sorrel and mat grass. Birds such as green woodpecker, tree pipit, turtle dove and several species of warbler have all been recorded here.

✳ **Reed Pond** near Lambley village is believed to have originally been the stew pond for the rectory or parsonage which had stood there since the 14th century. Whitethroat, mallard and reed bunting breed on the site and heron and kestrels have also been seen here. Various traditional meadow plants grow here and the area attracts a diverse range of butterflies. Wildlife such as fox, mole, grey squirrel and the common shrew have all been recorded.

✳ **Sellers Wood** is a woodland nature reserve on the west side of Bulwell. Tree species include aspen, elder, wild cherry, rowan, ash and wych elm. The site also boasts a wide variety of plants including giant bellflower and early purple orchid. The ponds here are home to frogs, toads and newts. A number of different species of hoverfly have also been recorded including the rare Triglyphus Primus.

✳ **Skylark Nature Reserve**, close to the National Watersports Complex at Holme Pierrepont, was the first of its kind in the country to be laid out specifically for the benefit of wheelchair users. Situated in a disused gravel pit it attracts a wide range of wetland birds as well as skylark and lapwing. The site is also home to large numbers of dragonflies and damselflies. Butterflies seen here include meadow brown, common blue, small heath and orange tip. Various types of orchid are also found here and stands of Norfolk reed provide a habitat for frogs, newts and toads.

✳ **Spalford Warren** is an area of sand-blown heathland, which is one of the rarest habitats in the country. In addition to patches of heather, gorse and broom, more specialised sand-land plants are found here including slender trefoil, field mouse-ear and shepherd's cress. Common lizards have made this area their home and bird species recorded here include sparrow hawk, green and great spotted woodpecker, woodcock, coal tit and redpoll. Butterflies which frequent the area include the common blue and small heath.

✳ **Spa Ponds** is a wetland reserve. Three of the ponds are of mediaeval origin and many different types of dragonflies and butterflies have been recorded here. The site also attracts a number of different bird species include kingfisher and little grebe.

✳ **Strawberry Hill Heath** is a heathland nature reserve situated on the eastern outskirts of Mansfield. It was originally part of the Rainworth and Rufford forests which covered large tracts of land for a number of centuries. Woodland includes oak and birch but most of the area is covered with heather and bracken. This provides a rich habitat for reptiles and invertebrates and over 40 species of beetle have been recorded.

✳ **Teversall Pastures** is a grassland nature reserve which was established in 1983 and extended two years later. The reserve now covers around 6.5 hectares and is bounded by the River Meden and a disused railway. It is home to a wide range of flora. Meadowsweet, ragged robin water avens and lady's mantle grow in the damper areas while drier areas support yellow rattle, bulbous buttercup, glaucus sedge, quaking grass and blown oat grass.

✳ **Tresswell Wood** is one of the best examples of oak, ash and maple woodland in Nottinghamshire. It is a part of a ancient woodland, and flowering plants include sweet woodruff, wood sorrel, primrose and wood anemone. Woodland birds recorded here include woodcock, jay, nuthatch and two species of woodpecker. In summer blackcap, garden warbler and spotted flycatcher can be seen. The ponds on the site support plants such marsh marigold, yellow iris and water crowfoot. Amphibians such as the great crested newt, the smooth newt and more than a dozen species of water beetle have been recorded. In 1995 the wood was selected as the site for the reintroduction of the dormouse into Nottinghamshire.

✳ **Walkeringham Nature Reserve** is located in the far north-east of the county between Gringley-on-the-Hill and Misterton. A former landfill site, it now boasts a remarkably interesting mixture of habitats including woodland, hedgerow, pond and grassland. The area attracts a wide range of birds, particularly in the breeding season and the common lizard, grass snake, brown hare, stoat, weasel and water vole have all been recorded here.

✳ **Wilford Clay Pit** is located in the middle of the Compton Acres housing estate in West Bridgford. It was previously used by the Wilford Brick Company for the excavation of brick-making clay. Today it provides a variety of habitats including marshland pools, calcareous grassland and areas of scrub and woodland. The site contains a variety of trees including oak, ash, field maple, goat willow, hawthorn and bramble. Mammals such as fox, rabbit, weasel and vole make their home here as well as freshwater invertebrates and amphibians. Birds which have been recorded here include moorhen, reed bunting, willow and sedge warblers, kingfisher, tits and many more common garden species.

✳ **Wilwell Farm Cutting** is a grassland nature reserve situated on the outskirts of Nottingham between Wilford and Ruddington. The reserve is one of the best wildflower sites in the county with over 230 species recorded here, some of which are rare within Nottinghamshire. Large numbers of butterflies and moths are also attracted to the area. Over 90 species of wild birds have been recorded here including a variety of tits and wagtails. Sparrow hawks, owls and woodpeckers are sighted regularly. Foxes, rabbits and squirrels also inhabit the area.

✳ **Woodthorpe Meadow Nature Reserve** is a small area of mixed woodland and grassland believed to be a remnant of old Sherwood forest. The area attracts a diverse range of wildlife including grey squirrels, foxes and owls.

Rivers and Waterways

✳ The River Trent is one of Britain's major rivers with an overall length of around 170 miles. It dominates the waterways of Nottinghamshire and all but one of the other rivers within the county are its tributaries. From its source between Biddulph and Biddulph Moor in Staffordshire, it flows through and gives its name to Stoke on Trent and Burton upon Trent. It enters the county at Redhill where the borders of Leicestershire, Derbyshire and Nottinghamshire meet. After being diverted along the Cranfleet Cut the river meanders past Thrumpton and Barton in Fabis, both of which once had ferries across the river. At Attenborough a nature reserve has been created from former gravel workings. The river is joined by the Beeston Canal near Beeston Rylands before flowing through Nottingham. It remains a freshwater non-tidal river as far as Newark. After leaving Nottinghamshire the Trent eventually joins the River Ouse at Trent Falls to form the Humber Estuary.

✳ The Trent is unusual among English rivers in flowing north for the second half of its route. It is also unusual for its tidal bore, the Trent Aegir. Although the Aegir can reach a height of 1.5m it cannot travel much beyond Gainsborough as the shape of the river reduces it to little more than a ripple.

✳ Nottingham Riverside Festival is held each year on the Victoria Embankment. It regularly attracts over 100,000 visitors to three days of entertainment including music and dancing.

✳ The last sturgeon recorded in the Trent was caught near Holme in 1902. It was 8½ft long and weighed 250lb.

✳ In the late 18th and early 19th century passenger steamers ran a regular service from Trent Bridge to Colwick. Today trips are still available from Nottingham and Newark.

✳ Several coal fired power station were constructed along the banks of the Trent in Nottinghamshire. Some of these have been demolished in recent years but a number still remain including those at Staythorpe and Ratcliffe.

✳ To celebrate its centenary in 1984 Nottinghamshire County Council opened the 84-mile Trent Valley Way, a footpath following the route of the river through the county. Starting at Cuckney this long distance path continues to West Stockwith where it links up with the Cuckoo Way along the Chesterfield Canal.

✳ The River Devon enters the county across its Leicestershire boundary near Bottesford. It joins the much larger River Smite near Staunton Grange before continuing its way northwards past Cotham and Hawton. It passes under the

Ratcliffe on Trent Power Station.

Fosse Way before entering the Trent just before Newark. The mouth of the river forms a marina which is popular with a wide variety of pleasure craft.

✳ The River Erewash rises in Kirkby-in-Ashfield but is partly culverted as it flows south westward from the town. It surfaces to the north of the Kirkby Woodhouse and flows roughly westward between Pinxton and Selston. From here it becomes the approximate boundary between Derbyshire and Nottinghamshire, flowing south between Langley Mill and Eastwood. The river continues south between Sandiacre and Stapleford until at Toton it turns east and flows into the River Trent at the Attenborough Nature Reserve near Long Eaton.

✳ The River Idle has its source at the confluence of the River Maun and the River Meden near Markham Moor. From there it flows north through Retford and Bawtry before entering the River Trent near Misterton.

✳ The River Leen is a tributary of the River Trent. It rises in the Robin Hood Hills just outside Kirkby-in-Ashfield. It then flows though the grounds of Newstead Abbey before skirting Hucknall and passing through Bestwood Country Park. It follows the route of the Leen Valley through Nottingham where it enters the Trent opposite Wilford.

✳ The River Maun has its source near Sutton in Ashfield. From here it flows through Mansfield, Edwinstowe and Ollerton. It becomes known as Whitewater near Walesby and joins the River Meden for a short distance before diverging again. The two rivers finally meet near Markham Moor where they become the River Idle.

✳ The River Soar has its source near Hinckley in Leicestershire but flows through Nottinghamshire for much of its course. The river enters Nottinghamshire at Stanford-on-Soar but is not navigable here and it is joined by the Grand Union Canal or Loughborough Navigation It passes close to Normanton-on-Soar, Sutton Bonnington, Kingston-on-Soar and Ratcliffe-on-Soar before joining the River Trent near Trent Lock.

✳ The Nottingham Canal ran from the River Trent at Meadow Lane to the Cromford Canal near Langley Mill. The main purpose of the canal was to carry coal cheaply from the hinterland and to provide an outlet for collieries such as those of Lord Middleton at Bilborough, which were being undercut by competitors already served by the Erewash canal which had opened in 1777. While the Nottingham Canal was being constructed the Trent Navigation Company built an artificial channel, the Beeston Cut, to bypass the river from Trent lock to Beeston. There it met the Nottingham Canal which therefore became the part of the river-through-route. Where the Beeston Cut met the Nottingham Canal, the canal company installed a chain across the navigation to prevent boats from passing without paying a toll. The junction is still known as the Lenton Chain today. Several small branch canals were also constructed to link the canal to coal mines and other industrial enterprises. These smaller branches were often served by tramways. The Bilborough Cut for example left the main line above Wollaton locks and ran level to a wharf in Bilborough Wood. From here tramways ran to Bilborough and Strelley collieries. Passengers were also carried on the canal. In September 1797 a packet boat commenced a twice weekly service between Nottingham and Langley Mill. Fares charged were five shillings for the best cabin and three shillings for the second. In 1818 the canal suffered something of a catastrophe when 21 barrels of gunpowder stored in a warehouse near Wilford Street Nottingham exploded killing two men and completely destroying the warehouse. According to one contemporary account 'the shock was so tremendous as to be heard many miles distant from Nottingham'. The canal enjoyed about 50 years of reasonably profitable life, co-operating usefully with both the Cromford and Grantham canals. From the 1840s the canal began to suffer considerably from railway competition. Despite this trade continued well into the 20th century, though mostly short haul in the area of Nottingham itself. The Lenton to Langley Mill section of the canal was closed in 1936 and filled in after World War Two. Today the south section is part of the River Trent Navigation and the north section is a nature reserve. A Nottingham Canal Society was formed in 1976 and achieved some success in preserving a stretch of the canal at Trowell.

Castle Marina, Nottingham.

* The Chesterfield Canal was an early yet ambitious venture to link the town of Chesterfield with the River Trent. It was promoted by a several landowners and industrialists who wanted to gain access to the River Trent. The first public meeting was held at the Red Lion in Worksop on 24 August 1769. James Brindley was engaged to make a survey and prepare plans and estimates. He proposed a route running from Chesterfield to Northwood past Shireoakes and Worksop to East Retford and thence to the Trent at West Stock. Construction of the canal began in 1771. The first major engineering challenge was the construction of a tunnel through the magnesium ridge at Norwood before opening up the rest of the canal. When this was done with the first year of operation traffic on the canal comprised of 42,379m tons of coal, 7,569 tons of stone, 4,366 tons of corn, 3,955 tons of lime, 3,862 tons of lead and 1,544 tons of iron together with much smaller quantities of pottery, ale and other sundry items. By 1795 the company was able to pay a modest dividend of six per cent and a modest prosperity was maintained until the middle of the 19th century. In addition to the cargoes already mentioned the Chesterfield canal also played its part in the history of our nation. During the Napoleonic Wars armaments manufactured in and around Chesterfield were taken by canal boats to West Stockwith, and from there by river to Hull where they were transferred to waiting ships for speedy passage to our armies in Europe. Early in 1840 the first cargo of Anston stone for the new Houses of Parliament was carried to West Stockwith for transhipment. Approximately 250,000 tons were

transported in total. Tonnage reached its peak in 1848 but by this time the canal had already been taken over by the Manchester, Sheffield and Lincolnshire Railway and within 10 years the amount carried had fallen to only 110,761 tons. In 1871 the first effects of mining subsidence was felt at the Norwood Tunnel ands although £21,000 was spent on repairs over the next 35 years the Royal Commission of 1906 reported that only 40 boats were operating on the canal and none beyond the tunnel on the Chesterfield side. In 1908 part of the tunnel collapsed bringing an end to almost all the traffic beyond Shireoaks. The last commercial traffic was from the brickyards at Walkeringham to West Stockwith and this finally ceased in 1955. Within a few years the canal became derelict and largely impassable. Fortunately this decline was halted and reversed. In 1961 the canal was saved from abandonment by a group of enthusiasts and it is today navigable between West Stockwith and Worksop.

✳ The Erewash Canal was opened in 1779 and ran from the River Trent in Nottinghamshire to a junction with the Cromford Canal at Langley Mill in Derbyshire. The main purpose of the canal was the transportation of coal from collieries in Derbyshire to Nottingham via the River Trent. Trade was slow to develop but new pits were sunk and within a few years a network of tramways had been constructed to bring coal to the many wharves along the line of the canal. In 1792 the canal carried 70,000 tons of coal but with the opening of the

Trent Lock at the entrance to the Erewash Canal.

Cromford, Derby and Nutbrook canals this had increased to 270,000 tons by 1808. Other goods were of course carried on the canal including limestone, lead, iron, millstones, chalk and marble. This growth in trade brought prosperity for the shareholders. In 1826 dividends rose to an amazing peak of 74 per cent and six years later the £100 shares had a market value of £1,300 each. The value of these shares fell rapidly, however, with the growth of railway competition. Despite reductions in tolls, traffic rapidly declined and by the 1860s all that remained was some through traffic from other canals and the coal brought by rail to the Long Eaton basin to be transhipped for the short journey down the canal and then on to the Trent. Traffic had virtually ceased by the end of World War Two and nationalisation in 1947 did nothing to reverse the fortunes of the Erewash Canal. Closure came in 1968 when the Transport Act of that year defined it as a 'remainder waterway'. To prevent it becoming derelict the Erewash Canal preservation and Development association was formed. Thanks to the hard work of these enthusiasts the Nottinghamshire and Derbyshire county councils were persuaded to finance the restoration of the canal to cruising standard and in 1973 the ECPDA itself completed the restoration of the Great Northern Basin at Langley Mill.

✳ The Grantham canal was opened in 1797 and followed a meandering route across the Vale of Belvoir from Grantham to the River Trent at West Bridgford. Traffic on the canal was mainly upwards, in coal, coke, lime, building materials and foodstuffs to villages along the line of the canal, to Grantham and to places beyond to which goods were distributed by wagon. Downwards, the canal transported corn, malt, beans, wool and other agricultural products, Grantham and Harby acting as collecting points for a wide area. A Saturday passenger service from Cotgrave to Nottingham was also inaugurated in April 1798 although it is not known for how long it operated. In common with other canals in the area from the mid-19th century the Grantham Canal suffered from railway competition. By 1905 traffic on the canal had declined to 18,802 tons, mainly in manure (8,256), road stone (16,116) as well as plaster and coal on short hauls. Regular trading ended in 1917 but some boat movements continued until 1936 when the Grantham Canal was finally abandoned. Some restoration work has been carried out in recent years.

✳ The Trent and Mersey Canal was one of the first major canals to be constructed in this country and ran for part of its length through Nottinghamshire. The Construction began officially on 26 July 1766 when the first sod was ceremonially cut by Josiah Wedgewood, the famous pottery owner. The canal was finally completed in May 1777 but unusually the occasion was not marked by any lavish celebration. For much of its life the canal was a considerable commercial and financial success. Goods such as coal, iron ore, stone, flint, clay lime, pottery, salt, corn, cheese and timber were all transported along the canal. In addition, from the ports came such items as beer, wine, sugar, tobacco and cotton. Nor was traffic confined to long distance hauls. The canal served many small communities along its length in a variety of ways. This commercial success led, of course, to considerable financial gain for the shareholders. After the completion of construction work and the payment of debts the dividends began to increase substantially. As a result shares soon began to change hands at a considerable premium. In 1806 the £100 shares were selling at £840 and the annual dividend was 40 per cent. Between 1820 and 1831 the dividend reached a phenomenal 75 per cent! This prosperity was soon to end with increased competition from the railways and a slow period of decline set in. In 1846 the Trent and Mersey canal was amalgamated with the North Staffordshire Railway Company, and although the canal fared better in the hands of a railway company than many others, the heyday of the Trent and Mersey Canal was over. Traffic, however, continued until well after World War Two.

The Armed Forces in Nottinghamshire

The Army
The Sherwood Foresters

✴ The history of the Sherwood Foresters can be traced back to 1741 when Colonel
D. Houghton raised the regiment which subsequently became the 45th Foot. The
regiment won its first battle honour at Louisburg in Canada in 1758. In the
following year the Regiment fought at the battle of Brooklyn in the West Indies and
then in Brazil. In 1782 the regiment was authorised to adopt the title of 1st
Nottinghamshire regiment, thus establishing the connection with the county. In
1808 it fought as part of Wellington's army in Portugal and Spain during the
Peninsular War, where the Regiment gained 14 battle honours and the nickname
'old Stubborns'. The Battle of Badajoz was the most notable of these honours and
is still celebrated on 6 April each year. As a consequence of the army reforms of
1881 the Nottinghamshire and Derbyshire regiments were merged. The 45th
(Nottinghamshire) Regiment became the 1st Battalion and the 95th (Derbyshire)
Regiment became the 2nd Battalion of the Sherwood Foresters. During World War
One the Sherwood Foresters raised 32 battalions. These fought with great
distinction in Flanders, France, Gallipoli and Italy and a total of nine Victoria
crosses were awarded to members of the regiment. At the outbreak of World War
Two the 1st battalion was serving in Palestine. The 2nd Battalion was sent to France
as part of the British Expeditionary Force and was later joined by 1/5th, 2/5th and
9th Battalions. All took part in the fighting leading to Dunkirk. Meanwhile the 8th
Battalion took part in the ill-fated Norwegian campaign. Unfortunately, the 1/5th
Battalion were made prisoners of war after the fall of Singapore. In North Africa
the 2nd and 5th Battalions fought with the First Army while the 14th Battalion took
part in the Battle of El Alamein. Later in the War all three battalions took part in
the fierce fighting of the Italian Campaign. In the post war period the regiment
served in Germany, Egypt, Libya, Malaya and Cyprus. In 1971 the Sherwood
Foresters was amalgamated with the Worcestershire Regiment. The regiment was
again amalgamated on 1 September 2007 and became the 2nd Battalion, The
Mercian Regiment (Worcestershire and Sherwood Foresters).

✴ During World War One the Sherwood Foresters lost 11,409 men. Nine
members of the regiment were awarded the Victoria Cross and more than 2000
others received other decorations, honours and distinctions.

✴ In World War Two a total of 26,940 officers and men served in the Sherwood
Foresters, of whom 1,520 were killed or died of wounds and about three times
that number were wounded.

✳ The war memorial of the Sherwood Foresters is located in the Derbyshire village of Crich. It takes the form of a lighthouse tower and stands on the summit of a 1,000ft hill. It was dedicated in 1923 in memory of the 11,409 men of the Sherwood Foresters who gave their lives in World War One. Later a plaque was added to commemorate the 1,520 men who gave their lives in World War Two.

The Navy

✳ HMS *Caunton* was a coastal minesweeper named after the village of Caunton. The ship's crest and lifebelt were placed in St Andrew's Church in the village.

✳ HMS *Nottingham* is the name given to four different ships that have seen service in the Royal Navy between 1703 and 2010.

✳ The first HMS *Nottingham* was a fourth ship of the line launched in 1703. With an armament of 60 guns and a crew of 365 she was part of the fleet which captured Gibraltar in 1704. The ship also saw action in the Battle of Cabrita Point in March 1705 and in the Mediterranean in 1711. Rebuilt in 1719 and again in 1745 the ship fought in a number of naval engagements before being sunk as a breakwater in 1773.

✳ The second HMS *Nottingham* which served in the Royal Navy from 1796 until 1799 was a 67 ton river barge which had been converted into a gunboat by the addition of two 18 pounder guns and a 32 pound carronade. This vessel never fired a shot in anger and was sold in 1780.

✳ The third HMS *Nottingham* was a Town Class light cruiser which was launched in 1913 and commissioned in 1914. With a crew of 433, the ship had 2in thick armour plating and was armed with six, 9in guns, one 13 pounder anti-aircraft gun and two 21in torpedo tubes. She first saw action in the Battle of Heligoland Bight in 1914 and the Battle of Dogger Bank in January 1915. She was sunk by a German submarine during the Battle of Jutland with the loss of only a few hands.

✳ The most recent and last HMS *Nottingham* was a Type 42 destroyer powered by two Rolls-Royce Olympus gas turbines and armed with one twin Sea Dart missile launcher and a Mk 8 automatic gun. Launched in 1978 and commissioned in 1983 she was something of an unlucky ship throughout her career. On its maiden voyage four members of the crew were lost in a drowning incident in Oporto. Four years later on 7 July 2002 she ran aground on Wolf Rock near Lord Howe Island, 200 miles off the coast of Australia. A massive hole was torn down her side, flooding five of her compartments and nearly causing the ship to sink. After repairs taking almost two years to complete, HMS *Nottingham* was re-launched on 7 July 2002 and returned to service in July 2004. Despite the huge cost of the refit (around £39 million) in April 2008 the ship was placed on a state of 'Extended Readiness' at Portsmouth and her crew dispersed. She was finally decommissioned on 11 February 2010.

✼ Photographs, mementos and models commemorating the last two ships to bear the name HMS *Nottingham* may be found in display cabinets in the foyer of the Council House in Nottingham.

✼ During World War Two a number of towns and villages raised money during Warship Weeks.

The RAF
✼ No 504 (County of Nottingham) Squadron was formed on 26 March 1928 at RAF Hucknall, Nottinghamshire, in a light bomber role. It played an important role in the Battle of Britain, flying Hawker Hurricane fighter aircraft against German bombers. Throughout the remainder of World War Two the squadron operated from a number of airfields in both Britain and abroad. They were involved in interdiction raids across occupied France as well as escorting heavy bombers on raids against enemy targets. In March 1945 the squadron was re-equipped with Gloster Meteor Jets but the war ended before they saw any action. A few months later the squadron was withdrawn from active service. It was reformed at RAF Syerston in 1947 and served as a night fighter and day fighter unit as well as undertaking a training role. The squadron was finally disbanded in 1957 after its standard had been presented to St Mary's Church, Wymeswold. After a gap of over 40 years, on 1 January 1997 the squadron was reformed in an offensive support role. One of its duties is airfield protection and members of the squadron have recently been deployed to Afghanistan.

Military Airfields
✼ RAF Balderton, two miles south of Newark, opened in 1941 and acted as a satellite station, first for RAF Finningley and later for RAF Syerston. The Royal Canadian Air Force moved here towards the end of 1941 and their Hampden bombers were used to attack naval and industrial targets during the early years of the war. During 1943 and 1944 the airfield was used for trials of the new Meteor jet fighter. In September 1944 aircraft from Balderton took part in Operation Market Garden, the unsuccessful attempt to capture the bridge over the Rhine at Nijmegen. During 1944 and 1945 Lancasters of Bomber Command flying from Balderton took part in night time raids on Germany. The base ceased to be operational before the end of the war but was not finally closed until 1957.

✼ RAF Bircotes near Bawtry was opened in 1941 and was used for operational training. Ansons, Hampdens, Hurricanes, Lysanders, Manchesters, Martinets and Wellingtons all flew out of Bircotes until it was closed to flying in 1944.

✼ RAF Blidworth, near Mansfield opened in 1941 and served only for the storage of fighter aircraft. It closed in 1945.

✳ RAF Gamston near Retford opened in 1942 as a training base. Oxford trainers were replaced by Wellington bombers in 1943. The station closed in 1945 but reopened in 1953 as a training school, flying meteor and vampire jet aircraft. RAF Gamston finally closed in 1957.

✳ RAF Hucknall first opened during World War One as a training ground and remained so for most of the war. In 1928 No 504 (City of Nottingham) squadron was formed here as a cadre unit of the Special Reserve. It became part of the Auxiliary Air Force in 1936 and was equipped with a number of different aircraft. The squadron continued to be based here until August 1939. For most of World War Two RAF Hucknall was used for training and maintenance. Both during and after the war the airfield was used by Rolls-Royce for testing its engines in a variety of aircraft and the famous flying bedstead made its first flights from here in 1953 and 1954. In 1957 the RAF terminated its involvement with Hucknall but Rolls Royce continued to use the airfield for ground and flight testing. Flight testing here ended in 1971.

✳ RAF Langar was opened in 1942. No 207 squadron, operating Lancaster bombers from here, took part in a number of raids over occupied Europe. During the Sumer of 1943 Langar was one of a number of bases to be used for the storage of Horsa gliders intended to be used in the D Day landings. The American Army Air Force used the base from 1943 until 1944. It was used

Hawker Hurricane at Hucknall Airfield.

briefly as a training base to convert pilots to bomber aircraft such as the Lancaster and Halifax but by the end of the year it had ceased to be operational. From 1951 until 1963 it was used by the Royal Canadian Air Force, largely as a supply depot. A number of transport aircraft also operated out of the airfield.

✻ RAF Newton was established in 1936 and in 1940 Wellington bombers from this station attacked the battleship Gneisenau in Brest harbour. In 1941 it became part of Flying Training Command and a large number of Polish airmen were trained here. In the years after the war RAF Newton was used for a variety of roles including the Royal Air Force School of Education, the RAF Police School, the Management Training Squadron and the Air Cadet Training Squadron. Many thousands of air cadets also learned to fly gliders here.

✻ RAF Orston was opened in 1941 as a satellite for RAF Newton. It was used as a training base and closed soon after the end of the war.

✻ RAF Ossington opened in 1942 and was used for the training of aircrew for bomber aircraft, later being used to train bomber crews to fly transport aircraft. The airfield closed in August 1946.

✻ RAF Syerston near Newark on Trent was opened in December 1940 as an operational bomber station. Two Polish squadrons flying Wellington bombers operated from here in 1941 making raids on the oil storage tanks at Rotterdam as well as other strategic targets. Later in the year the Polish squadrons were replaced by the Royal Canadian Air Force who briefly operated Hamden bombers from here, attacking a wide range of naval and industrial targets. The station was temporarily closed while new runways were constructed. RAF Syerston reopened as a heavy bomber station in May 1942 and Lancasters from here took part in many of the most important raids of the war, including the first shuttle-bombing raid by Bomber Command, the raid on Hamburg and the attack on the Research and Development station at Peenemunde. The bomber squadrons left in November 1943 and for the remainder of the war Syerston was used for training, a role which it maintained until 1971.

✻ RAF Tollerton began its existence in 1930 and the Flight and Test Establishment was founded here in 1931. The Nottingham Flying Club moved here in the same year and in 1937 the RAF began to train its Volunteer Reserve here. A year later Field Aircraft Services Ltd of Croydon built a large hangar in order to operate part of their repair and servicing organisation from here. During the war it was used largely for flying training and by Field Aircraft Services for the repair and overhaul of large numbers of RAF aircraft.

✻ RAF Winthorpe near Newark was opened as a satellite for RAF Swinderby. Two Polish squadrons made their home here during World War Two.

Recipients of the Victoria Cross with connections to Nottinghamshire

Francis Wheatley, Ruddington, 1st Rifle Brigade, Crimean War, 12 October 1854
Francis Wheatley was the first Nottinghamshire man to be awarded the Victoria Cross. Born at Ruddington in 1822, he was educated locally and enlisted into the Rifle Brigade as a private soldier. He saw service in Malta, South Africa and the Crimea. He was present at the Battles of Alma, Inkerman and the Siege of Sebastapol. It was during the Siege of Sebastapol that Francis Wheatley displayed his great courage. He was awarded the Distinguished Conduct Medal for gallantry in the trenches on 11 October 1854, and the following day his actions were recognised by the award of the Victoria Cross. He was occupying a section of the trenches defending Sebastapol when a live Russian shell fell among the men. Without hesitation Wheatley seized hold of the shell and attempted to knock out the fuse with the butt of his rife. When this attempt failed with great courage and presence of mind he somehow managed to heave it over the parapet of the trench. It had scarcely fallen outside when it exploded. Wheatley's courage and quick thinking undoubtedly saved the lives of many of his comrades. He was decorated by Queen Victoria at the first investiture of the Victoria Cross at Hyde Park on 26 June 1857. He died in London on 21 May 1865 and was buried in a common grave, which remained unmarked until a headstone was erected in 2001.

Robert Humpston, Nottingham, 2nd Battalion Rifle Brigade
Robert Humpston was born in Derby in 1832 and later enlisted in the 2nd Battalion the Rifle Brigade. He first saw service in the Crimea and was present at the battles of Alma and Inkerman. He received his Victoria Cross in recognition of his actions at Sebastapol where, along with two other riflemen, he charged a Russian rifle pit in broad daylight. He was decorated by Queen Victoria on 26 June 1857 at the first investiture at Hyde Park. He remained in the army and later saw service in India, where he was involved in the suppression of the mutiny. On his discharge from the army he returned to Derby, where he died on 22 December 1884. He was buried four days later in an unmarked grave in Nottingham General Cemetery. The grave remained unmarked for over 100 years, but funds were eventually raised for a headstone which was unveiled on 8 September 2007 in the presence of the Lord Mayor of Nottingham and two of Robert Humpston's direct descendants.

William Raynor, Plumtree, Bengal Veteran establishment, Indian Army, 11 May 1857
William Raynor is believed to have been the oldest recipient of the Victoria Cross. Born at Plumptree in 1795 and educated locally, he joined the East India Company in 1813. He was posted to the Bengal European Regiment serving in India and quickly won promotion, achieving the rank of Sergeant Major in 1818 and becoming a Sub-Conductor of Ordnance in 1819. He was later commissioned from the ranks. When the Indian mutiny broke out in 1857 he was serving in the Bengal Veterans Establishment. On 11 May of that year Lieutenant Raynor and nine other soldiers defended the magazine of the fort for more than five hours against large and vastly superior force of rebels and mutineers. When the enemy

finally scaled the walls and with no relief in sight, Lieutenant Raynor ordered the detonation of the contents of the magazine. Only Raynor and two other soldiers survived, but many of the enemy were killed. Raynor finally made his way back to Meerut and safety. His award was gazetted on 18 June 1858. He died less than three years later on 13 December 1830 at Ferozepore, India, and was buried the following day in the local cemetery.

Samuel Morley, Radcliffe on Trent, 2nd Battalion Military train, 15 April 1858, Azimgurh, Indian mutiny

Samuel Morley was born at Ratcliffe-on-Trent in 1829 and began his military career with the 8th Hussars. Having served briefly in the Crimea, he returned to England and transferred to the Military Train. He was something of a rogue and was frequently in trouble and went absent without leave on a number of occasions. He was court martialled twice and served two terms of imprisonment. It was during his service in India that he was awarded the Victoria Cross for his part in saving the life of Lieutenant Hamilton. The lieutenant had been unhorsed and was surrounded by the enemy when Private Morley, together with Farrier Murphy came to his assistance and fought off the attackers. Initially, only Murphy was awarded the VC but following an enquiry ordered by Lord Paget he received his medal from Queen Victoria on 9 November 1860. After his discharge in 1870 he returned to Ratcliffe on Trent and found employment at the local gas works. When he died in 1880 the city of Nottingham paid for an inscribed headstone which can still be seen in the general cemetery, Nottingham.

Anthony Clarke Booth, Carrington, 80th Regiment, 12 March 1879, Zulu War

Anthony Booth was born in the Carrington district of Nottingham on 21 April 1846. On leaving school he was apprenticed to a local tailor. At the age of 18 he joined the South Staffordshire Regiment. He had a varied career, and his quick temper led to his being reduced in rank on a number of occasions. He won his Victoria Cross during the Zulu Wars in South Africa. On 12 March 1879 the Zulus launched an attack on a British encampment on the banks of the Intombi River. Sergeant Booth rallied a few men on the south bank of the river and covered the retreat of 15 soldiers and others over a distance of three miles. His citation stated that, 'had it not been for this non-commissioned officer not one man would have escaped'. Booth was originally recommended for the Distinguished Conduct Medal but following the intervention of Lord Chelmsford, the commanding officer, this was changed to the Victoria Cross. He received other gifts in recognition of his bravery and was presented with a silver revolver by the officers of the regiment. He never returned to Nottingham and died at Brierley Hill, Staffordshire less than a year after retiring from the army.

William Thomas Marshall, Newark, 19th Hussars, 28 February 1884, Battle of El Teb, Sudan

William Marshall was born at Newark on 5 December 1854 and educated privately. In 1873 he joined the 19th Hussars. His regiment was sent to Egypt and he first saw action at the battle of Tel-el Kebir on 13 September 1882. He continued to serve in Egypt and took part in the Sudan Campaign of 1884. It was during a cavalry charge at the battle of El-Teb that Quartermaster Sergeant Marshall won his VC for conspicuous bravery in saving the life of Lieutenant Colonel Barrow. The colonel had been unhorsed and severely wounded and was surrounded by the enemy. William Marshall stayed behind and dragged the colonel through the enemy back to the regiment. His award was gazetted on 21 May 1884 and only a few months later he was commissioned as Lieutenant and Quartermaster. He served with distinction in the Boer War and retired from the army in 1907. He died on 11 September 1920 and was buried with full military honours.

Harry Churchill Beet, Bingham, Sherwood Foresters, 22 April 1900, Boer War
Harry Beet was born at Brackendale Farm, Bingham, on 1 April 1873. He was educated locally and joined the Nottinghamshire and Derbyshire Regiment in 1892. Two years later he sailed with his regiment to India where he took part in the Punjab Campaign between 1897–98. The regiment was next posted to South Africa and it was here, during the Boer War, that Harry Beet was to win the Victoria Cross. As a corporal in the 1st Battalion Mounted Infantry he received the award for his part in saving the life of one of his comrades. On 22 April at Wakkerstroom, Corporal Beet remained behind with a wounded comrade. He administered first aid and fought off the Boers until nightfall when assistance arrived. He received the Victoria Cross from the Duke of York (later King George V) at Natal on 4 August 1901 and was later propmoted to Sergeant by Lord Kitchener for his service in the field. After leaving the regular army in 1903 he continued to serve in the reserves as a member of the South Notts Hussars. He emigrated to Canada in 1906 and joined the Saskatchewan light Horse at the outbreak of World War One. He saw service in Europe and was commissioned in January 1916. At the outbreak of World War Two he enlisted once again but was discharged because of his age in March 1942. Not to be deterred he then joined the Royal Canadian mounted police and spent the remainder of the war guarding Japanese prisoners of war. He died in 19467 and was buried with full military honours at Vancouver Veterans cemetery. His Victoria Cross and other campaign medals are displayed in the Regimental Museum at Nottingham Castle.

Charles Ernest Garforth, Beeston, 15th (kings) Hussars, 2–3 September 1914, Mons
Born at Willesden Green, London, in 1891 Charles Garforth joined the Territorial Army at the age of 18 and transferred to the 15th (King's Hussars) regiment two years later. After a period of training he was posted to South Africa where he remained until 1913. On the outbreak of World War One Garforth sailed with his regiment to France and was involved in fierce fighting on the Western Front. He was recommended for the Victoria Cross no fewer than three times. On three separate occasions he risked his own life to rescue

comrades under fire. Shortly after winning the Victoria Cross, Corporal Garforth was captured and became a prisoner of war and it was not until 19 December 1918 that he received his medal from King George V. After his discharge from the army he found employment at Chilwell Ordnance Depot. He served as an ARP instructor in World War Two and died at his home in Beeston on 1 July 1973.

Captain Charles Vickers

Charles Geoffrey Vicars was born at Nottingham in 1894, the son of a wealthy lace manufacturer. He was educated at Oundle School and Merton College, Oxford, where he served in the Officer Training Corps. In September 1914 he was commissioned into the 7th Battalion, the Nottingham and Derbyshire Regiment (Robin Hoods). He was posted to France and was involved in fighting at Ypres and the battle of Loos. He was awarded the Victoria Cross in October for the conspicuous bravery which he demonstrated at the Hohenzollern Redoubt. When all of his men had been killed and wounded and with only two men left to pass the mills bombs (grenades) he held a barrier for some hours against attacks from the front and flanks. He ordered a second barrier to be built, even though in doing so he cut off his own retreat. Despite being severely wounded, he survived and was presented with his Victoria Cross by King George V at Buckingham Palace on 15 July 1916. On his return to Nottingham he was honoured with a civic reception and the presentation of a gold watch. After the war he qualified as a solicitor and practised locally with the firm of Slaughter and May. During World War Two he became Deputy Director General of the Ministry of Economic Warfare and a member of the joint intelligence committee to the Chief of Staff. He was knighted in 1946 and continued to make important contributions to public life. He died in 1982, and his Victoria Cross and other medals are displayed in the Regimental Museum in Nottingham Castle.

Wilfred Dolby Fuller, Greasley, Grenadier Guards, 12 March 1915, Neuve Chappelle

Wilfred Fuller was born at East Kirby, Greasley in 1893. On leaving school he worked briefly at Crown Farm Colliery, Mansfield, before enlisting in the Ggrenadier Guards at the age of 18. He was posted to France shortly after the start of World War One and was soon promoted to lance-corporal. He won the Victoria Cross at Neuve Chappelle on 12 March 1915 when he single handedly forced the surrender of around 50 enemy soldiers. His citation described how, 'seeing a party of the enemy endeavouring to escape along a communication trench, he ran towards them and killed the leading man with a bomb (grenade); the remainder (nearly 50) finding no means of evading his bombs surrendered to him'. He was presented with the Victoria Cross by King George V at Buckingham Palace on 4 June 1915 and remained in the country to assist with the recruiting campaign. He was also honoured locally. A civic reception was held in his honour at Mansfield and he was presented with an illuminated address and a gold watch. He was discharged from the army on medical grounds in 1916. He moved to Frome in Somerset where he served with the police until his retirement in 1945 on the grounds of ill health. When he died at the age of 55 his funeral was attended by 100 guardsmen and 60 police officers.

Walter Richard Parker, Stapleford, Royal Navy Marines, 30 April–1 May 1915, Gallipoli

Born at Grantham in 1881, Walter Parker joined the Royal Marine Light Infantry shortly after the outbreak of World War One. He won the Victoria Cross during the Battle of Gallipoli for his bravery in rescuing comrades under fire. He was himself seriously wounded and was discharged from the Royal Marines on 17 June 1917. He did not receive his Victoria Cross until the following month. On his return to civilian life he found employment at the Chilwell Ordnance Factory. He died at his home in Stapleford on 28 November 1936 and was buried with full military honours in the local cemetery.

James Upton, the Meadows, Sherwood Foresters, 9 May 1915, Rouges Bancs, France

James Upton was born in the Meadows district of Nottingham in 1888 and has the distinction of being the first man from Nottingham to win the Victoria Cross. At the age of 18 he joined the Nottinghamshire and Derbyshire regiment and after training was posted to India. Soon after the outbreak of World War One the regiment was posted to France. On 9 May 1915 during fierce fighting at Rouges Bancs Corporal Upton displayed tremendous courage in rescuing wounded while exposed to heavy rifle and artillery fire. During a whole day James Upton displayed great courage in rescuing wounded comrades while under almost constant fire from the enemy. One wounded man was killed by a shell while being carried by Upton and when he was not actually carrying the wounded he was engaged in providing first aid while fully exposed to enemy fire. He received his Victoria Cross from King George V at Windsor Castle on 24 July 1915. He was also honoured with a civic reception in Nottingham where the Mayor presented him with an illuminated address and a purse of gold. After his discharge in 1919 he settled in Middlesex and served as a Major in the Middlesex Regiment of the Home Guard during World War Two. He died at Edgware Hospital in 1949. His Victoria Cross and campaign medals are on display in the Regimental Museum in Nottingham Castle.

Samuel Harvey, Basford, York and Lancaster Regiment, 29 September 1915, Hohenzollern redoubt, France

Although Born in Nottingham in 1881, Samuel Harvey moved with his family to Ipswich while still a schoolboy. He joined the army in 1905 and served in India for seven years. He then left the regular army but re-enlisted at the outbreak of World War One. He was involved in some of the fiercest fighting on the Western Front and was wounded three times. He won his Victoria Cross at Big Willie trench on

29 September 1915 where he volunteered to fetch boxes of grenades which were needed to repulse and enemy attack. His communication trench was blocked with wounded and so he was forced to cross and recross open territory under constant enemy fire. He succeeded in bringing no fewer than 60 boxes of grenades before he received a head would. His citation stated that it was mainly due to his cool bravery in supplying bombs that the enemy was eventually driven back. In later life he fell upon hard times and for a while lived in the Salvation Army Hostel in Ipswich. He died on 24 September 1960 and was buried a few days later with full military honours.

John Joseph Caffrey, Nottingham, York and Lancaster, 16 November 1915, Ypres, Belgium

John Caffrey was born in Ireland in 1891, but his family moved to Nottingham while he was still young. He commenced his military career with the 7th Battalion, The Nottingham and Derbyshire Regiment (the Robin Hoods) but transferred to the York and Lancaster Regiment in 1910. He was posted to France at the outbreak of World War One and was involved in many of the battles which took place on the Western Front. He was awarded the Victoria Cross for most conspicuous bravery near La Brique on 16 November 1915 when he made three journeys 'under close and accurate fire' to rescue fallen comrades. According to the citation he 'risked his own life to save others with the utmost coolness and bravery'. Following his discharge he found employment in a number of capacities, and after a period of unemployment he was found a post as assistant public administrator at the Council Offices at Shakespeare Street. During World War Two he served as a Company Sergeant Major with the Sherwood Foresters. He later moved to Derby and died there in 1953. He was buried in Wilford Cemetery, Nottingham.

William Hackett, Sneinton, Royal Engineers, 22–23 June 1916, near Givenchy, France

William Hackett was born in the Sneinton district of Nottingham in 1873. After leaving school he became a miner. He moved to Yorkshire after losing his job at a local pit. He was above the age for normal military service when war broke out but probably because of his mining experience was accepted into the Royal Engineers. He was sent to France as part of the 254th Tunnelling Company. The idea behind tunnelling was to blow up enemy trenches form below and was extremely dangerous. In June 1916 he and four others were tunnelling towards enemy lines when the Germans exploded a mine. After working for 20 hours a hole was made through fallen earth and broken timber and Sapper Hackett helped three of his comrades to escape. A fourth, Private Thomas Collins, was seriously wounded and Hackett refused to leave him until they could both be rescued. The rescue squad toiled for a further four days but eventually the gallery collapsed and both men were buried alive. For this act of self-sacrifice Sapper Hackett was posthumously awarded the Victoria Cross. The medal was presented to his widow by King George V at Buckingham Palace on 29 November 1916.

Albert Ball, Lenton, Sherwood Foresters attached to the Royal Flying Corps, April–May 1917, and Western Front
Albert Ball is probably one of the most famous of the Nottinghamshire holders of the Victoria Cross. Born in Lenton in 1896, he was educated at Nottingham High School and Trent College, Long Eaton. At the outbreak of World War One he joined the ranks of the Derbyshire and Nottinghamshire Regiment (the Robin Hoods) before transferring to the Royal Flying Corps. He was posthumously awarded the Victoria Cross for his actions between 26 April and 6 May 1917. During this period Captain Ball took part in 26 aerial combats, destroying 11 enemy aircraft. On one occasion he fought six enemy planes single-handed. He was finally shot down and died on 7 May 1917. He is buried in Annoeullin in Northern France (see also Nottinghamshire Notables).

William Henry Johnson
William Johnson was born at Worksop in 1890. After leaving school he was employed at Manton Colliery. At the outbreak of World War One he enlisted in the Derbyshire and Nottinghamshire Regiment and was sent to France. He served with gallantry and distinction and was quickly promoted to sergeant. It was towards the end of the War that he won the Victoria Cross. On 3 October 1918 at Ramicourt in France, his platoon was held up by a nest of machine guns at very close range. Sergeant Johnson worked his way forward under very heavy fire and single-handed charged the post, bayoneting several gunners and capturing two machine guns. He was severely wounded but continued to lead his men forward. After this first attack the platoon was again held up by machine gun fire. Once again Sergeant Johnson rushed forward and attacked the machine gun post single-handed. According to the citation with wonderful courage he bombed the garrison, put the guns out of action and captured the teams. He showed throughout the most exceptional gallantry and dedication to duty. During World War Two he served in the Home Guard until ill-health forced him to retire. He died on 23 April 1945 and was buried with full military honours at Redhill Cemetery, Nottingham.

Robert James Bye, Warsop, Welsh Guards, 31 July 1917, Yser Canal, Belgium
Robert Bye was born at Pontypridd in 1889 and enlisted in the Welsh Guards on 3 April 1918. He proved to be an outstanding soldier and was soon promoted to sergeant. He was awarded the Victoria Cross during the Battle of Ypres for leading attacks on a number of enemy blockhouses, killing, wounding or capturing over 70 enemy soldiers. Bye was discharged from the Welsh Guards on 1 February but re-enlisted with the Derbyshire and Nottinghamshire Regiment just over six months later. He served with them until 1925 when he settled in Nottinghamshire and found employment as a miner in a number of different collieries. During World War Two he served as a Sergeant-Major in the Nottinghamshire and Derbyshire Regiment but was discharged on medical grounds in 1941. He was a member of a number of local organisations and died at Worksop on 23 August 1962. He was buried with full military honours at Worksop Cemetery.

Harry Nicholls, the Meadows, Grenadier Guards. 21 May 1940, River Escaut, Belgium

Harry Nichols was born in Nottingham on 21 April and after being educated locally he found employment with Burrows Adding machines in Arkwright Street. At the age of 19 he joined the 3rd Battalion, The Grenadier Guards. He was a keen sportsman and enjoyed swimming football and boxing. In 1938 he won the Heavyweight Championship of the British Army at the Albert Hall. Soon after the outbreak of World War Two, he was sent to France as part of the first draft of the British Expeditionary Force. It was in May 1940 during the withdrawal of the British Expeditionary Force near the river Escaut in Belgium that Harry Nicholls won his Victoria Cross. Although suffering from a shrapnel wound, he led his section in a counter attack against the advancing Germans. According to the citation, Lance Corporal Nicholls seized a bren gun and dashed forward towards the machine guns firing from the hip. He succeeded in silencing first one machine gun and then two others, in spite of being again severely wounded. He then engaged the German infantry massed behind, causing many casualties and continued to fire until he had no more ammunition left. It was believed at first that Nicholls had been killed and his Victoria Cross was presented posthumously to his wife by King George VI at Buckingham Palace on 6 August 1940. In fact he had been wounded and after treatment was transferred to various prisoner of war camps. It was at Stalag XXA Prison Camp that he was told of his award by the Camp Commandant, apparently on the orders of Adolf Hitler. After his repatriation at the end of the war he was awarded his VC personally by King George VI. He never really recovered from the wounds received and he died in Leeds in 1975. His body was returned to Nottingham and buried with full military honours at Wilford Cemetery.

Robert St Vincent Sherbrooke, Oxton, Royal Navy, 31 December 1942, off North Cape, Norway

Robert St Vincent Sherbrook was born at Oxton Hall, near Newark, on 8 January 1901. He attended the Royal Naval College at Osborne. He saw service in World War One and was later sent to study at Cambridge University. He enjoyed a successful naval career and as captain of HMS *Cossack* he won the DSO during the second battle of Narvick. Almost three years late in December 1942 he was awarded the Victoria Cross for his part in saving an important convoy bound for Murmansk in Russia. As the captain of HMS *Onslow* he was the senior officer in command of the four destroyers escorting the convoy. On the morning of 31 December 1942 off the North Cape the convoy was attacked by a German cruiser Admiral Hipper, with an escort of destroyers. Without hesitation Captain Sherbrooke went on the attack, sending half his force against the destroyers while he took on the Hipper. Every time the enemy withdrew Sherbrook pressed home the attack. The engagement lasted about two hours but after about 40 minutes the *Onslow* was hit and Sherbrooke was seriously wounded in the face, losing the sight of one eye. Even then he continued to direct the ships under his command until further hits on his own ships forced him to disengage, but not until he was satisfied that the next senior officer had assumed command. It was only then that he agreed to leave the bridge to receive medical attention. He insisted on receiving reports of all the action until the convoy was out of danger. His citation recorded that by his leadership and example the convoy was saved from danger and brought safely to its destination. Sherbrooke permanently lost the sight in his eye but returned to active duty in June 1943 as Commanding Officer of the Royal Naval Air Station, Arbroath. He was promoted to Rear Admiral in 1951 and retired due to ill health in 1954. He became High Sheriff of Nottinghamshire in 1958 and later became Lord Lieutenant of the county. He died at Oxton Hall on 13 June 1972 and was buried in the local churchyard. The flag from HMS *Onslow* is displayed in the parish church.

The Victoria Cross Memorial
The Nottingham and Nottinghamshire Victoria Cross Memorial was unveiled on Friday 7 May 2010. Standing in the grounds of Nottingham Castle the memorial is made from rough hewn granite, polished and engraved on one side only. The names of 20 recipients of the Victoria Cross who were either born in Nottingham or Nottinghamshire, or laid to rest therein are recorded.

Markets, Malls and Fairs

✳ Market Days in Nottinghamshire

Arnold	Tuesday, Friday and Saturday
Beeston	Friday and Saturday
Bingham	Thursday
Bulwell	Tuesday, Friday and Saturday
Clifton	Friday and Saturday
Eastwood	Thursday and Friday
Hucknall	Friday
Kirkby in Ashfield	Friday and Saturday
Mansfield	Monday, Thursday, Friday and Saturday
Newark	Monday, Wednesday, Friday and Saturday
Nottingham Victoria Centre	Monday to Saturday
Nottingham Market Square	Specialist Craft Markets during August and December
Ollerton	Wednesday, Friday and Saturday
Retford	Thursday and Saturday
Sneinton	Monday and Saturday
Sutton in Ashfield	Tuesday, Friday and Saturday
Worksop	Wednesday, Friday and Saturday

✳ Nottingham City Markets

Bulwell Market is an ancient and popular retail market which is held in the Market Place every Tuesday, Friday and Saturday from 9am to 4pm. Over 50 stalls sell a variety of goods including books, crafts, a wide range of fresh food and an array of clothing and fashion accessories. A flea market is also held every Wednesday morning.

Hyson Green Market, located adjacent to its own tram stop, is held at Radford Road, Hyson Green every Wednesday from 9am to 2.30pm. This vibrant community market with its 40 plus stalls sells a wide range of beautiful fabrics as well as Asian and Caribbean food and a variety of other goods.

Clifton Market on South Church Drive first opened in 1981. Held on Fridays and Saturdays each week from 9am to 4pm its 40 stalls offer a wide range of goods for sale. These include fresh produce, crafts, clothing, hardware and a range of everyday essentials.

St Ann's Market is located on Robin Hood Chase, off St Ann's Well Road, close to the city centre. Open every Tuesday from 9am to 2.30pm, it benefits from a vibrant multicultural atmosphere and from close links with the local community. Its 20 stalls sell a variety of goods and it was for many years renowned for its excellent range of food stalls.

Sneinton Market has been trading on its present site, close to the city centre, for over 100 years. Stalls on the market feature a wide range of products ranging from fresh fruit and vegetables to clothes, shoes and cards. After a period of decline and the threat of closure it was successfully re-launched in 2006. At the time of writing plans were well advanced for the redevelopment of the Sneinton Market area to create a new public space that will be a venue for markets, gatherings, events, performances, festivals and community use.

The Victoria Centre Market is on the first floor of the Victoria Centre opposite the John Lewis store. It is the largest and only indoor market in the city with over 200 stalls which trade from 9am to 5pm from Monday to Saturday. It attracts around 3 million shopping visits every year.

✳ A return made to quarter sessions in 1780 listed 10 market towns in Nottinghamshire. These were Bingham, Blythe, Mansfield, Newark, Nottingham, Ollerton, East Retford, Southwell, Tuxford and Worksop.

✳ The Old Market Square in Nottingham is the largest such square surviving in the country and covers an area of about 22,000sq m. Created in the 11th century, for hundreds of years it provided a home for both an open air market and the annual Goose Fair. In 1927 the market was moved to an area on King Edward Street and was later relocated to the Victoria Centre. The Goose Fair was held there the last time in the same year and has since been held on the Forest. The Square was redesigned to complement the new Council House and became a favourite meeting place for local people and for many years it was known affectionately as Slab Square. It underwent another considerable facelift between 2005 and 2007. The new square includes a dramatic water feature with jet fountains and waterfalls. These can be turned off if required to allow an amphitheatre-style seating area to be created for shows and concerts. The area becomes a market again in December each year when a traditional German Market is held here. It remains an important meeting place for local people and visitors alike, and thousands gather here to see in the New Year each year.

✳ The Exchange Building in the old Market Square, Nottingham was built in 1724 at a cost of £2,400, the architect being Marmaduke Pennel, who was also the Mayor for the year 1724–25. The building contained a number of public rooms including one which was known as the ballroom. On the north side of the exchange was the police office, where the magistrates' courts were held every Tuesday and Friday morning. Underneath the Exchange and facing the Market Place were four shops, while most of the ground floor was laid out in extensive shambles (butchers' stalls). The Council House replaced the Exchange in 1929.

✳ The layout of Nottingham Market Place in the middle of the 18th century was described in *The Nottingham Date Book* as follows: 'A structure known as the

The Old Market Square, Nottingham.

Malt Cross stood in the centre between Sheep Lane and St James' Street; its base was 4ft high, upon which rest six pillars covered with a tiled roof...Within this cross and around it sat those, on market days, who sold china and earthenware; and it was from this structure that all proclamations or declarations of war or peace were read, in the face of the full market: it was also the usual resort of labourers waiting for employment. The Exchange, then called The New Change then presented a red brick front, supported by 10 stone pillars forming a piazza...In front, were the stalls of fishmongers and dealers in hard-wares. Farmers and contractors occupied a large space in front of the Malt cross...The gardeners took up their station in the middle of the Long-row up to Chapel bar. In The Sands (more in the centre, parallel with the Row) was the market for horses. The dealers in swine were to be met with on the South Parade, a dirty and generally noisome swamp. The other parts of the spacious area were covered with miscellaneous merchandise.'

✳ The Lace Market in Nottingham was never a market where lace was sold but it was here that many of the lace manufacturers built their offices and warehouses as well as carrying out some of the industrial processes and accepting orders from the trade. Some manufacturers also built substantial homes in the area. Many of these still stand and the whole district forms an important conservation area in the centre of the city.

✳ Farmers Markets

Beeston	– Stoney Street on the fourth Friday of each month
Bingham	– Market Place on the third Saturday of every month
Mansfield	– Buttercross market on the third Tuesday of each month
Nottingham	– City Square on the third Friday of each month
Retford	– Town Hall Yard on the third Saturday of each month
Southwell	– Market Place on the second Friday of each month
Wollaton	– Co-op Store Trowell Road on the first Saturday of each month

✳ A cattle market was established in Burton Street, Nottingham in 1855. It remained there for 30 years until the site was used for the erection of a new guildhall. A new cattle market was, therefore, built on a site at Eastcroft extending to Meadow Lane. The site remains, but it is no longer a cattle market, but auctions are held here every Saturday morning selling a variety of goods from furniture to bicycles and a range of bric-a-brac.

✳ Mansfield Cattle Market was established in 1806. Initially it was held on the second Thursday of each month for 'All kinds of fat and lean stock'. For many years this was held on Westgate around the old Market Cross but in 1877 a new purpose built cattle market was opened next to Tichfield Park, now the site of the Water Meadows swimming baths.

✳ Mansfield was granted a charter to hold a market by Henry III in 1227 but this was repealed a few years later. In 1337 Richard II granted the town the right to hold a fair. This was originally held over four days at the feast of Saint Peter and Saint Paul. By the 18th century Mansfield also had two major fairs in Autumn; one for winter provisions such as cheese and another, the Statute Fair for the hiring of servants on a 12-month contract.

✳ In 1897 Herbert Simpson was fined two shillings and sixpence in Mansfield Police Court for shouting too loudly to advertise his potatoes in the market and failing to be quiet when asked by the police, contrary to the bye-laws. After the verdict he said, 'I'll get a barrel organ – it will be all right then'.

✳ In 1739 Nottingham possessed 5 apothecaries, 15 attorneys, 40 bakers, 1 banker (Mr Smith), 30 barbers, 4 basket-makers, 1 bell founder, 1 bird-cage maker, 3 bleachers, 3 booksellers, 2 brass-founders, 3 braziers, 11 bricklayers, 65 butchers, 3 button makers, 7 carpenters, 9 carriers, 10 chandlers, 1 coach maker, 3 collar-makers, 1 confectioner, 7 coopers, 1 cork-cutter, 1 counsellor, 4 curriers, 3 cutlers, 3 distillers, 5 drapers, 3 druggists, 1 dry-salter, 3 dyers, 2 fellmongers, 4 fishmongers and ironmongers (then one business) 1 file cutter, 20n gardeners, 1 grass-manufacturer, 12 glovers, 3 goldsmiths, 4 dealers in hats, 3 hair-pickers, 41 innkeepers, 24 joiners, 1 lead manufacturer, 2 mat-makers, 12 mercers, 1 miller, 3 milliners, 1 nailor, 9 plumbers, 2 printers, 3 painters, 2 paviours, 6 physicians, 1 pin manufacturer, 12 plasterers, 2 potters, 91 pot or ale houses, 2 rope makers, 7 saddlers, 30 shoemakers, 3 smiths, 4 soap-boilers, 4 stay makers, 1 stone cutter, 3 surgeons, 3 tanners, 52 tailors, 2 tinmen, 4 pipe makers, 3 dealers in toys, 3 turners, 2 upholsterers, 5 weavers of linen, 2 wheelwrights, 2 wooden heel makers, and 3 wool combers.

✳ The Victoria Centre was opened in 1972 on the site of the old Nottingham Victoria Railway Centre. It houses over 120 shops including major retailers such as the House of Fraser, Boots, Next and John Lewis. In addition to a wide range of retail units the Centre also accomodates a large indoor market, cafés, restaurants and a bus station. A large tower block was constructed over the Centre, this provides 464 flats and 36,000sq ft of office space.

✳ The Broadmarsh Shopping Centre (now known at Westfield Broadmarsh) was opened in 1972. It houses over 80 stores including Argos, Bhs and Boots. Plans are currently in hand for a major redevelopment of the site.

✳ The Rosemary Centre in Mansfield occupies the building previously known as Lawn Mills which was established in 1906 by the Cash family. It was used to prepare cotton which was then sent for weaving elsewhere. Today it is a shopping centre which houses a number of stores including Iceland, Argos Bewise, Lloyds Pharmacy and Domino's Pizza.

✳ The Four Seasons Shopping Centre in Mansfield is a modern indoor shopping mall which was opened in 1974. It contains over 50 stores nestled on one level. Its larger units include Boots, Debenhams and Primark but the centre also houses a wide range of shops retailing everything from books and cards to electrical goods, toys and holidays.

✳ The Exchange Arcade is part of the Council House Building on Old Market Square. It was opened in 1929. Today it is an upmarket shopping mall which is home to a range of popular boutiques, a gallery and jewellers.

The Exchange Building.

✱ The Flying Horse was one of Nottingham's oldest inns and the present building dates from the Tudor period. It closed as a pub in 1987 to reopen, fully restored, as a shopping arcade. Today it houses stylish boutiques as well as a few specialist retailers.

✱ The first Co-operative society in the county was formed in Nottingham in 1863 by Thomas Bayley and Benjamin Walker. It was at first called the Lenton Industrial and Provident Society but later changed its name to Nottingham Co-operative Society. By the early years of the 20th century it had around 13,000 members and over 50 branch outlets. In 1916 it opened a department store in Parliament Street. The society continued to grow and following mergers with other local societies became known as Greater Nottingham Co-operative Society.

✱ By the 1930s there were around 20 societies in the Nottingham District Association of the Co-operative Union. The three largest being Mansfield, Hucknall and Pleasley. Smaller societies existed at Annesley, Radcliffe-on-Trent, Ruddington, Selston, Stapleford and Warsop Vale.

✱ The Mansfield Co-operative Society was established in 1864. It opened a small shop in Leeming Street, paying a nominal rent of £12 per annum to the landlord of the Masons Arms.

✱ The Brewhouse Yard Museum contains a number of reconstructed shops. These include an Edwardian grocery shop and a Victorian chemist. A 1920s shopping experience is recreated in a row of shops including a barbershop, pawnshop, ironmongers, cobblers and music shop.

✱ Nottingham has over 1,000 shops covering 2.7 million sq ft of store space. Over 25 million shoppers visit Nottingham each year.

✱ Retford was granted its first charter, the right to hold a fair, by Henry III in 1246. This was extended in 1275 by Edward I to allow a Saturday market; a tradition which continues today.

✱ According to the Showman's Guild, June features what are known as the Nottingham festive fairs. The main week of these consists of five fairs at various locations in and around Nottingham, the largest of which is James Mellor's fair at Clifton.

✱ In 1337 Richard II granted a fair to the town of Mansfield. This fair was originally held over four days at the Feast of St Peter and St Paul. The patron saints of the parish. From the 11th century the fair took place in July and is remembered by many for its famous Gooseberry Pork Pie.

* In the 18th century Mansfield had two major autumn fairs; one for winter provisions such as cheese, and another, the Statute Fair or 'Stattis' for the hiring of servants on a 12-month contract. These fairs were held in the Market Place until the 20th century.

* Nottingham Goose Fair is one of the largest and best known fairs in Britain. It was first held in 1284 when King Edward I granted the burgesses of Nottingham a charter to hold an annual fair. Historically the Goose Fair has been associated with not only geese but also food of all kinds, especially cheese and a host of general goods as well as livestock and horses. Although primarily a trading fair where local people could buy and sell goods it is likely that entertainers such as minstrels, acrobats and jugglers would have provided entertainment. During the 19th century the Goose Fair became more important as a source of entertainment for local people. Although merry-go-rounds were initially banned, as the years passed more spectacular amusements including steam powered roundabouts like the 'Gallopers' and attractions such as the cakewalk were introduced. Eventually the fair became almost exclusively a funfair. In 1880 Goose Fair was reduced to just three days starting on the first Thursday in October. After hundreds of years, in 1927 the Goose Fair was held in the Market Square for the last time. It's increasing size coupled with the growth of traffic and the resulting congestion meant that a much larger site was needed. The decision was made to move to the Forest Recreation Ground where it is still held. Today Goose Fair attracts over 500 rides, stalls and other attractions. Nottingham Leisure Services Committee works closely with the Showman's Guild to ensure a successful and well organised event each year. Meticulous planning is needed to assemble all the attractions safely and efficiently. The larger rides arrive from 7.00am on the Sunday before Goose Fair. Other rides are gradually allowed on site over the next few days with the smaller stalls finally setting up after 2pm on the Wednesday. The official opening ceremony takes place at 12 noon on the Thursday. The Lord Mayor of Nottingham rings a pair of silver bells, known as the Goose Fair Bells, after the Chief Executive and Town Clerk have read the proclamation in the presence of the Sheriff of Nottingham and other civic dignitaries. For three days thousands of people enjoy all the fun of the fair but on the Saturday the showmen work through the night to dismantle the stalls and rides. Many then travel on to Hull Fair, a hotly contested rival to Nottingham's Goose Fair.

* Newark Antiques Fair is the largest antiques fair in Europe with over 4,000 stalls. Held on the Show Ground at Newark on six occasions during the year it attracts tens of thousands of visitors many of them from overseas.

Food and Drink

* The Bramley Apple originated at Southall. In 1909 the first Bramley apple tree grew from pips planted by a young girl, Mary Ann Brailsford. The cottage and garden were later bought by Matthew Bramley, a local butcher. In 1856 a local nurseryman, Henry Merryweather asked if he could take cuttings from the tree and start to sell the apple. Bramley agreed but insisted that the apple should bear his name. The first recorded sale of the variety is in Henry Merryweather's account book which records that on 31 October 1862 he sold 'three Bramley apples for 2/- to Mr Geo Cooper of Upton Hall'.

* For many years Worksop was famous for the growth of liquorice. It was first cultivated by the monks at Worksop Priory for medicinal purposes. Later local people grew the plant in liquorice gardens. Liquorice was used mainly as a sweetener and to mask the unpleasant taste of some medicines. John Harrison in his *Survey of Worksop* in 1636 wrote; 'I cannot here omit that thing wherein this town excels all others within the realm and most noted for: I mean the store of liquorish that grows there and that of the best'. The industry died out around 1750 with the arrival of sugar cane from the West Indies. Mr Brampton, a Slack Walk nurseryman was one of the last to grow it. Today one of the pubs in Worksop is called the Liquorice Tree.

* Marshall Talleyrand of France who was held prisoner in Nottingham in the early 18th century is reputed to have been the first person to cultivate the celery which grew wild in the Lenton area. It is also said that he taught the Nottingham bakers to make French rolls.

* Cock-on-a-stick was a toffee lollipop that was sold at Nottingham Goose Fair for over 100 years. For over 50 years they were produced by Ray Whitehead whose grandfather, Ben Whitehead, started the tradition towards the end of the 19th century. Describing the process by which they were made Ray Whitehead explained: 'I start making the cocks in June and I take my time, it's a slow process. To make them you have to boil glucose and sugar to 200 degrees Fahrenheit and then pour when it's malleable. We then add colour. We pull the toffee and it turns white. Lay it in stripes and pull portions off, cut each piece and shape it and add a flourish to the tail'.

* Mushy peas and mint sauce is another traditional food available at Goose Fair.

* Brandy Snaps are a traditional confectionary sold at fairs such as Nottingham Goose Fair. Sharp and Nicklass is a Nottingham family baker and biscuit manufacturer that has been making brandy snaps since 1888 and exports them to Ireland and Australia.

* Mansfield Toffee is made from butter, Demerara sugar, vanilla essence and chopped hazelnuts. It was a traditional fairground treat and popular at Halloween and Bonfire parties.

✳ During World War Two Nottingham Egg Week was organised to encourage people to donate eggs to Nottingham General Hospital so that they could be pickled for future use.

✳ Between the two world wars Nottingham had feeding stations for poor children with the average cost of a meal being 3d. Commonly the menus included potatoes, pie, stews, soups and a sort of corned beef hash.

✳ A Nottingham chef has been campaigning recently for people to make dandelions part of their diet. Claire Tutley, chief lecturer at the Nottingham School of Cookery described the herb as good traditional food. Some of the recipes which Claire has cooked up include dandelion soup, dandelion blossom pancakes and dandelion egg salad.

✳ Eglintine Vineyard was established in 1979 on south facing slopes in the parish of Costock. It takes its name from the smallest of the wild English roses which grow along the hedgerows in parts of the countryside. There are about 5,000 vines, the main variety being the Madeleine Angevine which is well suited to the local climate. The wines are produced in a purpose built winery and include sweet, sparkling and dry white wines, rose, red wine and a cherry wine as well as mead from locally produced honey.

✳ A cheese weighing half a ton passed through Nottingham in 1957 on its way to the London Dairy Show. It was 4ft in diameter and 3ft deep. To mark the occasion the Lord Mayor was given a 40lb cheese which he donated to Portland Training College for the Disabled.

✳ Nottinghamshire once boasted nine breweries but one by one they were subject to mergers or take-overs and have disappeared. The last to close was Hardy and Hanson at Kimberley in 2006. Other well known Nottinghamshire breweries included, the Nottingham Brewery, Home Brewery, Shipstone's and Mansfield Brewery.

✳ Microbreweries have replaced these traditional breweries to produce a wide range of real ale for the people of Nottinghamshire.

✳ Springhead is Nottinghamshire's largest independent brewery. Their bottled beers

Hardy and Hanson's Brewery at Kimberley.

are available nationally and regionally in Morrison's, Waitrose, the Co-op, and Asda and Tesco supermarkets. Gift packs of its most popular beer, Roaring Meg, are also available in some National Trust properties.

✳ A £2 million micro-brewery is to be built at the University of Nottingham to boost its teaching and research in brewing science. Due to be opened in 2011 the new facility will be used to research new technologies for the brewing industry to try and cut the amount of energy needed in the production process.

✳ Nottingham Express Transit has produced a 'Beer by Tram' guide showing the pubs that may be visited on the route of the tram from Hucknall to Station Street in the city centre. A total of 25 pubs are listed including the Green Dragon at Hucknall, The Orange Tree at Trent University and the Vat and Fiddle in Station Street.

✳ The Nottingham Robin Hood Beer and Cider Festival has been an annual event in the city since 1977. Originally sited in the Victoria Leisure Centre it moved to Nottingham Castle in 2007. As well as beer, cider and perries, country wines, a wide variety of food and snacks are also available. Entertainment includes live music and morris dancing.

✳ Stilton Cheese is a traditional blue cheese which can only be made in the three counties of Nottinghamshire, Derbyshire and Leicestershire. Originating in the village of Stilton in the 18th century, there are now just six dairies in the whole world licensed to produce Stilton. Together they produce over one million Stilton cheeses each year. In Nottinghamshire the cheese is produced in Cropwell Bishop and Colston Bassett.

✳ A survey carried out by the British Cheese Board in 2005 reported that Stilton cheese seemed to cause unusual dreams when eaten before sleep, with 75 per cent of men and 85 per cent of women experiencing 'odd and vivid' dreams after eating a 20-gram serving half an hour before sleeping.

✳ Colwick Cheese takes its name from the village of Colwick near Nottingham. Rennet was used to curdle the skimmed milk and when it had set sufficiently firmly, the curd was transferred to a muslin lined mould to drain. A traditional Colwick cheese was shaped like a shallow bowl about 7in deep and 5in in diameter. It was commonly sold on market stalls with each cheese presented on a fresh cabbage leaf. Colwick cheese was popular throughout the 19th and early 20th century. In the 1920s Samuel Colton and Sons were one of the largest manufactures of Colwick in the county and during the summer months almost 40,000 cheeses were sold each week. Its popularity declined, however, and commercial production finally ceased in 1993.

✳ Pyclets are thick yeast pancakes cooked on a griddle and contained within a metal ring. A typical pyclet is pale, lightly flecked with golden brown and honeycombed with a mass of little holes. The underside is smooth and golden brown in colour. In other parts of the country pyclets are called crumpets.

✳ Gotham, Newark, Mansfield, and Welbeck all have puddings named after them. The ingredients of Welbeck Pudding include Bramley apples, apricot jam, cornflower, milk, eggs and sugar.

✳ Tripe was for many years a popular dish locally, being cheap, nourishing and easily digested. In the 19th century tripe shops flourished all year round serving piping hot food to be eaten on the spot, or carried home in a basin covered with a cloth. At Goose Fair stalls sold hot tripe to the crowds enjoying all the fun of the fair.

✳ Haslet is a dish which is also served in neighbouring counties. Similar to faggots it contains pig's liver, belly pork, onions and seasoning. Cooked in the shape of a large bun it is served cold and cut into slices. It was popular until the 1950s when it was often made and sold at specialist pork butchers.

✳ Nottingham Veal Cake was a traditional recipe which was popular in the 19th century. Cheap to produce the ingredients included knuckles of veal and hard boiled eggs.

✳ HP Sauce was invented and developed by Frederick Gibson Garton. A Nottingham grocer. He chose the name HP because he claimed to have heard a rumour that it was served in the restaurant at the House of Commons. In 1903 bottles of HP Sauce, with pictures of the Houses of Parliament on the label, appeared in food stores for the first time.

✳ John Roe from Calverton developed a particularly fine plum in the 18th century. Named the Johnny Roe it is still grown locally.

✳ Nottingham batter pudding is a recipe which utilises local Bramley apples.

✳ Nottingham Blewitts is a traditional recipe using blewits (a variety of wild edible mushroom). The recipe involves cooking the blewits with milk and onions and serving them with mashed potato.

✳ Nottingham Pie is made with sweetened hot-water pastry and filled with gooseberries set in a clear apple jelly. They were once popular at Mansfield Fair.

✳ Nottingham Roast Goose is a traditional recipe in which the skin of the goose is rubbed with salt and pepper and the cavity filled with a stuffing of chopped cooking apples, sage and breadcrumbs.

✳ The Southwell Galette is a scrumptious pastry confection of hazelnuts, sultanas and bramley apple.

✳ Thaymar Dairy Ice Cream is produced at Houghton Park Farm near Bothamsall.

✴ The diet for inmates at Nottingham Workhouse in 1797 was: Breakfast – Sunday, Tuesday, Friday, Milk pottage; Monday, Wednesday, Saturday, water gruel; Thursday bread and gruel. Dinner – Sunday, Tuesday, Friday, broth, beef and potatoes; Thursday, puddings and sauce made of water, ale and sugar. Supper – every day except Thursday, bread and beer; Thursday, bread, cheese and beer. Children and sick persons are sometimes indulged with puddings and flour hasty puddings. At Thursday's supper about 2¾ of cheese are allowed each adult and a proportionate quantity for children.

✴ A butcher's bill paid by Mr Hustwaite of St James Street in Nottingham in 1748 listed the following purchases:

1748		£	s	d
Oct 18	A Leg of Mutton, 6lb at 2½d	0	1	3
Oct 19	A Calves's Head	0	0	9
Oct 22	A Saddle of Mutton	0	2	2
Oct 29	Beef, 7 ½ lb at 3d	0	1	10½
Nov 1	A Leg of Veal, 7lb at 2d	0	1	2
Nov 2	A Leg of Mutton	0	1	4
Nov 6	Beef, 8lbs at 3d	0	2	0
		0	10	6½

✴ At around this time (the middle of the 18th century) the price of provisions in Nottingham were generally as follows: Wheat, 28s to 32s per qr; barley, 16s; rye, 14s; oats 7s to 10s; beans and peas, 16s to 30s (extremely fluctuating); malt, 24s. Beef, veal, mutton, ham and pork, on average 2 ½ d per lb; butter from 4d to 6d per lb; cheese, 3d per lb; eggs 30 to 50 for 1s ; fowls, per couple, 1s 4d to 2s; pigeons, per dozen, 1s 4d to 1s 6d. A goose, green, 1s; stubble, 1s 6d; Christmas, 2s to 2s 6d. Ducks, per couple, 8d to 1s and 1s 6d; a turkey, from 2s to 3s: rabbits per couple, 6d to 8d; peas, green per peck, 4d to 6d.

✴ According to a recent history of Nottingham the poor survived during the inter-war years on a diet of cow heel, pig's head, chap and trotters, sheep's head, the heads and tails of fish and 'speck jocks' (bruised fruit). They shopped at markets, bought left over cuts of meat, stale bread and broken biscuits. In contrast, affluent families dined on expensive cuts of meat and luxury fruit and vegetables delivered by Burton's on Smithy Row or Skinner & Rook on Clumber Street.

✴ The OXO cube is manufactured by Premier Foods in Worksop. The best known flavour of stock cube is still the original beef flavour but the company also produces other flavours. In 2009 the company announced that the traditional cube would be replaced by an x-shaped block. Because of the foil packaging, however, it still has the external appearance of a cube.

✴ Ruddington Village Museum is home to the world's oldest fish and chip shop. Dating back to the early years of the 20th century, it was originally located in a cottage on the corner of Ruddington High Street and the Green, and remained open until 1941. For 40 years it lay untouched until it was rediscovered and installed in the museum. The actual fryer dates back to 1904–05 and is coal fired.

✳ Sat Bains and his wife Amanda run Nottingham's restaurant, Sat Bains with Rooms, which in 2003 was awarded the city's first-ever Michelin star. He also appeared in the BBC TV programme *The Great British Menu* in 2007.

✳ Nottingham's first vegetarian restaurant, the Savoy Café in St James Street, was opened in 1904. The founder, Alfred Martin, had been advised by his doctor not to eat meat and as a consequence he and his family converted to vegetarianism.

✳ In a 2006 Frequency of Overseas Dishes (FOOD) study by MSN, Nottingham emerged as Britain's international food capital with six restaurants representing different world cuisines for every square mile.

✳ Professor Don Grierson of the University of Nottingham led the team that produced the first genetically engineered tomato. The tomato was the first genetically modified plant food to be approved on both sides of the Atlantic.

✳ On 20 July 2001 a Nottingham Restaurant entered the record books by building the world's tallest poppadom tower. Staff at the Curry Lounge on Upper Parliament Street used 1,052 poppadoms to build a 151cm tower, breaking the previous record of 148cm.

✳ Nottingham had the first ever organic sugar beet crop grown in the UK. A Newark factory began slicing the organic sugar beet crop on the night of 30 November 2001.

✳ The Food for Life Catering Mark was launched by Prince Charles in February 2009 during a visit to Nottingham. Open to caterers in both the public and private sectors the Mark has three tiers; gold, silver and bronze. To achieve the Gold standard the caterer's menu has to be 75 per cent freshly prepared 50 per cent local and 30 per cent organic.

✳ Nottingham University Hospital scooped a Food for Life award in 2009 after revamping its menu to include an array of dishes from pasta carbonara and roast lunches to fish and chips and goat curry.

✳ Chillies are grown at Clumber Park. A firm called Gringley Gringo cultivates two acres of land for growing chillies which are then processed into a range of sauces and pastes. The company won a National Trust Fine Farm Produce Award in 2010.

✳ The largest manufacturer of pork pies in the country is the Nottingham firm of Pork Farms.

First, last, biggest, oldest, best!

✳ According to the Nottingham Date Book the town's first tiled roof was constructed at the Unicorn Inn on Long Row.

✳ Nottingham was the first city to install Braille plates for blind people in its shopping centres.

✳ Centre Parcs created their first UK holiday village in Nottinghamshire in 1987.

✳ In AD1180 Nottingham became the first city in England to record an earthquake.

✳ Nottingham Goose Fair is the oldest, biggest and best three day Fair in Britain.

✳ The Screen Room in Hockley features in the Guinness Book of Records as the world's smallest cinema with just 21 seats.

✳ The first 'talkies' in Nottingham were shown at the Elite Cinema on 24 June 1929.

✳ The William Smith Building in Keyworth, opened in 2010, is the largest wooden-framed open plan office in the UK. It is owned by the British Geological Survey.

✳ The first woman to hold the office of Sheriff of Nottingham was Councillor Mrs C.M. Harper. She was appointed on 9 November 1931.

✳ By the early years of the 20th century Raleigh had become the largest cycle works in the world. In 1919 they were producing around 100,000 cycles a year.

✳ The hamlet of Kersall, originally a Quaker settlement, boasts the best-kept phone box in the world.

✳ Possibly the first church bells to ring out over Nottinghamshire were heard soon after 1023 when Alfred, Archbishop of York, presented two bells to Southwell Church. The building of the Minister began later in the century.

✳ Nottingham's oldest hotel is the Comfort Hotel in George Street, formerly the George. Built around 200 years ago it has seen a range of celebrities pass through its doors. Stars have included Richard Burton and Elizabeth Taylor. Charles Dickens stayed here in 1852 and the hotel has also seen a number of royal visits.

✳ The streets of Nottingham were first lit by oil lamps in 1762. The illumination provided was, however, poor as the globular glass bottoms of the lamps were so thick and opaque as render them almost useless.

✳ Thomas Hammon is credited with producing the first piece of machine-made lace in 1768.

✳ The earliest gas works in Nottingham was established in 1818 in Butchers Close and Island Street, off London Road. By 1819 lamps had been erected on Hollowstone, Drury Hill, Bridlesmith Gate and six in the Market Place.

✳ Nottingham's first steam powered fire engine was demonstrated in Great Market Place in 1864. Spectators watched as a 1in hose projected water 130ft into the air.

✳ Nottingham Police took delivery of their first motorcycle in 1910. It was ridden by PC 103 Dench. In the same year the force recruited their first police dog.

✳ The first edition of the *Nottingham Evening Post* was published on 1 May 1878. It comprised four broadsheet pages and sold for a halfpenny.

✳ Nottingham's first electricity supply was provided in 1894. A Corporation generating station in Talbot Street used coal-fired boilers to drive generators which supplied electricity to premises in and around the city centre. Demand was low to begin with and did not reach 1,000 kilowatts until 1899.

✳ The Camellia House at Wollaton Hall claims to be the world's first iron framed building. It was restored in the early 1970s following an appeal by David Bellamy, the naturalist and TV personality.

✳ Eric Irons who was born in Jamaica came to Nottingham in 1947. In 1962 he became the country's first black magistrate.

✳ Nottingham had the country's first children's library. It was founded in 1882 by Samuel Morley, a local MP and benefactor.

✳ In 1993 Councillor Mohammed Ibrahim became Nottingham's first Asian Lord Mayor.

✳ The first meeting of the new Nottinghamshire County Council took place on 1 April 1889. The first chairman of the County Council was Lord Belper who held office for 25 years.

✳ George Miller became the first blind chairman of Nottinghamshire County Council in 1991. With Selina, his German Shepherd guide dog by his side he promised to promote the interests of the disabled.

❋ The first stocking machine was invented by William Lee, a Calverton clergyman, in 1589.

❋ Mail coaches first ran between Nottingham and London in 1784. They left London at 6pm reaching Nottingham at 6pm the following day.

❋ In 1797 Joseph Raynor was appointed Nottingham's first Postmaster. The postal business at the time was, however, so small that he was able to run a successful seeds man's business in his spare time at his shop and post office in High Street.

❋ The first pillar post boxes were erected in Nottingham on 24 September 1857, and post men in uniform first appeared in the streets on 24 May 1858.

❋ Nottingham's first public telephone box was installed in Theatre Square in 1908.

❋ Nottingham's first hospital was the General Hospital, erected by public subscription in 1781 on a site which was then just outside the borough boundary. It remained a voluntary hospital until 1948 when it became part of the National Health Service. The building of the Queens Medical Centre resulted in its closure.

❋ In 1878 Nottingham opened the first Museum of Fine Art outside London. The Castle Museum and Art Gallery still has a fine collection of paintings including works by local artists such as Dame Laura Knight.

❋ The first aeroplane to visit Nottingham was piloted by Paul de Lesseps. He landed at Colwick on 30 September 1910.

❋ The last execution in Nottingham took place on 10 April 1928.

❋ Notts County is the world's oldest football club. It was founded in 1862.

❋ The earliest game of cricket to be played in Nottingham was in 1771 with a match against Sheffield.

❋ The first Cricket Test March against Australia was played at Trent Bridge Cricket Ground in 1899.

❋ The Trent Bridge Library holds the biggest collection of cricket books in the UK.

❋ The first local man to ascend in a balloon was a certain Mr Sadler who, in 1813, left Canal Wharf and descended at Pickworth, a distance of some 33 miles. His son also made a name for himself as a balloonist and on 23 November 1823 made an ascent from the grounds of Nottingham Castle. Around 2,000 people paid 2s each for their vantage point. An estimated 7,000 people looked on from outside the grounds. On 3 August 1836 a number of ladies and gentlemen paid a certain Mr Green 10s 6d each for a tethered balloon flight. A bolder spirit, Mr Saywell paid Green 25 guineas and soared with him as far as Edwalton at a height of 2,400ft. By seven o' clock in the evening Green was back in Nottingham bringing his balloon with him on the top of his chaise. He visited Nottingham again in 1847 and made a flight to Staunton Harold Hall.

✳ Nottingham's Market Square is the largest in Britain and covers an area of 5.5 acres.

✳ The first public tram service to run in Nottingham was a horse-drawn service operated by the Nottingham and District Tramway Company Ltd. They commenced service on 17 September 1878 with two services; one from St Peter's Church to Trent Bridge via Carrington Street and Arkwright Street and another from Saint Peter's Church to London Road via Carrington Street, Arkwright Street and Station Street.

✳ Nottingham's first electric tram route, Sherwood – Market Place, opened on 1 January 1901.

✳ Tom Barton launched a bus service in 1908 running from Long Eaton to Goose Fair and back again. It had a maximum speed of 12 miles per hour.

✳ Nottingham established the first police forensic laboratory in 1934. It also sent the first radio message by police car in 1932.

✳ Nottinghamshire had the first wooden railway track in the country. Two miles of wooden rails connected with the coal mines at Strelley and Wollaton.

✳ The first public park in Nottingham was the Arboretum. Designed in 1850 it retains much of its original layout.

✳ Feargus O'Connor was the first and only Chartist ever to become a Member of Parliament. Elected as MP for Nottingham in 1847, his statue stands in the Arboretum.

✳ Nottingham's first telephone exchange was in Bottle Lane. The first telephone directory was issued in 1885. It had 170 subscribers listed.

✳ The idea of having a Christmas tree in the Market Square first came about in 1958 and then on 17 December of that year the first one was erected.

✱ Nottingham's first purpose built cinema, the Victoria Electric Palace in Milton Street, opened on 24 March 1910.

✱ Nottinghamshire CCC won the County Cricket Championship for the first time in 1907.

✱ The first rugby international to be played in Nottingham took place at Meadow Lane on 6 December 1911. England beat the Australians five points to three.

✱ Shin protectors for football players were invented in Nottingham in 1880.

✱ The first aerial press photograph was taken over Nottingham in 1910.

✱ Nottingham had the first high pressure water supply in the country. The Trent Waterworks Company opened in 1831 and provided a constant high pressure supply which prevented contamination from entering the mains supply.

✱ The first ever live webcast of a Nottinghamshire County Council meeting took place on Thursday 16 May 2002.

✱ Nottingham Trent University created the world's first virtual reality catwalk for its fashion students.

✱ The first zebra crossing in Nottingham was put into operation between the Mechanics Institute and Victoria Station in April 1935.

✱ The blockbuster film, *Robin Hood Prince of Thieves*, starring Kevin Costner received its UK premier at the Showcase Cinema in Nottingham on 18 July 1991.

✱ The Post Office Speaking Clock service was first used in Nottingham on 28 October 1939.

✱ Britain's first traffic court was held in Nottingham on 14 April 1930.

✱ One of the first municipal car parks outside London was opened in Nottingham in 1933. A parking space for 80 vehicles was created next to the Central Bus Station on Huntingdon Street. Drivers were charged one shilling a day and were allowed to leave and return as often as they liked.

✱ The first parachute mine dropped by the German Luftwaffe fell on Winthorpe airfield in 1940.

✱ The world's longest running theatrical production opened at Nottingham's Theatre Royal on 6 October 1952. *The Mousetrap* then went on a Provincial Tour before opening at the Ambassador's Theatre in November.

✳ The largest inland dry dock in Britain is at Newark. Barges were once built here but it is now used mainly for the repair, renovation or maintenance of privately owned craft.

✳ Aspire is a work of art constructed on the Jubilee Campus of Nottingham University. It is a 60m high red and orange steel sculpture and is the largest free standing public work of art in Britain, taller than Nelson's Column and the Angel of the North. The sculpture weighs 854 tons and cost £800,000 which was donated by an anonymous benefactor. The name Aspire was chosen in competition which was open to staff and students at the university.

✳ The tallest building in Nottingham is the Victoria Centre which stands at 256ft. It was built in 1972.

✳ BBC Radio Nottingham went on air for the first time on 31 January 1968.

✳ Paul Smith opened his first shop in Nottingham in March 1970.

✳ Elton John played live on the opening night of the Royal Concert Hall on 27 November 1982

✳ One of the earliest home video recorders was designed and made in Nottingham in 1963 by the Nottingham Electronic Valve Company. They marketed the Telcan video recorder for £62, a considerable amount of money at the time.

✳ The Annual Conference of the Labour Party was held in the Albert Hall, Nottingham, on 23 January 1918.

✳ In April 1999 the Asda supermarket at Sutton in Ashfield held the UK's first blessing and reception in a supermarket. It had been unable to obtain a ceremony licence.

✳ New College in Nottingham is the second largest in Europe with more than 50,000 full and part-time students.

✳ Students at Clarendon College of Further Education made a sherry trifle weighing 3.13 tonnes including 91 litres of sherry at the Forest Recreation Ground, Nottingham on 26 September 1990.

✳ In October 1985 students from Nottingham University squeezed 27 people into a Ford Sierra car.

✳ The Little John Bell, which hangs below the dome of Nottingham Council House clock has the deepest tone of any bell in Britain and weighs 10.5 tonnes.

✳ Nottingham's first Pagan Pride parade took place on Sunday 1 August 2010. It is the only event of its type outside London.

✳ Nottinghamshire Library Service was founded in 1919. Within a year book lending had risen to over 44,000 volumes.

✳ Nottingham city's first police woman was appointed in July 1919 despite objections of some members of the watch committee. Miss Plumtree was appointed originally on a three-month trial which was later extended. Unfortunately she caught flu and after an absence of two weeks the committee stopped her pay and later suspended her.

✳ Traffic Wardens appeared on the streets of Nottingham for the first time on 20 January 1963.

✳ Nottinghamshire police began using hand held radar guns to catch speeding motorists in 1974.

✳ Nottingham's first park and ride service was introduced in November 1972. The service which operated only on Saturdays, picked up passengers from the Forest recreation ground and dropped them off near the Theatre Royal. A second park and ride service took passengers from a car park at County Hall to Maid Marion Way.

✳ The *Nottingham Evening Post* made newspaper history in 1976 when it became the first newspaper in Britain to publish articles 'set' by journalists. The electronic editing and typesetting equipment was developed in collaboration with International Computers Ltd.

✳ Nottingham's first Robin Hood Festival took place in 1990, when over 2,000 people crowded into the Old Market Square to watch as Robin Hood escaped the clutches of the Sheriff.

✳ In September 2010 research by the Campaign for Better Transport rated Nottingham as the least car dependent city in England with London, and Brighton and Hove, in second and third place respectively.

What's in a name?

Place Names

✱ Most settlements in Nottinghamshire date from before the Norman Conquest. Their names give us some idea of when and why they were first founded and something of the physical environment at that time. Place name elements in Nottinghamshire are generally the same as those found throughout the Midlands and include the following:

Place name ending	Meaning	Example
Anglo-Saxon		
First Phase of settlement		
ham	homestead	Bingham, Welham
Second phase		
borough, bury	fortified settlement	Woodborough, Fledborough
bridge	bridge	East Bridgford
ford	crossing place	Basford
ton	enclosure of land	Laxton, Balderton
Later clearing, drainage and establishment of smaller or linked settlements		
cot, cote	outlying hut	Bramcote, Bulcote
field	clearing in wood	Mansfield, Bassingfield
ley	clearing	Kimberley, Lambley
mere	lake	Gibsmere
stoc, stoke	daughter settlement	East Stoke
stow	holy place	Edwinstowe, Broxtowe
wich,wick,wike	dairy farm	Papplewick, Colwick
worth or worthy	an enclosure	Babworth, Rainworth
Scandanavian Period (circa AD800–1100)		
beck, slack	stream	Welbeck, Holbeck
by	settlement or homestead	Bilby
thorp(e)	daughter settlement	Winthorpe, Owthorpe
thwait	clearing	Huthwaite

Street Names

✱ In Nottingham, and other similar towns, street names often originate with the trades or occupations carried on there in the Middle Ages. These include:

In Nottingham

Fletcher Gate – Not the street of the fletchers or arrow makers but the flesh-hewers or butchers. Some of the shambles (butchers stalls) were situated here.

Lister Gate – The street of the listers or dyers.

Barlock Road – It was built in the 1920s and took its name from the Barlock Typewriter Company which had built a new factory there.

Fisher Gate – Where the men who fished in the Trent and Leen made their homes.

Elsewhere

Tetheringrass Lane at Beckingham indicates that animals were once tethered here for grazing.

Tinker's lane at Besthorpe suggests that a maker and/or seller of pots and pans once lived here.

Tenter Lane in Mansfield indicates that cloth was stretched here on frames after the fulling process had taken place.

The Rope Walk at Leake, although a modern name, refers to the Ellis rope works which was here from 1974 to 1987.

Saversick Lane in Southwell was where the soap makers carried on their business.

At Newark Stodmare Street a stud mare was stabled and offered for selective breeding for a fee.

Theaker Lane in the village of Scaftworth takes its name for from the dialect word for thatcher.

✱ Sometimes streets are named after people or significant events. In Nottinghamshire there are streets, roads, avenues and crescents named after military heroes such as Lord Nelson and the Duke of Wellington; writers and poets such as Shakespeare, Tennyson, Wordsworth and other well known figures including William Gladstone, John Wesley, Florence Nightingale, William Hogarth and Nel Gywnn! Many of these streets were named long after the deaths of the people they commemorate but in the Victorian and Edwardian eras when large scale public housing was being developed streets were often named after contemporary heroes or personalities. In Nottingham, Albert Street was named after Prince Albert, Queen Victoria's consort; and Zulu Road, Chard Street, and Durnford Road all commemorate the Zulu War of 1879.

✱ Some streets are named after local Nottinghamshire personalities and these include:

Coates Avenue in Hucknall is named after Eric Coates, the composer.

Lovelace Walk (also in Hucknall) is named after Ada Lovelace who made a major contribution to the development of computer programming.

Brandreth Drive in Giltbrook commemorates Jeremiah Brandreth, the 'Nottingham Captain' who led the Pentrich Revolution.

Lord Byron, the famous poet, is commemorated in Byron Court, Stapleford, Byron Crescent, Awsworth and Byron Street in Hucknall.

Sir Richard Arkwright who invented the water frame and established a cotton mill in Nottingham in 1769 is remembered in Arkwright Street and Arkwright Walk, both in Nottingham.

D.H. Lawrence, the author of *Sons and Lovers*, *The Rainbow* and *Lady Chatterley's Lover* has streets named after him in Breaston, Awsworth, Colwick, Eastwood and Brinsley.

William Booth, the founder of the Salvation Army who was born in Nottingham, is remembered in William Booth Road in the city.

Cranmer Street in Nottingham refers to Archbishop Cranmer. Born at Aslockton.

✳ Not surprisingly several streets in Nottinghamshire are named after Robin Hood. These include Robin Hood Drive in Hucknall, Robin Hood Close in Eastwood, Robin Hood Road in Arnold and Robin Hood Way in Nottingham.

✳ Several streets throughout the county are named after saints but this is often because of their proximity to churches with the same dedication. Particularly popular are roads or streets named after St Alban, St Andrew, St James, St Mary and St Peter.

✳ Other street names are associated with important buildings such as mill, castle, church or abbey. In Nottinghamshire these include:

Mill Lane in Newark

Castle Gate in Newark

Slaughterhouse Lane in Newark

The Spital in Gonalston (named after the hospital built nearby by William de Heriz)

✳ Street names often change over time. The following examples are taken from Nottingham

Canal Street was Leen-side

Carlton Street was Swine Green

Clumber Street was Cow Lane

Market Street was Blowbladder Street

Milton Street was Boot Lane

Park Row was Butt-dyke

The Poultry was Cuckstool Row

Sussex Street was Turncalf Alley

✳ Nottingham City council now issue guidelines for the names of new streets and buildings. These include the following points:

Names of living persons are not normally permitted

Names should not sound like existing ones within the Nottingham city area

They should not be difficult to pronounce or spell

If possible names should reflect the past history of the area

Names that could be considered advertising will not be accepted

Names that could be considered offensive will not be accepted

Schools

School names reflect a whole range of criteria which have changed over the years. The majority are still named after the village, street or general locality in which they are situated. Church schools are invariably named after saints and often share the same name as the local parish church. Catholic Schools, which tend to have a wider catchment area serving several churches, are often given a different name to any of the parishes which they serve. There has been a trend in recent years to name them after some of the Catholic martyrs of the Tudor period. A significant member of schools are named after famous people or local worthies although in recent years there has been a trend away from naming schools after living persons.

Schools named after lesser known saints include the following:

✜ The Becket School at Nottingham is a Catholic secondary school. It is named after Thomas Becket who was Chancellor to Henry II. After a violent quarrel between the two men he was murdered on the steps of the altar of Canterbury Cathedral.

✜ St Margaret Clitherow Primary School is named after a Catholic Martyr who lived in York. After being accused of harbouring a priest she refused to plead and was crushed to death. She was later canonised by the Catholic Church.

✜ The Blessed Robert Widmerpool School is named after Robert Widmerpool who came from Nottingham. He studied at Oxford University before working as a tutor for the sons of the Earl of Northumberland. He was arrested for giving aid to a Catholic priest and was hanged, draw and quartered during the reign of Elizabeth I.

✜ St Edmund Campion school is named after another Catholic martyr. A Jesuit priest, he returned to England in 1580 and led a hunted life preaching and ministering to Catholics in secret. He was eventually caught and after being tortured he was hanged, drawn and quartered.

✜ St Philip Neri with St Bede Catholic Primary School at Mansfield is unusual in being dedicated to two saints. St Philip Neri was an Italian priest who was born at Florence in 1595 and was noted for his personal spirituality. He underwent numerous ecstatic religious experiences and many miracles were attributed to him. Saint Bede was an Anglo-Saxon saint and scholar who was responsible for the first history of the English people.

✜ St Giles Special School is named after a Greek saint of the same name, he is regarded as the patron saint of disabled people, outcasts and the poor.

✜ St Swithun's C of E Primary School in Retford is named after a ninth-century bishop of Winchester. Early chroniclers ascribed a number of miracles to him but he is best known for the legend that if it rains on St Swithun's Day (15 July) it will rain for a further 40 days.

Schools named after famous people or local worthies include the following:

✳ Bishop Alexander School at Newark is named after Bishop Alexander who was Bishop of Lincoln during the reigns of Henry I and Stephen. He was known for his ostentatious and luxurious lifestyle and is sometimes known as Alexander the Magnificent.

✳ Annie Holgate School is named after Annie Elizabeth Holgate, a teacher, who entered local politics and became Chair of the Education Committee.

✳ Colonel Frank Seeley School at Calverton is named after Frank Evelyn Seeley who was born in 1846. The son of Sir Charles Seeley he gained a BA degree at Cambridge University before joining the family business at Babington Colliery. He went on to become Chairman of the Company.

✳ Robert Miles School at Bingham is named after Robert Miles, the rector of Bingham from 1845 to 1883. A wealthy and forthright evangelist, he was responsible for restoring the local church and for building Bingham Church School, which was opened in 1846 (Now used as a church hall).

✳ Dean Hole School at Caunton is named after the Reverend Samuel Reynolds Hole, son of the squire of Caunton. He was made a curate in 1844 and was inducted into the living at Caunton in 1850. He remained in the parish until 1887 when he was made Dean of Rochester. Known locally as Dean Hole he was buried in Caunton Churchyard in 1904. He was nationally famous as a rose grower and judge, founder of the National Rose Show (1858) and as the author of *A Book of Roses* (1869).

✳ Ethel Wainwright Primary School at Mansfield is named after Ethel Wainwright, a strong supporter of women's suffrage who was elected as the first female councillor in Mansfield in 1920. Four years later she was appointed as the first female magistrate in the area. Throughout her public life she was involved in the welfare and education of young people. During her 32 years of service, first as Chairman of the Local education Committee and later of the West Notts Divisional Executive she had a significant impact on education in the area.

✳ Garibaldi School at Mansfield is named after the Italian patriot and freedom fighter who successfully won independence for Italy in the 19th century.

✳ George Spencer School at Broxtowe is named after George Spencer who was Member of Parliament for Broxtowe from 1918 to 1929.

✳ Harry Carlton School at East Leake is named after a local parish, rural district and county councillor. Carlton Crescent is also named after him.

✳ John Blow Primary School at Newark is named after the composer and organist who was born in Nottinghamshire (probably at Newark) in 1649. He became a Doctor of Music and in 1685 was named as one of the private musicians of James II. He was responsible for 14 services and over a hundred anthems including music for the coronation of James II. He died in 1708 and was buried in Westminster Abbey.

✳ Richard Bonington Primary School at Gedling is named after Richard Parkes-Bonnington, the famous 19th-century landscape painter. Born in Arnold in 1802, his first paintings were exhibited in the Paris Salon in 1822. Two years later he won a gold medal at the Paris Salon along with John Constable and Anthony Vandyke Copley Fielding. He died of tuberculosis at the early age of 25.

✳ Robert Mellors School is named after Robert Mellors, the noted antiquarian who was also an alderman and chairman of Nottinghamshire County Council Education Committee, during the early years of its existence. He was prolific writer on the local history of the Nottingham area in the early part of the 20th century.

✳ Robert Miles Infant and Junior schools are named after the Revd Robert Miles, a wealthy and forthright evangelist. He became rector of Bingham in 1845 and was responsible for building Bingham Church School, now called Church House and used as a church hall.

✳ Robin Hood Primary School at Mansfield is obviously named after the famous mediaeval outlaw. Surprisingly it is the only county council school thus named although there is a city school with the same name.

✳ Sir Edmund Hilary Primary and Nursery School in Bassetlaw is named after the famous mountaineer who made the first successful ascent of Mount Everest.

✳ The William Lilley Infant and Nursery School is named after the William Lilley who was a member of the Board of Managers for many years.

✳ Walter Halls Primary School, between Mapperley and St Ann's, is named after a local politician and former Lord Mayor. Born in 1870 to a poor farm labourer, Walter Halls left school at the age of 10 to find work as a ploughboy, later working as a railway porter. After moving to Nottingham in 1913 he became involved in local politics and became Chairman of Nottingham Education Committee in 1934. From 1937–38 he was Sheriff of Nottingham and in 1938 he was made Lord Mayor. The school which is named after him was opened in 1939.

✳ The Henry Whipple Primary School at Beeston is named after Nottingham's first Director of Education.

✤ Hogarth Primary School in Mapperley is named after the 18th-century artist and caricaturist who is famous for such works as *Beer Street*, *Gin Lane* and *Marriage a la Mode*.

✤ Joseph Whitaker School in Rainworth is named after the famous naturalist and sportsman who lived at nearby Rainworth Hall.

Pub Names

✤ The Air Hostess in Tollerton takes its name from its proximity to Nottingham's civil airport though it is unlikely that any air hostesses ever flew out from here.

✤ The Black Diamond in Cotgrave refers to the coal that used to be mined at the nearby Cotgreave Colliery before its closure in 1993.

✤ The Blacksmith's Arms in Clayworth was once a blacksmith's shop. It became a pub in the 1870s when the local blacksmith, Thomas Parkinson, became the first landlord.

✤ The Boat Inn at Hayton takes its name from the canal boats which used to operate along the adjacent Chesterfield Canal.

✤ The Bramley Apple at Southwell takes its name from the famous type of apple which was first grown in Southwell in the 1840s.

✤ The Bromley Arms at Fiskerton takes its name from Lord Bromley who lived at East Stoke Hall. According to local legend he wanted to hunt on both sides of the river so bought this pub and named it after himself.

✤ The Cadland takes its name from a racehorse of that name which won both the Derby and the 2,000 Guineas in 1828. The horse was owned by the Duke of Rutland and trained in an area close to Chilwell known as 'The Flats'.

✤ The Cardinal's Hat may be named after Cardinal Woolsey, who served Henry VIII as his chancellor. He stayed at Southwell in 1530 and visited Newark on several occasions before being arrested on a charge of treason.

✤ The Sir John Cockle refers to an old legend in which King Henry II, while hunting in Sherwood Forest, lost his way and was entertained by a poor miller who did not recognise him. He fed the king on venison but when he discovered who he was entertaining he feared for his life. The king, however, knighted him and made him overseer of the forest.

✤ The Court in St Peters Gate, Nottingham, occupies the former County Court building. It was opened in 1993.

✳ The Cranmer Arms in Aslockton is named after Archbishop Cranmer who was born in the village.

✳ The Crusader in Clifton commemorates Sir Gervase Clifton who was killed while fighting in the Third Crusade. His body lies in the local church.

✳ The Cuckoo Bush inn at Gotham refers to one of the stories told about the Wise Men of Gotham. It is said that they constructed a hedge around a cuckoo to prevent it flying away as part of a ruse to persuade the King not to tax the village.

✳ The Cricketers Arms in Kirby-in-Ashfield, commemorates local cricketing heroes Harold Larwood and Bill Voce.

✳ The Dukeries in Edwinstowe takes its name from the local area which encompasses the ducal estates of Welbeck, Clumber and Thoresby.

✳ The Ferry Inn, Wilford, takes its name from the ferry that used to operate nearby.

✳ The Framesmith's Arms in Bulwell takes its name from the craftsmen who made the stocking frames used in the area to manufacture hosiery.

✳ The Forest Folk in Blidworth takes its name from a book called *The Forest Folk*, written by James Prior Kirk. The story is set in 19th-century Nottinghamshire and much of it is written in local Nottinghamshire dialect. A unique feature of the pub is a stained-glass window commemorating the life of the author.

✳ The Gardeners in Cossal takes its name from the fact that it was built on land previously occupied by allotments. It opened in 1959 and its signboard depicted a gardener resting on his spade.

✳ The Goose Fair in Bulwell was opened in 1982. It commemorates the famous Goose Fair which has been held at Nottingham since the 13th century.

✳ The Fairway at Keyworth takes its name from the nearby Stanton-on-the-Wolds Golf Club.

✳ The Fellows Morton and Clayton in Nottingham is named after a famous canal carrying company which operated fleets of narrow boats on the English canals in the 18th and 19th centuries. The building previously served as a warehouse and part of it was for a short period Nottingham Canal Museum.

✳ The Ferry Boat at Laneham enjoys a riverside setting and takes its name from the fact that a ferry existed here from the 13th century until the Victorian era.

The Festival Inn, Trowell.

- The Festival Inn, Trowell, is named after the Festival of Great Britain held in 1951. Trowell was chosen to be the official festival village because it combined the strength of modern industry with the peaceful beauty of the countryside. The village had no pub or restaurant at this time but one was built there in 1956. To mark Trowell's unique role in the Festival of Britain it was called the Festival Inn.

- The Flying Bedstead at Hucknall is named after the flying bedstead, the name given to a experimental vertical take-off and landing vehicle which flew from the nearby Hucknall airfield in 1954.

- The Gooseberry Bush in Peel Street Nottingham reflects the fact that it was built on the site of the former maternity hospital.

- The Greasley Castle in Eastwood is named after the fortified manor house built by Nicholas Cantelupe in the 14th century.

- The Great Northern Inn was once owned by the London and North Eastern Railway Company (LNER). Its name reflects this fact.

- The Headstocks in Cinderhill commemorates the mining heritage of the area and in particular the colliery headstocks that once stood at the nearby Babington Colliery.

- The Johnson Arms in Lenton was originally known as the Abbey Tavern. In 1904 it was purchased by Frank William Johnson who demolished it. In the same year he rebuilt the pub and named it after himself.

✳ The Ling Forest public house in Mansfield was built in an area once covered by an area of woodland known as the Ling Forest. Ling is another word for heather.

✳ The Man of Iron in Stapleford relates to the iron industry which used to be important in the area. The old Stanton Iron Works is only a few miles away. Interestingly, a 19th-century report stated that the workers there were more prone to drunkenness than colliers or other workers but declared that this was caused by 'the very great thirst caused by their occupations'.

✳ The Man of Trent at Clifton has a sign showing a fisherman. It indicates the fact that the river is popular with fishermen and a number of angling clubs fish there.

✳ The Dame Agnes Mellors in St Ann's is named after Agnes Mellors, a wealthy and well connected widow who founded Nottingham High School in the 16th century.

✳ The Old Cross in Stapleford refers to the ancient Saxon cross which stands in the nearby St Helen's churchyard. It dates from the early 11th century and is one of the best preserved Saxon crosses in Nottinghamshire.

✳ The Four Bells in Woodborough takes its name from the four bells in the belfry of the nearby St Swithun's Church.

✳ The Peveril in St Ann's is named after William Peverel, a wealthy and influential Norman landowner who was the first governor of Nottingham Castle.

✳ The Pilgrim Fathers in Scrooby commemorates the fact that many of the Pilgrim Fathers came from the Scrooby area.

✳ The Jester in Sneinton Dale may refer to William Wallet an actor and clown who performed before Queen Victoria in 1844 and for many years styled himself the Queens Jester. He lived for many years in Beeston and was buried in the General Cemetery in Nottingham.

✳ The Mill in Woolpack Lane. Nottingham is built on the site of Richard Arkwright's original horse-powered cotton spinning mill.

✳ The Muskham Ferry refers to the ferry that operated here until the 1940s. It was previously known as the Newcastle Arms.

✳ The Newcastle Arms at Basford refers to the Duke of Newcastle who not only owned extensive lands in the county but also served as Lord Lieutenant of Nottinghamshire.

✳ The Old General in Hyson Green is named after local rogue and eccentric Benjamin Mayo who was well known in Nottingham in the first half of the 19th century.

✻ The Packet Inn at Retford takes its name from the packet boats which used to operate on the nearby Chesterfield Canal. Packet boats were fast passenger boats which plied the canals.

✻ The Palmerston Arms is named after the famous Victorian Prime Minister. His wife came from nearby Beauvale.

✻ The Pauncefort Arms takes its name from the Pauncefort family who lived at nearby Stoke Hall. In 1889 Lord Pauncefort was appointed the first British Ambassador to the USA.

✻ The Railway Inn, Mansfield, takes its name from its close proximity to the former Mansfield Railway Station which was closed in 1963.

✻ Robin Hood is a popular pub name in many parts of the country including Nottinghamshire where the name is found in It is of course named after the famous Nottingham outlaw who robbed the rich to give to the poor.

✻ The Colonel Hutchinson public house at is named after Colonel John Hutchinson who was Governor of Nottingham Castle during the Civil War between King and Parliament. He was one of the regicides who signed King Charles I death warrant.

✻ The Royal Children in Nottingham is named after the children of Princess Anne, the daughter of James II. She and her children sought refuge in Nottingham at the time of the Glorious Revolution and became popular in the neighbourhood. According to some accounts the royal children were accommodated at the inn.

✻ The Savile Arms in Eakring takes its name from the Savile family who owned the Rufford Estate just a few miles from Eakring.

The Royal Children Public House.

* The Will Scarlet in Hucknall takes its name from the member of Robin Hood's band of outlaws. He appears in many of the Robin Hood stories and according to legend is buried in the churchyard at Blidworth.

* The Sherwin Arms at Bramcote is named after the Nottinghamshire family which served the community for many years, including several times as mayor of the city of Nottingham.

* The South Notts Hussars in West Bridgford takes its name from the South Notts Hussars Yeomanry Field regiment RA (TA). Originally formed in 1794 the regiment saw service in the Boer War and was part of the British Expeditionary Force that was sent to France at the outbreak of World War One.

* The Starting Gate in Colwick is so named because it stands on the site of the former straight mile starting post on Nottingham Racecourse.

* The Trent Bridge is unusual as a pub name in that the Trent Bridge Cricket ground is named after the pub and not the other way around.

* The Tiger Moth in Tollerton was built on the edge of Tollerton airfield and takes its name from the famous tiger moth two-seater training aircraft which was one of a number of different types of trainers used at the airfield in the 1930s and later.

* The Trip to Jerusalem is possibly the oldest pub in Nottingham. Its name comes from the legend that soldiers on the way to the crusades stopped there for a drink.

* Tuck's Habit in Bramcote is named after the friar who was part of Robin Hood's band of outlaws. Friar Tuck was famous for his great appetite and it is not surprising that the pub named after him serves food.

* The Mill in Woolpack Lane, Nottingham, is built on the site of Richard Arkwright's prototype horse powered cotton spinning mill of 1770. The pub sign shows an image of Sir Richard Arkwright.

* The Narrow Boat, on Canal Street, Nottingham, is named after the narrow boats which operated on the local canals during the 18th and 19th centuries.

* The Spinning Jenny in Meadow Way, Nottingham, is named after the machine invented by James Hargreaves which allowed operators to spin as many as a hundred threads at a time. Hargreaves later established a cotton mill in Nottingham.

Strange and unusual deaths

✴ A tragic case of a mother and child being burnt to death occurred in December 1834 at Lambley. Five-year-old Samuel Culley was burned to death when his cradle fell into the fire. His mother was also severely burned and died in the General Hospital in Nottingham a few days later.

✴ A young boy was run over and killed by a stagecoach at Stapleford in 1833. Thomas Bramley, who was nearly five years of age, was playing on the turnpike road in front of his father's house when the Times stagecoach came down the hill. The coachman called out to him but the little boy ran in front of the coach and was trampled by the horses. He died within the hour.

✴ William Peach died in 1848 after having been entangled in a corn threshing machine. The nine-year-old boy had gone with some friends to watch a threshing machine at work in the stackyard of a local farm. Unfortunately, his smock became entangled in the spindle and he was drawn up into the machinery. He suffered dreadful injuries and was found to be dead by the time he was extricated from the machine.

✴ William Spittal, a farmer from Widmerpool, was gored to death by a cow in 1843. Visiting a neighbouring farmer he had been holding a gate open when one of the cows, instead of passing through, rushed at him. He was gored so badly that he died from his injuries less than 24 hours later.

✴ A number of cases of accidental poisoning were recorded in the 19th century. On Saturday 18 June 1864 the three-year-old daughter of Mr and Mrs Braithwaite from East Leake died after licking a saucer containing a mixture of sugar mastic and arsenic which had been placed in the kitchen/cheese room for the purpose of killing flies. According to a report in the *Nottingham Review* the poor girl was soon seized with violent pains and retching and died after enduring great suffering. In another case a four-month-old baby was given sulphuric acid in mistake for laudanum by her 11-year-old sister.

✴ An unusual death occurred in 1852 as part of a baptism ceremony. On 29 January William Barnes, the leader of a group of Lattter Day Saints, drowned near the swing bridge at Trent Lock when conducting a baptism by immersion. He fell off the lock wall and drifted into the middle of the river. He shouted for help but attempts to save him failed and he was not seen again that night. His decomposed body was discovered about 500yd downstream a few days later.

✴ Another drowning occurred in May 1845. Israel Knightly and a group of friends went hunting for bird's nests. As they were crossing over the lock gates of the number-12 lock on the Nottingham Canal, Israel caught his foot on a stump near the lock gate and fell head first into the water where he was drowned.

✳ Several coal mining accidents were reported in the local press during the 19th century, many involving the death of young boys. In 1833 a nine-year-old boy was killed by a roof fall at the pit owned by Barber, Walker & Co. at Watnall. Edmund Varley was employed to drive an ass and was doing so when a roof fall buried both him and the ass. He was rescued within five minutes but it was found that he was crushed about the lower parts of his body. He died a few days later.

✳ Factories were also dangerous places. Machines were generally unguarded and young children were employed in a range of occupations. In 1834 11-year-old Samuel Oxspring was killed when he became entangled in machinery at Mr Cox's Bleach Works at Basford.

✳ Sometimes children visited their parent's workplace to deliver messages or food. In December 1865, four-year-old Robert Moult was killed in an accident at Mansfield Gas Works which he visited with the intention of collecting his father's breakfast tin. In order to reach his father Robert attempted to cross a lake of pitch. Although it was glazed over it had not set and he fell through badly burning himself. Medical assistance was rapidly obtained but the unfortunate boy died a few days later.

✳ The coming of the railways also resulted in a number of accidents. On 22 June 1866 an old woman called Julia Hingley was stuck by a train while crossing the railway at a place called Tenter Lane Crossing near Mansfield. The old lady was very deaf but had good eyesight so the cause of the accident remained something of a mystery. The jury recommended that a gate should be put up at the side of the railway for the safety of the public. A more gruesome accident had occurred a few years earlier at Aslockton when Thomas Lane, a 70-year-old rag collector, was knocked down when crossing the line just 120yd from Aslockton Station. The body of the deceased was found in a much mangled state. Both his legs had been severed and a portion of his body and clothes were lying on different parts of the ground. The body had to be inspected by the coroner's jury at this time and according to a report in the *Nottingham and Newark Mercury* it presented a most shocking spectacle.

✳ On 8 May 1840 a young man named Hind was killed at the railway below Beeston Station. He was collecting tickets after the train had started, and slipped at the steps. The Leicester train being just behind passed over him taking off his head and one arm. He was later taken to the Victoria Hotel where an inquest was held.

✳ Windmills were also the cause of a number of accidents. The unguarded machinery in the mills presented an obvious hazard but the revolving sails caused the death of a number of children as a consequence of being struck on the head. Joseph Paling, the five-year-old son of the miller at Sneinton died in this way in March 1839 when he was struck by a sail. Although the mill was only running at three quarters speed his skull was completely smashed-in and a piece of bone was found on the windmill sail.

✳ There were rare instances of people being killed after being struck by lightning. In 1825 John Hemsley, a farm worker at Ruddington, was struck by lightning after taking shelter under a tree. He was dead when found and it was noted that his lips were swollen and his face discoloured. A similar accident took place in 1846 when two farm labourers were struck by lightning when working in a field at Ratcliffe on Trent. It was reported that the hair of both their heads was much singed and their flannel waistcoats were considerably scorched.

✳ Children also died in more unusual circumstances. In 1845 Fanny Radford died after falling into a cauldron of hot broth in the workhouse kitchen at Mansfield. The inquest heard how she was badly scalded up to the middle of her body after climbing on to the top of the copper and falling in. She died a few hours later.

✳ Drunkenness was frequently a contributory cause of accidents during the period but in 1851 two men died from excessive drinking. Henry Thrall, William Ball and John Guyler were installing a pump to empty a cesspit at a house in Sherwood where they were provided with beer and a variety of spirits including whiskey, rum, gin and brandy. Left alone for a while they drank to excess and before long Thrall became insensible and had to be carried home where he soon died, leaving a wife and eight children. Guyler was also taken very ill and died a few days later. Only Ball, who had taken much less alcohol, survived.

✳ People also died of choking on food, and during the 19th century there are reports of people dying as a result of choking on a variety of objects including a nutshell, an apple and a piece of turnip. There are also reports of children dying as a result of drinking boiling water from a kettle spout. This was the cause of death of four-year-old Elizabeth Herring at Lowdham in 1844.

✳ Wells were still used to provide fresh water and accidents sometimes occurred when sinking new wells, alongside falls into wells. In 1834 two-year-old James Wright fell into a well in the yard of the National School at Beeston. He was rescued by a pot hawker but died the following day from bruises and inflammation of the lungs.

✣ There were, of course, accidental deaths in people's home. In 1834 a charwoman died after falling down the cellar steps of the house she had been cleaning. Mary Spencer was working at the house of Richard Butler in Ratcliffe on Trent when she mistook the cellar door for that of the kitchen and fell to the bottom of the steps. She was unconscious when found and died a few hours later. It was noted that Mr Butler's mother, his wife and several other people had fallen down the same steps. A verdict of accidental death was recorded.

✣ Probably the most unusual death recorded in Nottinghamshire in the 19th century was caused by a balloon accident. On Monday 24 August 1863 a Grand Fete was held in the grounds of Basford Hall. One of the attractions was a balloon ascent by a local aeronaut Henry Coxhill. Unfortunatel, there were problems in inflating the balloon and Hall proposed to make an unmanned flight. At this point a local man, James Cambers volunteered to take his place as he was lighter and had previous experience of ballooning. Although the ascent was a success the balloon later crashed in Arnold, killing Chambers.

✣ The Duke of Newcastle died following a hunting accident in July 1701. The *Nottingham Post* recorded; 'Tis said his grace being a stag hunter, his horse fell on his shoulder, yet for the present he felt no harm. When the stag was killed, finding himself worse, getting into a coach he ordered to be driven home, fell into convulsions and died'.

✣ In May 1795 Thomas Pelham Clinton, Third Duke of Newcastle, caught whooping cough. On 18 May he died when a blood vessel ruptured, the result of vomiting induced by a cure prescribed for his ailment. He was only 43 years old and had been Duke for only 15 months.

✣ In 1806 a 17-year-old soldier was killed in a duel at Basford. His opponent, Ensign Butler, was later accused of murder.

✣ Ten people were killed in an explosion in 1818 when gunpowder being unloaded from a canal barge in Nottingham was accidentally ignited.

✣ A man called Lupton died in a bare-knuckle fight at Mapperley Plains in May 1835. He was fighting a rival for the affections of a local servant girl. A contemporary account reported that the fight had lasted for two hours by the time Lupton was rendered insensible. He died shortly afterwards.

✣ Inspector Isaac Phelps of Nottingham police died in 1839 after being bitten by a rabid dog he was trying to rescue. He must have been a popular man for a subscription raised more than £500 for his widow and nine children.

✳ Walter Montgomery, the former manager of the Theatre Royal in Nottingham, committed suicide while on honeymoon in 1871.

✳ Arthur Shrewsbury, the Nottinghamshire and England cricketer, shot himself in 1903 because he was wrongly convinced that he was suffering from an incurable disease. The post mortem found no evidence of any disease.

✳ The weekend of 13 and 14 November 1915 saw a freak run of accidental deaths in Nottingham. An errand boy was knocked down by a taxi in Gregory Boulevard, a confectioner was hit by a car in Arkwright Street and a 44-year-old woman fractured her skull falling downstairs at the County Club in Bridlesmith Gate. A further fatality occurred when a window cleaner fell from a window in Union Street.

✳ An elderly man died after running into a brick wall in Sneinton in 1932. A witness saw the 74-year-old gathering speed as he walked down a hill with a small dog. At the bottom of the street he ran straight into a wall and died in hospital 12 days later.

✳ Caretaker Solomon Beardsley was killed when the boiler exploded at Eastwood Council School in 1920. The Education Committee agreed to pay £200 in full discharge of their liabilities.

✳ Ann Webster from Calverton was frozen to death on 11 February 1772. Returning from Nottingham market, she was caught in a blizzard and died with her horse only a mile from home. Two other travellers, Thomas Rhodes and John Curtis suffered a similar fate on the road to Mansfield.

✳ In November 1851 a Rufford gamekeeper was killed in a battle between four poachers and 10 keepers.

✳ In October 2007 a 23-year-old man from Hucknall died after being hit by a Nottingham Tram when he stepped out in front of it at Weekday Cross. His death was the first such fatality since the opening of the new tram service.

Epitaphs and Memorials

Epitaphs appear in a variety of forms. Some which were originally inscribed on tombstones or church walls have disappeared over time but are still described in old books or documents. A survey of the inscriptions in Greasley Churchyard was undertaken in 1910 and some of the epitaphs recorded here are taken from that survey. The Nottingham Date Book and various antiquarian histories are also valuable sources of information.

✤ Thomas Booth was a famous poacher and deer taker who died in 1752. The stone marking his internment in St Nicholas burial-ground, Nottingham, bore the following inscription:

Here lies a marksman, who with art and skill,
When young and strong, fat bucks and does did kill.
Now conquered by grim Death, (go render tell it!)
He's now took leave of powder, gun and pellet.
A fatal dart, which in the dark did fly,
Has laid him down, among the dead to lie
If any want to know the poor slave's name,
Tis old Tom Booth, – Ne're ask from whence he came
He's hither sent; and surely such another,
Ne're issued from the belly of a mother.

Unusually this epitaph was written before his death and Old Tom was so pleased that he had it engraved on a stone some months before its service being required.

✤ Old David, a local balladeer was also something of a self-publicist. When he died in 1827 a local newspaper published the following epitaph:

Here rests his head upon the lap of earth,
A minstrel old, in Nottingham well known –
In Caledonia was his humble birth,
Old England makes his aged bones her own.

Numerous his verses were, his life was long.
Wide as a recompense his fame was spread;
He sold for halfpence, (all he had) a song,
And by them earn'd (twas all he wished) his bread

If further you his merits would disclose,
Or draw his frailties from his cold abode,
Go by his life (wrote by himself) which shows,
His service to his country and his God

✳ The churchyard of St Luke, Hickling, contains a number of 18th-century slate headstones including the following, to John Smith, dated 1725:

This world's a city full on crooked streets
Death is the market-place where all men meets
If life were merchandise yt men could buy
The rich would often live and the poor men die.

✳ Epitaphs frequently praise the virtues of the deceased. Wilfred Ellis caused the following memorial to his wife to be erected in Shelford, St Peter and Paul in 1761

With Wit Well-natur'd, learned, yet not in vain,
Devout yet cheerful, and resign'd in Pain;
With polish'd manners, and a Taste refin'd,
With female softness, but manly Mind;
Such my ELIZA was, and shall no Verse;
Record these Virtues, or adorn her Hearse?
Forbid it Justice, Gratitude, and Shame,
He who best knew, attests them with his Name

✳ Occasionally the verses on tombstones are ingeniously devised to spell out the name of the deceased. The following tribute to Henry Hanley, buried at St Michael and All Angels in Bramcote, in 1582 is a good example:

Heaven holds that soule who took such care
Everlasting feasts for others to prepare
Nature nere taught to do such excellent things
Reason forbids such acts as damage brings
Yet these (fruits of faith) by Hanley done
Hanley will make to live when wee are gone
And let his name immortall bee though dead
Never forgotten who soules and bodies fedd
Live Hanley's name the basis sure was good
Your house is richer downe than when it stood

✳ John Barton of Holme was a Newark wool merchant. When he died the following verse was inscribed on his memorial window:

I thank God and ever shall
It is the sheep hath paid for all

✳ William Morris was the landlord of the Three Crowns Inn. He died in 1800, aged 70, and is buried at Arnold. The concluding lines of his epitaph read;

Thee Crowns on Earth adorn'd my Name, One Crown immortal now I claim.

✳ The following epitaph to a stonemason is found in St George's Church in Barton-in-Fabis:

Thomas STONE, stone cutter, died 12th Sep 1726 aged 63
Here lyeth one that all may see

A true emblem of their mortality
Whos business was on other tombs to write
And oft on them verse for to recite
But now heaven we hope has took his flight

✳ Other occupations are also mentioned in epitaphs. Joseph Marlow who died in 1829 and was buried in Greasley churchyard definitely pursued a military career as a young man for this epitaph reads:
When I was young in wars I shed my blood,
Both for my King and my Country's good;
In older years my care was Chief to be
Soldier to him who shed his blood for me

✳ Edward Marshall died on 22 January 1844, aged 82, and was buried in the churchyard of St Mary Magdalene, Newark. His military career was outlined on his tombstone as follows:
He enlisted at Newark on 9th June 1778, into the 30th Regiment of Foot, and served during the America War, he afterwards joined the 14th regiment of Infantry, and served in the Indies and on the Continent, after being promoted as sergeant in the last named regiment, was discharged at his own request August 24th 1792. He was subsequently appointed Trumpeter to the Newark troop of Yeoman Cavalry on the formation of that Corps in 1794, which appointment he retained to the time of his death.

✳ Another soldier whose military career was described in detail was John Flinders. Buried in Gedling churchyard, his tombstone read:
He served his country 62 years as a soldier, 34 of which he was a gunner in the Royal Artillery, 22 years in the 8th or King's own regiment of foot, 6 years in the 22nd regiment (General Lambton's). While in the 8th regiment he was in six battles and two sieges :- Dettingen, Fontenoy, Falkirk, Culloden, Rackoo, Val Stirling Castle, and Begen-op-Zoom.

✳ In contrast George Lee, who died in 1819 aged 19, was clearly the victim of a mining accident:
Take warning of my fate Ye Miners All
And be prepared for Death's tremendous call;
Tho' now in perfect health and youthful bloom
You may be brought to an untimely Tomb
By damp, foul air, or fatal fall live me
Receive the summons of Eternity

✳ Another victim of a mining accident was Charles Braddow who is buried in St Helen's churchyard, Pinxton. He was killed in an explosion at Pinxton Collierty on 22 March 1825. His epitaph read:
The wild fire proved my fatal destiny

✱ Elizabeth Cliff from Burton Joyce suffered a tragic death in 1835. The inscription on her headstone read:

This monumental stone records the name
Of her who perished in the night by flame
Sudden and awful, for her hoary head;
She was brought here to sleep amongst the dead.
Her loving husband strove to damp the flame
Till he was nearly sacrificed the same,
Her sleeping dust, tho' by thee rudely trod,
Proclaims aloud, Prepare to meet thy God

✱ Another reference to an occupation, or perhaps a hobby, was recorded some years ago in St Mary's Churchyard, Nottingham:

HERE lies John Mills, who over hills
Pursued the hounds with hollow
The leap though high from earth to sky
The huntsman we must follow

✱ At Bingham Church the Parish Clerk is remembered in the following epitaph:

Beneath this stone lies Thomas Hart, Years fifty-eight he took the part of Parish Clerk
Few did excel, correct he read and sang so well
His words distinct, his voice so clear
Till eighteen hundred and fiftieth year
Death cut the brittle thread, and then a period put to his amen
At eighty-two his breath resigned to meet the fate of all mankind
The third of May his soul took flight to mansions of eternal light
The bell for him with awful tone his body summoned to the tomb
Oh! May his sins be all forgiven and Christ receive him into heaven.

✱ Another parish clerk, Robert Smith of Ratcliffe-on-Soar died in 1782, aged 82 years. The epitaph on his headstone read:

Fifty-five years it was and something more,
Clerk of this parish he the office bore,
And in that space, 'tis awful to declare,
Two generations buried by him were!

✱ Some people lived less blameless lives and the following epitaph was written by Lord Byron on the death of John Adams, a carrier of Southwell:

JOHN ADAMS lies here, of the Parish of Southwell
A Carrier who carried his can to his mouth well,
He carried so much, and he carried so far,
He could carry no more so was carried at last;
For the liquor he drank, being too much for one,
He could not carry off so he's now carri-on

✳ Others had more interesting and exciting lives. The graveyard of Greasley, St Mary contains the grave of Benjamin Drawwater who was ship's surgeon on one of Captain Cook's voyages. His epitaph reads:

UNDERNEATH
LIES INTERRED THE MORTAL REMAINS OF
BENJ. DRAWWATER, GENTLEMAN OF
MANSFIELD, LATE OF EASTWOOD
WHO SUDDENLY DEPARTED THIS LIFE ON
THE 2ND JUNE 1816 IN THE
88TH YEAR OF HIS AGE
IN HIS PROFESSIONAL DUTY HE HAD
ACCOMPANIED THE GREAT CIRCUMNAVIGATOR
COOK IN THE YEARS 1772–1775,
HIS VIRTUES WERE COMMENDABLE
AND EXEMPLARY AND WERE HIGHLY
ESTEEMED BY FRIENDS AND RELATIONS
AND HIS SURVIVING FAMILY
HE WAS A PIUS AND GOOD CHRISTIAN
HE LIVED RESPECTED AND DIED
LAMENTED

✳ In the churchyard of St Lawrence, Wollaton there is a tombstone to Lord Middleton's gamekeeper, William Barlow, who died in 1842. It is made of slate and a verse recalls his occupation:

He oft in life with death did sport
Till death itself his life cut short
Few could excel him with a gun
Except grim death, who misseth none

✳ John Walker from East Bridgford was an engineer and palisade maker who died on 22 September 1832, aged 36 years. The epitaph on his tombstone read:

Farewell my wife and father dear;
My glass is run, my work is done,
And now my head lies quiet here.
That many an engine I've set up,
And got great praise from men,
I made them work on British ground,
And on the roaring seas;
My engines's stopp'd, my valves are bad,
And lies so deep within;
No engineer could there be found
To put me new ones in.
But Jesus Christ converted me,
And took me up above,
I hope once more to meet once more,
And sing redeeming love.

✻ Dan Boswell, the King of the Gypsies, died in 1827 and was buried in the churchyard of St Helen's Selston. His epitaph read:

I've lodged in many a town,
I've travelled many a year
But death at last has brought me down
To my last lodgings here

✻ Very rarely murders are mentioned on gravestones. Isaac Beardsley was brutally murdered for not closing a gate in Nottingham. The following inscription was recorded in the graveyard of St Mary the Virgin:

Marc Stop passenger to ponder on this stone and think how soon the cruel deed was done. A wicked wretch pursued my life to slay, Because to shut a gate I would not stay, so he pursu'd 'till me he overtook, just by a gap on t'margin of a brook and fear' it is he firmly did intend, to my short life to put a final end. In memory of Isaac Beardsley who departed this life 9th November in ye 12th year of his age

✻ In contrast there are a few memorials which recognise acts of courage and self sacrifice. The following memorial is to be found on a wooden panel in the church of St Peter and St Paul in Shelford:

IN MEMORY OF WILLIAM J LAMIN
SOMETIME CHURCHWARDEN OF THIS PARISH
WHO GAVE HIS LIFE IN AN EFFORT
TO RERSCUE A BOY FROM DROWNING
AT WHATTON IN THE VALE, 1930
ERECTED BY HIS FELLOW FARMERS

✻ Longevity is sometimes a cause for comment in epitaphs. Charles Maltby who died in 1821 aged 90 is recognised in the following verse:

With successful industry he passed through life,
Attached to his children, his friends and his wife;
And reached the advanc'd age of ninety you see
Having lived an example of Oeconomy

✻ Richard Greensmith who was buried in the same churchyard seems to have outlived his entire family for his epitaph reads:

Now this weary world I leave
Pale death he doth me call,
And now I go in hopes to meet
My wife and children all.

✻ Infant mortality was commonplace in the 18th and 19th centuries. According to *White's Directory of Nottinghamshire* of 1853 the churchyard at Sibthorpe contained a gravestone erected to the memory of four children by the name of Hall who died in infancy. The inscription at the foot of the stone read; 'The cup of life just with their lips they pressed, They found it bitter and declined the rest. Averse then, turning from the face of day, They softly sighed their little souls away'.

✴ A personal warning may sometimes be encountered as in the following examples from Greasley churchyard:

1740
Remember Man as thou goes by,
As once thou art so once as I,
And as I am so thou must be,
Prepare thyself to follow me

1778
Stop passenger, awile and weigh
Whose line is shortest, thine or mine;
If God has tain my Soul today
Tomorrow he may call for thine;
The only difference then will be;
That thou has one day more than me

✴ Married bliss is frequently mentioned in gushing terms even to the present day and the following inscriptions are typical:

1782
We joined in mutual love,
And so we did remain;
Till parted were by God above
But hopes to meet again

1837
Two of the best friends are dead,
And they have laid them here,
Tread lightly on their hallowed bed
For death hath made it dear

✴ References to people escaping from the jaws of death are much less common. Hercules Clay remarkably survived when his house in Newark was destroyed by canon fire during the Civil War. His remarkable escape is alluded to in this monument in the Church of Mary Magdalen in Newark:
Sacred to the memory
Of HERCULES CLAY, Alderman of Newark
Who died in the year of his Mayoralty
Jan i, 1644

On the 5th of March, 1643,
He and his family were preserved
By the Divine Providence
From the thunderbolt of a terrible cannon
Which had been levelled against his house
By the Besiegers
And entirely destroyed the same
Out of gratitude for this deliverance
He has taken care
To perpetuate the remembrance therof
By an alms to the poor and a sermon,
By this means
Raising to himself a Monument
More durable than Brass
The thund'ring Canon sent forth from its mouth the devouring Flames
Against My Household Gods, and yours O Newark
The Ball, thus thrown Involved the House in Ruin;
But by a Divine Admonition from Heaven I was saved

✻ Even more unusual are memorials to lives saved. The following inscription is taken from a small brass plate in St Swithun's Church, Woodborough:

On May 26th 1966
Two Provost jet aeroplanes
Collided in mid-air and
Crashed within the confines
of the village
Thanks be to God
No-one was hurt

✻ Epitaphs to animals are rare but Lord Byron was so fond of his dog that he had this monument erected in the grounds of Newstead Abbey:

BOATSWAIN MONUMENT
Near this spot are deposited the remains of one
Who possessed Beauty without Vanity
Strength without Insolence
Courage without ferocity
And all the virtues of man without his vices
This praise which would be unmeaning flattery
If inscribed over human ashes
Is but a just tribute to the memory of
BOATSWAIN, a DOG
Who was born in Newfoundland May 1803
And died at Newstead Nov 18 1808

✳ Sometimes epitaphs are written or suggested during a person's lifetime. A contemporary of Robert Lowe wrote the following epitaph:

Here lies poor old Robert Lowe,
Where he's gone to I don't know
If to the realms of peace and love,
Farewell to happiness above;
If haply to some lower level,
We can't congratulate the devil

Lowe was delighted and promptly translated it into Latin!

✳ Perhaps the last comment on epitaphs should be left to Brain Clough who once said:

'I want no epitaphs of profound history. I contributed. I hope they would say that, and I hope somebody liked me.'

Government and Politics

Local Government

✻ With the exception of the City of Nottingham, Nottinghamshire has a two tier system of local government comprising the county council and seven district/borough councils.

✻ Nottinghamshire County Council is a first tier local authority. In 2010 it spent £697 million in providing services – 65 per cent of the money coming in the form of government grants, the remaining 35 per cent from Council Tax. The County Council is responsible for services such as:

Schools
Homes for old people
Meals on wheels
Children's homes
Social workers
Libraries
Roads and street lighting
Waste and recycling
Country parks
Trading standards
Registrars for births deaths and marriages
Community safety
Emergency management
Youth offending service
Welfare rights

✻ Nottinghamshire Police Authority is an independent body responsible for monitoring the work of Nottinghamshire police Force. It exists to ensure an efficient and effective police service for the whole of Nottinghamshire. The Authority has 17 members; seven Nottinghamshire County Councillors, two Nottingham City Councillors and eight independent members. The Police Authority has a number of specific responsibilities including:

Setting and monitoring the police budget
Appointing the Chief Constable and senior police officers
Consulting with local people about policing
Setting local policing priorities and targets for achievement
Monitoring police performance against the targets set by the authority
Publishing a three year strategy and annual policing plan to tell local people
    what they can expect from their police service and report the achievements
Monitoring the Best Value programme of reviews

County Council Elections

✳ Elections to Nottinghamshire County Council are held every four years. The last county council elections took place on Thursday 4 June 2009. The results were as follows:

Conservative Party – 36 seats
Labour Party – 13 seats
Liberal `democrats – 9 seats
Mansfield independent Forum – 4 seats
Selston Area Independents – put people First– 1 seat
Independent – 2 seats
UK Independence Party – 1 seat
1 vacancy – Mansfield South Division

District Councils

✳ There are seven district/borough councils in Nottinghamshire. These are:

Ashfield District Council
Bassetlaw District Council
Broxtowe District Council
Gedling Borough Council
Mansfield Borough Council
Newark and Sherwood District Council
Rushcliffe Borough Council

✳ These Borough/District councils are responsible for a wide range of services including housing, council tax collection, pest control, refuse collection, parking, entertainment and leisure centres:

✳ Ashfield District Council was formed on 1 April 1974 and comprises the former urban districts of Hucknall, Kirkby-in-Ashfield, together with the parishes of Annersley, Felley and Selston which were part of Basford Rural District Council. The council headquarters are at Kirkby in Ashfield.

✳ Bassetlaw District Council has two main population centres, the market towns of Worksop and Retford, which are home to the majority of its 107,713 residents. The Council headquarters are in Worksop.

✳ Broxtowe District Council was formed on 1 April 1974 following the amalgamation of the former Beeston and Stapleford District Council, part of Basford Rural District Council and Eastwood Urban District Council. In 1977 the Council was granted Borough status and the first mayor was elected. The Borough is divided into 21 wards represented by 44 councillors. Elections for the full council are held every four years. The headquarters of the Council are in Beeston. Other important towns within the Borough are Eastwood, Stapleford and Kimberley.

✷ Gedling is a district council with borough status. It has a population of around 112,000. It covers an area of 46.3 square miles and includes the towns of Arnold and Carlton as well as smaller settlements such as Burton Joyce, Calverton, Colwick and Ravenshead. The council headquarters are located at the Civic centre in Arnold.

✷ Mansfield District Council was created in 1972 following the merger of the Borough of Mansfield with the urban districts of Mansfield Woodhouse and Warsop. Unlike most English districts, the council is led by a directly elected Executive Mayor. The headquarters is at Mansfield Civic Centre.

✷ The District of Newark and Sherwood includes the towns of Newark-on-Trent, Southwell and Ollerton though the area is predominantly rural. It covers an area of 251.5 square miles and has a population of over 113,000. Its headquarters is in Newark and until 1995 it was known as Newark District Council.

✷ Rushcliffe Borough Council was formed on 1 April 1974 following the merger of West Bridgford Urban District, the Bingham District Council and part of Basford District Council. It is an affluent and semi-rural area covering 158sq miles and has a population of over 100,000. The largest town and the administrative centre of the Borough is West Bridgford, which has a population of over 36,000. Other towns and villages include Bingham, Ratcliffe-on-Trent, Cotgrave, East Leake, Keyworth, Ruddington and Tollerton. The Borough is home to both Trent Bridge Cricket Ground and Nottingham Forest Football Club. The council also owns Rushcliffe Country Park.

Nottingham City Council

✷ Nottingham City Council is a unitary authority which provides all local government services to its residents. Fifty-five councillors represent electors in the 20 electoral wards within the city. There are local elections every four years when all 55 seats are contested.

The Lord Mayor of Nottingham

✷ The office of mayor was created by Edward I in 1284. The first mayor was Roger de Crophill. The title was changed to lord mayor by Letters Patent announced by King George V at the opening of the new University College in the city on 10 July 1928. The Lord Mayor is the first citizen of Nottingham and his/her role is:

To act as the a-political figurehead of the city council; champion of the city of Nottingham and its people and symbolise the social cohesion of the city and its many cultures and faiths.

To help promote the diplomatic, business, commercial, cultural and educational life of the city

✷ The Lord Mayor presides over meetings of the full council and receives members of the royal family and other important visitors to the city. Each year the Lord Mayor nominates up to three charities and raises funds for those charities.

✳ Alderman William Trigg served the office of Mayor of Nottingham five times; in 1730, 1737, 1742, 1748 and 1754. He lived in a large house in high street and was one of the wealthiest men in the town.

Aldermen

✳ The office of Alderman was created as part of the Charter granted to Nottingham in 1449 by Henry VI. The office evolved over the centuries and in 1835, as a result of the Municipal Reform Act, it was declared that Aldermen were to be elected by the Councillors from among themselves or from persons who were eligible to be elected as councillors. Aldermen were elected for a period of six years. In 1974 with the reorganisation of local government the office of Alderman was abolished. Nottingham, as a district council and later as a unitary authority, appointed Honorary Aldermen who were former councillors who had given distinguished and long service to the Council. Their duties are mainly ceremonial.

Town and Parish Councils

✳ Town and parish councils make up a third tier of local government in some areas. Their functions include recreation facilities, parks and open spaces, cemeteries, public conveniences, car parks and village halls and community facilities. In Nottinghamshire there are:

151 Parish Councils
10 Town Councils
38 Parish meetings

Together these cover half the population of the county including all of rural Nottinghamshire and some of its towns. They range in size from around 20 residents to nearly 25,000.

Parliamentary Constituencies

✳ There are 11 parliamentary constituencies in Nottinghamshire. They are Ashfield, Bassetlaw, Broxtowe, Gedling, Mansfield, Newark, Nottingham East, Nottingham North, Nottingham South, Rushcliffe and Sherwood.

✳ Ashfield Constituency was created in 1955 but the boundaries have been significantly changed over the years. In the 2010 General Election the constituency included much of the district of Mansfield as well as Brinsley, Eastwood and Greasley members of Parliament have included:

1955	William Warbey	Labour
1966	David Marquand	Labour
1977	Tim Smith (by-election)	Conservative
1979	Frank Haynes	Labour
1992	Geoff Hoon	Labour
2010	Gloria De Piero	Labour

✳ Bassetlaw Constituency was created in 1885 and covers the north of Nottinghamshire. It includes the towns of Worksop and Retford as well as a number of smaller villages. Members of Parliament have included:

1906	Frank Hillyard	Liberal
1910	William Ellis Hulme-Williams	Conservative
1929	Malcolm MacDonald	labour
1931	Malcolm MacDonald	National Labour
1935	Frederick Bellinger	Labour
1968	Joe Ashton	Labour
2001	Joe Mann	Labour

✳ Broxtowe Constituency was created in 1918 but abolished in 1955. It was recreated in 1983. In the 2010 General election the constituency included Attenborough, Awsworth, Beeston, Chilwell, Cossall, Nutall, Strelley, Stapleford and Trowell. Members of Parliament have included:

1918	George Alfred Spencer	Labour
1929	Seymour Cock	Labour
1953	Will Warbey (by-election)	Labour

The constituency was abolished in 1955 and recreated in 1983

1983	Jim Lester	Conservative
1997	Nick Palmer	Labour
2010	Anna Soubry	Conservative

✳ Geldling Constituency was created in 1983 replacing the earlier Carlton constituency. Lying within the Greater Nottingham area it includes Arnold, Burton Joyce, Carlton, Colwick and Gedling. Members of Parliament have included:

1983	Sir Philip Holland	Conservative
1987	Andrew Mitchell	Conservative
1997	Vernon Coaker	Labour
2010	Vernon Coaker	Labour

✳ Mansfield Constituency was created in 1885. Since World War Two its Members of Parliament have included:

1941	Bernard Taylor (by-election)	Labour
1966	Don Concannon	Labour
1987	Alan Meale	Labour
2010	Tracy Critchlow	Conservative

✳ Newark Constituency was originally created in 19th century. The present constituency includes the towns of Newark-on-Trent and Southwell as well as the villages of Collingham, Sutton and Lowdham. Members of Parliament since World War Two have included:

1943	Sidney Shepherd (by-election)	Conservative
1950	George Deer	Labour
1964	Edward Stanley Bishop	Labour
1979	Richard Alexander	Conservative
1997	Fiona Jones	Labour
2001	Patrick Mercer	Conservative

✳ Nottingham East Constituency covers the north-eastern part of the City of Nottingham and includes the inner city areas of Hyson Green, St Ann's and Sneinton as well as the suburbs of Carrington, Mapperley and Sherwood. The present constituency was created in 1974. Members of Parliament have included:

1974	Jack Dunnett	Labour
1983	Michael Knowles	Conservative
1992	John Heppell	Labour
2010	Christopher Leslie	Labour-Co-operative

✳ Nottingham North Constituency was created in 1955. It covers the north-western part of the City of Nottingham. Its Members of Parliament have included:

1955	James Harrison	Labour
1959	Bill Whitlock	Labour
1983	Richard Ottaway	Conservative
1987	Graham Allen	Labour

✳ Nottingham South Constituency covers the southern part of the City of Nottingham and includes Clifton, Dunkirk and Lenton. Originally created in 1885, the constituency was abolished in 1974 and recreated in 1983. Since that time its Members of Parliament have included:

1983	Martin Brandon-Bravo	Conservative
1992	Alan Simpson	Labour
2010	Lilian Greenwood	Labour

✳ Rushcliffe Constituency was created in 1885. It includes the towns of West Bridgford and Bingham as well as a number of villages. Since the end of World War Two its Members of Parliament have included:

1945	Florence Paton	Labour
1950	Martin Redmayne	Conservative
1966	Tony Gardner	Labour
1970	Kenneth Clarke	Conservative

✳ Sherwood Constituency was created in 1983 and includes the towns of Hucknall and Ollerton as well as villages such as Blidworth, Clipstone, Edwinstowe, Calverton, Newstead and Woodborough. Its Members of Parliament have included:

1983	Andy Stewart	Conservative
1992	Paddy Tipping	Labour
2010	Mark Spencer	Conservative

2010 General Election Results

✳ In the 2010 General election held on 6 May, Nottinghamshire elected four Conservative and seven Labour Members of Parliament. The results for each constituency were as follows:

Ashfield

De Piero, Gloria	Lab	16,239	(34 per cent)
Zadozny, Jason	Lib Dem	16,047	(33 per cent)
Hickton, Gary	Con	10,698	(22 per cent)
Holmes, Edward	BNP	2,781	(5.8 per cent)
Ellis, Tony	Eng Dem	1,102	(2.3 per cent)
Coleman, Terry	UKIP	933	(1.9 per cent)
Smith, Eddie	Ind	396	(0.8 per cent)

Bassetlaw

Mann, John	Lab	25,010	(51 per cent)
Girling, Keith	Con	16,803	(34 per cent)
Dobbie, David	Lib Dem	5,570	(11 per cent)
Hamilton, Andrea	UKIP	1,779	(3.6 per cent)
Whitehurst, Grahame	Ind	407	(0.8 per cent)

Broxtowe

Soubry, Anna	Con	20,585	(39 per cent)
Palmer, Nick	Lab	20,196	(38 per cent)
Watts, David	Lib Dem	8,907	(17 per cent)
Shore, Mike	BNP	1,422	(2.7 per cent)
Cobb, Chris	UKIP	1,194	(2.3 per cent)
Mitchell, David	Green	423	(0.8 per cent)

Gedling

Coaker, Vernon	Lab	19,821	(41 per cent)
Laughton, Bruce	Con	17,962	(37 per cent)
Bateman, Julia	Lib Dem	7,350	(15 per cent)
Adcock, Stephen	BNP	1,598	(3.3 per cent)
Marshall, Dave	UKIP	1,459	(3.0 per cent)

Mansfield

Meale, Joseph	Lab	18,753	(39 per cent)
Critchlow, Tracy	Con	12,741	(26 per cent)
Wyatt, Michael	Lib Dem	7,469	(15 per cent)
Camileri, Andre	Mansfield Ind	4,339	(9 per cent)
Hamilton, David	UKIP	2,985	(6.2 per cent)
Hill, Rachel	BNP	2,108	(4.4 per cent)

Newark

Mercer, Patrick	Con	27,590	(54 per cent)
Campbell, Ian	Lab	11,438	(22 per cent)
Jenkins, Pauline	Lib Dem	10,246	(20 per cent)
Irvine, Tom	UKIP	1,954	(3.8 per cent)

Nottingham East

Leslie, Christopher	Lab Co-op	15,022	(45 per cent)
Boote, Sam	Lib Dem	8,053	(24 per cent)
Lamont, Ewan	Con	7,846	(24 per cent)
Wolfe, Pat	UKIP	923	(2.8 per cent)
Sardar, Parvaiz	Christian Party	125	(0.4 per cent)

Nottingham North

Allen, Graham	Lab	16,646	(49 per cent)
Curtis, Martin	Con	8,508	(25 per cent)
Ball, Tom	Lib Dem	5,849	(17 per cent)
Brindley, Bob	BNP	1,944	(5.7 per cent)
Marriott, Irenea	UKIP	1,338	(3.9 per cent)

Nottingham South

Greenwood, Lilian	Lab	15,209	(37 per cent)
Holland, Rowena	Con	13,437	(33 per cent)
Sutton, Tony	Lib Dem	9,406	(23 per cent)
Woodward, Tony	BNP	1,140	(2.8 per cent)
Browne, Ken	UKIP	967	(2.4 per cent)
Butcher, Matthew	Green	630	(1.5 per cent)

Rushcliffe

Clarke, Kenneth	Con	27,470	(51 per cent)
Khan, Karrar	Lib Dem	11,659	(22 per cent)
Clayworth, Andrew	Lab	11,128	(21 per cent)
Faithfull, Matthew	UKIP	2,179	(4.1 per cent)
Mallender, Richard	Green	1,251	(2.3 per cent)

Sherwood

Spencer, Mark	Con	19,211	(39 per cent)
Oldknow, Emilie	Lab	18,997	(39 per cent)
Moore, Kevin	Lib Dem	7,283	(15 per cent)
North, James	BNP	1,754	(3.6 per cent)
Parker, Margot	UKIP	1,490	(3.0 per cent)
Swan, Russ	Ind	293	(0.4 per cent)

European Parliament

✤ Nottinghamshire is part of the East Midlands Region of the European Parliament. MEPs are elected by a system of proportional representation and serve for five years. The last elections to the European Parliament were held on 4 June 2009 when the following MEPs were elected:

Roger Helmer	Conservative
Emma McClarkin	Conservative
Glenis Wilmot	Labour
Derek Clerk	UK Independence Party
Bill Newton Dunn	Liberal Democrats

✤ The total number of votes cast for each party was as follows:

British National Party	–	106,319
Christian Party 'Proclaiming Christ's lordship'	–	17,907
Conservative Party	–	370,275
English Democrats Party	–	28,498
Jury Team	–	7,362
Liberal Democrats	–	151,428

No2EU:Yes to Democracy	–	564
Pro democracy; libertas.eu	–	7,882
Socialist Labour Party	–	13,590
The Green Party	–	83,939
The Labour Party	–	206,494
United Kingdom First	–	20,561
United Kingdom Independence Party	–	201,984
Turnout	–	1,228,065
Electorate	–	3,312,944
Percentage Turnout	–	37 per cent

✳ Votes recorded for each political party in the Nottingham City Council Local Counting Area was as follows:

British National Party	–	4,469
Christian Party 'proclaiming Christ's Lordship'	–	914
Conservative Party	–	12,351
English Democrats Party	–	1,219
Jury Team	–	367
Liberal Democrats	–	6,412
No2EU: Yes to Democracy	–	564
Pro Democracy: Libertas.eu	–	296
Socialist Labour Party	–	841
The Green Party	–	4,599
The Labour Party	–	14,931
United Kingdom First	–	1,011
United kingdom Independence Party	–	6,56
Electorate	–	184,486
Verified Total	–	54,802
Turnout	–	29.7 per cent

Political Personalities

✳ **Kenneth Clarke** has been MP for the Rushcliffe Constituency since 1970. He was a minister throughout the 18 years of successive Conservative governments from 1979 to 1977. During that time he served as Paymaster General, Chancellor of the Duchy of Lancaster, Secretary of State for Health, Secretary of State for Education and Science, Home Secretary and Chancellor of the Exchequer. He served on the opposition front bench for a period after the Conservative defeat in 1997 but returned to the back benches in 1997. He became Shadow Secretary of State in 2009 and was appointed Secretary of State for Justice and Lord Chancellor in the coalition government formed in May 2010.

✳ **Frank Cousins** was a leading trade unionist in the 1960s and 1970s. Born at Bulwell in 1904, his family moved to Doncaster while Frank was still at school. After working down the pit for a period he eventually became a truck driver.

He became a member of the Transport and General Workers Union and became a full time official in 1938. He soon became involved with the Union and became its leader in September 1969. After his retirement from the union he became a founder member and chairman of the Community Relations Commission. He died in 1986.

✤ **Bill Derbyshire** was a well known local Conservative politician. Born in 1913, he left school at 13 and worked in a bakery before opening his own general store on Valley Road. He was elected to Nottingham City Council in 1954 and became Conservative leader 10 years later. He became Lord Mayor in 1965 and served as leader again from 1968 to 1972. He later became an alderman. After his retirement he moved to Skegness and then to Spain. He returned to Nottingham in the 1990s and died at home in Mapperley Park in 2000.

✤ **William Ewart Gladstone** began his parliamentary career as Member of Parliament for Newark. Elected in 1832, in December 1834 he was appointed as a Junior Lord of the Treasury in Sir Robert Peel's first ministry. The following month he was appointed Under-Secretary for War and the Colonies, an office which he held until the government's resignation in April 1835. Gladstone remained MP for Newark until 1845 before successfully seeking election in a number of other constituencies. He went on to become President of the Board of Trade, Chancellor of the Exchequer and Prime Minister on four occasions. Along with his great rival Benjamin Disraeli, he dominated British politics throughout the Victorian Era.

✤ **Geoff Hoon** was Member of Parliament for Ashfield from 1992 to 2010. Born in Derby, he was educated at Nottingham High School before going on to read law at Jesus College Cambridge. Only two years after his election to parliament he was appointed an opposition whip and in 1995 he joined the front bench team as opposition spokesman on Trade and Industry. Following Labour's election victory in 1997 he was appointed Under Secretary of State at the Lord Chancellor's Department before being promoted to the rank of Minister of State in the same department. After a brief period as a minister in the Foreign and Commonwealth Office he joined the cabinet in 1999 as Secretary of State for Defence. Following the 2005 General Election he served as Lord Privy Seal and Leader of the House of Commons. The following year he was appointed as Minister for Europe. Under Gordon Brown's premiership he was Chief Whip of the House of Commons and Parliamentary Secretary to the Treasury. He became Secretary of State for Transport in 2008, a post which he resigned in June 2009. He decided not to seek re-election in 2010.

✤ **Dennis Petit** was born in Birmingham in 1925 but moved to Nottingham as manager of Express Lifts. He was elected to Broxtowe Borough Council in the same year and became leader of the Labour Group on the Council. He was elected to Nottinghamshire County Council in 1973 and three years later was elected Labour group leader. When the Labour group took power in 1981 he became the leader of the County Council. In 1997 he was awarded a knighthood for services to local government and the community of Nottinghamshire. He retired from local politics in 2000.

✳ **Anne Yates** was the youngest ever member of the County Council when she was first elected in 1955 and in 1968 she became authority's first woman chairman. She was awarded the CBE in 1972 in recognition of her contribution to public service and played a significant role in helping to establish the National Watersports Centre at Holme Pierrepont in 1973. She retired in 1999 aged 86 after nearly 40 decades in politics. She died at Newark Hospital in February at the age of 93.

The Diocese of Southwell and Nottingham
✳ The Diocese of Southwell was created in 1884. It covered an area of 847 square miles including the whole of Nottinghamshire and a few parishes in South Yorkshire. It changed its name to the Diocese of Southwell and Nottingham in 2005, mainly to help people understand its locality in the UK. In 2010 the diocese contained 314 church buildings in 264 parishes served by 213 clergy. The seat of the Bishop is at Southwell Minster.

Bishops of Southwell

George Ridding	1884–1904	Formerly Headmaster of Winchester College
Sir Edwyn Hoskyns	1904–25	Previously Suffragan Bishop of Burnley
Bernard Heywood	1926–28	Appointed Bishop of Hull in 1928
Henry Mosley	1928–41	Formerly Bishop of Stepney
Frank Barry, DSO, DD	1941–64	Chaplin with the BEF in World War One
Gordon David Savage	1964–70	Formerly Bishop of Buckingham
John Denis Wakeling	1970–85	Chairman of the Archbishops' Council on Evangelism, 1976–79
Michael Whinney	1985–88	Formerly Bishop of Aston
Patrick Burnett Harris	1988–99	Bishop of Northern Argentina in the 1970s
George Henry Cassidy	1999–2009	Formerly Archdeacon of St Paul's Cathedral
Paul Roger Butler	2010–Present	Formerly Bishop of Southampton

✳ The Bishop is assisted by the Suffragan Bishop of Sherwood. The current incumbent is Tony Porter.

Royal Nottinghamshire

✣ Edwinstowe is reputed to be the original burial place of King Edwin of Northumbria.

✣ King Edward the Elder visited Nottingham around 920, having already sent in a dependable garrison, and ordered the repair of the defences. Studying the site himself, he ordered the building of a timber bridge, the first Trent Bridge, and of a fortification at its southern end.

✣ King Athelstan mustered his army at Nottingham in 934 before marching on to win the Battle of Brunanburh.

✣ William the Conqueror passed through Nottingham on his way North. He ordered the building of a castle.

✣ Geoffrey of Anjou, later to become Henry II, besieged Nottingham in 1153. As King he visited Nottingham on seven occasions between 1155 and 1185.

✣ Henry III is calculated to have made 13 visits to Nottingham between 1226 and 1264.

✣ Edward I stayed at Newstead Abbey in 1280 and 1290 as did his son in 1307 and 1315.

✣ Queen Eleanor, the wife of King Edward I, refused to stay at Nottingham Castle in 1257 because of the smell from coal smoke. She later died at Harby in 1290. Taking her body to Westminster, Edward erected 12 memorial crosses (Eleanor Crosses) marking where the cortège rested.

✣ King John visited Nottinghamshire on a number of occasions. He held court at Nottingham Castle and regularly hunted in Sherwood Forest. It was also from the battlements of the Castle that he ordered the hanging of 28 Welsh hostages in 1212. He died at Newark in October 1216.

✣ Edward III seized power from his mother, and her lover Roger Mortimer, on 19 October 1330 when he and a number of companions made their way secretly into Nottingham Castle. Mortimer was later put to death and the Queen was imprisoned for the rest of her life. As King he returned to Nottingham on a number of occasions and twice held a Parliament here.

✣ King Edward IV visited Nottingham on a number of occasions between 1469 and 1471 and ordered the erection of a great octagonal tower at the castle.

✳ Richard III also undertook building work at Nottingham Castle and held court here in 1483. It was from Nottingham, in 1485, that he set out to battle only to be faced with defeat and death at the Battle of Bosworth Field.

✳ Henry VII, and his army, was in Nottinghamshire in 1487. Having attended the Corpus Christi Day service at St Mary's Church in Nottingham he led his army to the Battle of Stoke. With this exception no Tudor monarch ever visited Nottinghamshire.

✳ King James I passed through Nottinghamshire in 1603 on his way from Edinburgh to his coronation in London. His wife Queen Anne and her eldest son, Prince Henry, followed shortly afterwards and spent the night at Wollaton Hall on 21 June. The banquet that night included eight fish, six capons, a dozen chickens and four pigs. During his reign he hunted regularly in Sherwood Forest staying at Rufford, Newstead and at Thurland Hall in Nottingham, the home of Sir John Holles.

✳ The future King Charles I stopped at Worksop on his way to London, where he was entertained by the 12-year-old William Cavendish. In 1634 King Charles I and Queen Henrietta Maria stayed at Thurland Hall in Nottingham on their way to Scotland.

✳ Nottinghamshire played an important role in the Civil War between Charles I and Parliament. It was at Nottingham that the King raised his royal standard on 22 August 1642. It was Newark, however, not Nottingham which became the Royalist Headquarters during the Civil War and it was here that the king surrendered to Scottish forces in May 1646.

✳ Queen Anne, the wife of James II, spent some time at Nottingham in 1668, when she stayed at the home of the Duke of Newcastle.

✳ The celebrations in Nottingham marking the coronation of King George III on 22 September 1761 were described as follows: 'The people of Nottingham joined heartily in the national festivity. The morning was ushered in by the ringing of bells. At 10 o'clock a crowded congregation attended St Mary's Church, where a Coronation anthem composed by Mr Wise, the organist was performed by a large choir. At noon, a great number of the respectable inhabitants met at the Exchange, and proceeding thence paraded the principal streets, with music and streamers, preceded by the Mayor and Aldermen in their scarlet robes, and the Sheriffs and Chamberlains and Common Council in their corporate habiliments, and also by the clergy in their canonicals, and numerous gentlemen on horseback. One of the most conspicuous features of the procession was the company of woolcombers, then a numerous body, who had streamers and a music band of their own…About two o'clock, the procession divided into sections. Some repaired to the inns where banquets had been provided; and others retired to arbours which had been erected in the streets for the purpose of convivial enjoyment, collections having been made among the wealthy with which to regale the needy. Several sheep were roasted whole in the market-place, and a splendid and universal illumination of the town at night, and a brilliant display of fireworks, closed the festivity.'

✳ A general holiday was called for Queen Victoria's Coronation in 1838. Celebrations included a civic procession from the Exchange to a service in St Mary's Church, festivities in the Park during the afternoon, and fireworks in the market place in the evening.

✳ In 1840 Queen Adelaide, the widow of William IV, travelled through Nottingham en-route to Harwood House near Leeds. She passed through the county again the following year, making a brief stops at Nottingham and Wollaton Hall.

✳ Queen Victoria passed through Nottingham in 1843 on her way to Belvoir Castle. On this occasion the Corporation marched in procession to the Midland Station to pay their respects. Queen Victoria never made an official visit to the town.

✳ The Prince of Wales was a regular visitor to Nottinghamshire where he enjoyed shooting and house parties. He visited Clumber and Shireoakes in 1861 and in November 1881 he visited the Duke of Portland at Worksop for four days of shooting.

✳ The Prince and Princess of Wales visited Nottingham in 1878 to open the Midland Counties Museum and Art Gallery in Nottingham Castle. In 1904 as King Edward VII and Queen Alexandra they paid a private visit to Rufford.

✳ King Edward VII and Queen Alexandra visited Worksop on 11 December 1905. Arriving by train the Queen was presented with bouquets by Miss Dorothy Allen and Miss Ida Kemp. A huge welcome arch was erected across Park Street to greet the royal couple.

✳ In June 1914 King George V and Queen Mary became the first reigning monarchs since Charles I to make an official visit to Nottingham. While in the city they visited the Forest and Wollaton Hall as well as touring a number of lace factories. They later visited Forest Town near Mansfield where they made an unexpected call to the home of Mr Mottishaw, a local miner. As part of the same tour they also visited Retford where they inspected a guard of honour in front of the town hall. On 1 December the King visited the National Shell Filling Factory at Chilwell. The King and Queen returned to Nottingham in 1928 to open new buildings at the University of Nottingham and later paid a visit to the Royal Agricultural Show at Wollaton Park.

✷ The Prince of Wales (later Edward VIII) visited Nottingham in 1923 to lay the foundation stone of the Memorial Gateway on Trent Embankment. During the visit he also toured the Boots factory on Island Street. In the same year he visited Worksop on his way by train to Welbeck Abbey.

✷ In 1926 the Duke of York (later King George VI) visited Nottingham to attend a meeting of the Industrial Welfare Society, of which he was president. He also toured the Raleigh cycle works in Lenton.

✷ Later in the same year King George V made a private visit to Nottingham to visit the Anglo-Scottish Sugar Beet Corporation's factory at Colwick.

✷ Princess Mary, the King's daughter, visited Nottingham in April 1927 when she officially opened the Nottingham Co-operative Society's new model bakery on Meadow Lane. After lunch at the Guildhall the Princess opened an extension at the General Hospital and a new wing at the Children's Hospital in Mapperley.

✷ Edward, Prince of Wales, purchased Grove Farm in Lenton in 1929. Parts of the buildings were converted into royal apartments and the Prince became a regular visitor here for several years.

✷ HRH Edward, Prince of Wales, visited Cropwell Bishop on 29 June 1932. Having been greeted by Alderman Derbyshire he reviewed a parade of ex-servicemen and met members of the local Women's Institute.

✷ King George V and Queen Mary visited Nottingham in July 1928 to open the new Nottingham University College. During the same visit the royal couple also attended the Royal Agricultural Show at Wollaton Hall.

✷ Nottingham Council House was officially opened by the Prince of Wales in May 1929.

✷ King George VI and Queen Elizabeth visited Nottingham in March 1943 to help boost wartime morale. After receiving an official welcome in the Old Market Square they visited Chilwell Depot, Wilford Power Station and Boots.

✷ Princess Elizabeth and the Duke of Edinburgh visited Nottingham in 1949 as part of the city's quincentenary celebrations. The royal couple toured exhibitions at the Broadmarsh and Guildhall and watched the primary schools' sports day at the Forest. After lunch at the Council House the princess was presented with a silver coffee set as a gift from the city.

✷ Queen Elizabeth, the Queen Mother, made an official visit to Mansfield on 24 July 1950. At that time she was still Queen in her own right as wife and consort of King George VI.

✴ Princess Margaret attended a service at the part built St Francis Church on the new Clifton Estate in 1956.

✴ Princess Alexandra toured the Boots site at Beeston on 5 June 1958. During the same visit she officially opened Nottingham and District Technical College.

✴ The present Queen has made a number of visits to Nottinghamshire. The first was on 6 July 1955 when she visited Birkin's before going on to the Royal Show in Wollaton Park. She came again in 1968 and in 1977 as part of the Royal Jubilee celebrations. On this occasion her engagements included a civic banquet and visits to the Queens Medical Centre and Trent Bridge Cricket Ground to watch the test match between England and Australia. At Mansfield they opened the new library and visited the Town Hall, here they signed the visitors book. Her last visits of the 20th century were in 1997 to mark celebrations for the centenary of Nottingham's city status and 1999 to open the University of Nottingham's new Jubilee campus.

✴ Queen Elizabeth II visited Worksop on 5 June 1981 to open the new Queens Building at the Town Hall.

✴ The Duchess of Kent opened new premises for Nottingham's College of Art and Design on 14 October 1969.

✴ The Duke of Gloucester opened the Broad Marsh Shopping Centre on 26 March 1975.

✴ Princess Margaret visited Sutton-in-Ashfield on 9 November 1983 to open the new Elbeo Factory and warehouse complex at Stoney Street. She was in Nottinghamshire again on 28 September 1988 when she opened an extension to Dawn House School at Rainworth.

✴ Prince Charles was admitted to the Queens Medical Centre in 1990 to undergo an operation to treat a fracture of his right arm. During his week-long stay he received hundreds of gifts and well wishes including a bottle of Shipstone's bitter and a giant card from Ritzy's nightclub. In the same year Diana, Princess of Wales opened the city's indoor tennis centre. She also visited the Nottingham and Nottinghamshire Society for the Deaf on Forest Road West which was celebrating its centenary.

✴ The Queen and Prince Phillip visited Nottingham again in 2002. As part of their Golden Jubilee celebrations they officially opened the Nottingham Ice Centre before watching a special ice gala which had been choreographed by Jayne Torville and Christopher Dean.

✴ Diana, Princess of Wales, made several visits to Nottinghamshire. In 1993 she came to Nottingham Playhouse to see members of the CandoCo Dance

Company for able and disabled people perform, before visiting a mental health project and Challenge House, the Red Cross care home in Beeston. Following her death in 1997 thousands of people queued for hours to lay floral tributes in front of the Council House and to sign the books of condolences. On the Saturday afternoon following the Princess's funeral in Westminster Abbey a memorial service was held in Old Market Square. Thousands turned out for a multi-faith service during which speakers included representatives of charities the Princess had helped.

✳ Princess Anne visited Nottingham in 1978 to open the newly refurbished Theatre Royal. Following the opening ceremony she attended a special variety show at which Max Bygraves topped the bill. She was in Nottinghamshire again in 1987 and 1982 visiting local knitwear factories in her capacity as president of the British Knitwear, Clothing and Export Council. Another visit took place in October 1989 when she called in on the premises on the Nottinghamshire Royal Society of the Blind in Radford. She also opened the new Nottinghamshire Archives building on 20 October 1992. In 1991 she visited Mansfield when her engagements included planting a tree to mark the opening of Riverside Walk. The Princess visited Mansfield again on 29 November 1999 to officially open the Water Meadows Swimming Baths and fitness centre.

✳ Prince Charles has made numerous visits to Nottinghamshire. On 20 February 2009 he visited Nottingham for the day. During his time in the city he launched a food accreditation scheme, visited the Boots pharmaceutical and beauty products company, met young people helped by the Prince's Trust and joined apprentices learning new skills at a construction college. He was in the city again on 9 September 2010 as part of a five day tour of Britain's sustainable living projects. While in Nottingham he launched the East Midlands sustainable business network, stopped off at a couple of rejuvenated faith centres, visited the home of a 70-year-old woman who had had solar panels installed and wandered around the Arkwright Meadows Community Garden.

✳ The Duke of Kent visited Ollerton on 17 June 2010 to tour the energy-saving and eco-friendly Sherwood Energy Village.

✳ Princess Anne visited Keyworth on 20 July 2010 to open the British Geological Survey's new science building.

✳ The Duke of Kent visited Portland College, Mansfield in November 2010 to help commemorate its 60th anniversary.

✳ Sophie, Countess of Wessex, visited Nottingham on 17 November 2010. After visiting the Childline Call Centre she went on to the University of Nottingham Samworth Academy at Bilborough.

This and That

✤ The Hemlock Stone is a startling and unusual geological feature which stands near to the summit of Stapleford Hill, adjacent to Bramcote Hills Park. The upper part of the Hemlock Stone is heavily impregnated with barium sulphate, a mineral which is resistant to weathering. Over millions of years erosion of the softer sandstone surrounding the pillar left it standing in isolation and carved it into its unusual shape. There are lots of legends surrounding the stone. According to one account the stone was thrown there by the devil, while others believe it was used by the druids. A modern myth suggested by local people is that the stone is actually a meteorite.

✤ Nottingham experienced a frightening earthquake in AD1110, the first to be recorded in England.

✤ In 1367 King Edward III recognised the quality of Nottingham alabaster work by ordering an altar-piece for St George's Chapel in Windsor from Peter the Mason.

✤ A great storm claimed the lives of several people in Nottingham in 1558. Hailstones up to 15in in circumference were reported and properties between Wilford and Lenton were damaged.

✤ Mansfield stone, the rock found beneath the town, lies on the boundary between layers of limestone and sandstone and so combines the properties of both. This excellent building stone has been quarried in the Mansfield area since mediaeval times and can be seen in many of the town's buildings as well as Southwell Minster.

✤ The Duke of Newcastle was awarded £21,000 compensation for the burning of Nottingham Castle in 1831.

The Hemlock Stone.

✳ The aurora borealis was observed in Nottinghamshire in 1957 and again in 1989 on 13 March.

✳ In 1593–94 an outbreak of bubonic plague claimed the lives of 138 people in Beeston. The bodies of those who died were buried in a mass grave at the eastern end of the churchyard.

✳ A terrible fire caused great damage to the village of Misson in 1652. A note in the parish register recorded: 'a lamentable Fire at Misson August 8th 1652. It being the Lord's Day the people being at church the fire totally burned down and consumed to the ground 48 dwellings, houses, stables and other buildings to the number of 364 bays of buildings with very much corn and hay which the inhabitants lately laid in – The damage amounted to £5069 12s and upwards'.

✳ The Millennium Monument in the Riverside Park, Newark, is built in the form of a sundial. Slate markers are sunk into the turf to mark the hours and each is inscribed with an event significant in Newark's history.

✳ The winter of 1947 is was one of the worst on record in Nottinghamshire. On 27 January the temperature fell to 29F and 4in of snow fell on Nottingham. Further snowfalls occurred over the next few days and on 7 February the *Nottingham Post* reported 8in of snow and the closure of five Nottinghamshire collieries. The end of February saw more blizzards and another 124in of snow. Scores of people were taken to hospital suffering from broken bones, a trolley bus crashed on Carlton Hill and villages south of the river were cut off by 10ft drifts. The big freeze ended in March but was followed by flooding.

✳ Hundreds of people in Nottinghamshire died in the 1918 influenza epidemic.

✳ Six people lost their lives on 31 July 1784 when a temporary ferry capsized at Wilford during a gale.

✳ A statue of a beekeeper can be found on High Road in Beeston. A play on the town's name.

✳ Nottingham has over 400 caves under its city centre.

✳ A giant statue of a golden hand stands in the Vicar Water Country Park to the South of Clipstone. It symbolises the miner's belief that all life and wealth is taken from, and grows from, the earth. It was commissioned for the Sustrans National Cycle Route.

✳ Nottingham is one of only six designated Science Cities in the United Kingdom. It received the designation in 2005 in recognition of the city's scientific assets and the importance of science and technology in helping to drive the local economy.

✳ The Whitley Electrical Radio Company was founded in Mansfield in 1920 by A.H. Whitely and began making valve and coil holders for the expanding radio industry. The company pioneered a magnetic moving coil loudspeaker under the name 'Stentorian'.

✳ One of the tallest sundials in Europe stands in Portland Square in the centre of Sutton in Ashfield. It is 10m high.

✳ The Sneinton Dragon stands at the junction of Manvers Street and Sneinton Hermitage. Standing 7ft tall with a wingspan of 15ft, it was designed and built by Robert Stubley, a local craftsman. The dragon was unveiled in November 2006 after residents of Sneinton told the Renewal Trust that they would like a piece of public art to represent their area of the city.

✳ A notice on a barn wall at Halloughton near Southwell reads:
HALLOUGHTON
ALL VAGRANTS
Will be apprehended by order of
The JUSTICES OF THE PEACE
J Nicholson Chief Constable

✳ Mansfield Building Society is one of the few independent building societies still existing in the UK. Founded in 1869 it now has assets of around £300 million. It operates from purpose built premises in Mansfield town centre with a small network of branch offices in the surrounding area.

✳ A tornado swept through Sneinton and Colwick on 1 November 1775. Witnesses described it as a huge black cone measuring about 20ft in diameter in the middle. A contemporary account recorded that it ripped thatched roofs from barns and cottages and tore up apple trees by the roots. No one was injured but one boy was blown from one field, over a hedge and into the next.

✳ Mahatma Ghandi visited Nottingham in 1931 to call on his nephew who was studying at University College. While in the city Ghandi also visited Ericson's factory.

✳ The 17th-century manor house at Bilsthorpe has a cupboard where Charles I is said to have hidden during the Civil War.

✳ The Scots Grey pub in Bulwell (now closed) was featured in a television programme entitled *The Ten Hardest Pubs in Britain*.

✳ Coddington was the home of Constance Painswick Smith who revived the custom of Mothering Sunday.

✽ The Flying Bedstead was an experimental vertical take off and landing device developed by Rolls-Royce at their Test establishment at Hucknall.

✽ When Queen Elizabeth II visited Nottingham to celebrate its centenary in 1997 she was photographed with 100 local residents whose collective birth dates represented every year between 1897 and 1997, from a great, great grandmother to a babe in arms.

✽ The Jarrow Marchers passed through Nottingham in October 1936. The men were served with supper by the Co-operative Society and then accommodated for the night at a Sneinton hostel as guests of the city council. In the morning they were provided with breakfast by Nottingham Conservative Party.

✽ Desperate Dan, the famous comic character was created by Nottingham artist, Dudley Dexter Watkins. He was a successful book illustrator but will be best remembered for his immortal cartoon characters including Lord Snooty, Biffo the Bear and of course Desperate Dan.

✽ Games Workshop, the creator of the War Hammer is based in Nottingham.

✽ The village green at Car Colston is reputedly the largest in England.

✽ Stone from Mansfield was used to build the House of Commons.

✽ In 1983 Nottingham City Council went into the record business with the release of a promotional record. The single, called *Nottingham,* was played by a group called Sheriff whose lead singer was Mick Vaughan who had once been a member of Paper Lace. Designed to boost tourism in the city, copies were distributed to travel writers and radio stations while others went on general sale.

✽ There are four 'Thankful Villages' in Nottinghamshire; Maplebeck, Wysall, Wigsley and Cromwell. These are villages from which all the young men that went off to fight in World War One returned safely.

✽ In 1860 while digging a grave in Littleborough, the sexton discovered a stone coffin. On raising the lid there was revealed the perfect body of a young woman wearing a garment fastened with a Roman style broach. Within an hour, however, she crumbled to dust before his eyes.

✽ In 1855 a man sold his wife in St Peter's Square, Nottingham for a shilling and a pint of ale.

✽ Nottingham schoolboy Walter Walker had a lucky escape in 1902 when he stumbled in front of a tram. The quick-thinking driver, realising that he did not have time to stop, saved the boy by lowering the lifeguard and scooping him to safety.

✷ General Dwight D. Eisenhower, victorious Allied commander in Europe (and later to become President of the USA), visited Nottingham in October 1945 to launch the Roosevelt Scholarship which enabled young people from Nottinghamshire to travel in the USA.

✷ Nottingham has won the Britain in Bloom four times, achieving Britain in Bloom, Champion of Champions in 2008.

✷ The Castle Barge is Newark's famous floating pub. Formerly a grain barge it was converted to its present form in 1980. It is moored on the edge of Newark by the bridge near the castle.

✷ The Beehive Inn at Maplebeck is claimed to be the smallest in Nottinghamshire with just two small rooms.

✷ Nottinghamshire was for many years one of the most important rice growing areas in the country.

✷ The Royal Show was held in Wollaton Park in 1995.

✷ When the registration of motor vehicles was first made compulsory in 1903 a total of 123 vehicles were registered in Nottinghamshire. These included nine steam engines, 40 powered bicycles and tricycles, and a number of motor cars.

✷ The village of Wellow has a 60ft-high maypole in the centre of the village green. This is one of only three permanent maypoles in England. Normally made from timber, Wellow's maypole is constructed from metal for greater durability. An annual May Festival is held on the green.

✷ The Japanese Garden and meditation Centre at North Clifton near Newark is featured in the AA's book, *Inspirational gardens around the world*. The natural landscape of Japan is recreated here in miniature form with mountains and hills, waterfalls and rivers.

✷ James Tenant, who cut the famous Koh-I-Noor diamond, was born at Upton.

✷ The custom of Gait letting still takes place each year at Sutton-on-Trent to determine grazing rights on the 300 acres of land bordering the river.

✷ Charles Dickens visited Nottingham in 1852 and stayed at the George Hotel. He visited the town again in October 1858 and February 1869.

✷ The bell Great Tom of Lincoln Cathedral was made by Oldfield's of Narrow Marsh in Nottingham in 1595.

✤ At Weston, on the Great North Road, love-lorn John Morris ran himself to death chasing a coach as it left the village. His grave is in the churchyard.

✤ A private garden in Nottinghamshire is home to an extremely rare collection of tall bearded iris. The garden in East Bridgford is unique in the East Midlands and contains over 500 hybrid iris.

✤ A Nottingham firm of coach builders, by the name of Stareys, built carriages for Napoleon.

✤ A local disturbance known as the Great Cheese Riot took place in Nottingham in October 1776. According to a contemporary account the farmers demanded from 28s to 30s per hundredweight, a price deemed highly excessive. The people were so exasperated that their violence broke like a torrent – cheeses were rolled down wheeler gate and Peck lane in abundance – many others were carried away – and the mayor, in endeavouring to restore peace, was knocked down with one in the open fair. The dragoons were summoned and acted with great vigour, in quelling the riot. One man, William Eggleson from Car Colston, while guarding some cheese, was killed on the spot by the fire of a dragoon, and others received injuries. A number of persons were apprehended on suspicion of being parties to the riot but all of them were afterwards liberated.

✤ The first National Census was taken in 1801. The data gathered for Nottingham revealed a population of 28,801 in the borough which, at that time, was confined to its ancient bounds and did not include areas such as Lenton, Radford, Basford and Sneinton. There were 157 alehouses in the town as well as seven wine and spirit merchants. When shopping for food local people were served by 38 butchers, 38 grocers and tea dealers, 42 bakers and six fish mongers; and for those with a sweet tooth there were four confectioners. The town also had 34 tailors, 20 woollen and linen drapers, and 34 boot and shoe makers. The health of the townspeople was cared for by 16 doctors, seven chemists and druggists, and two dentists.

✤ The Mary Potter Heritage Centre opened in Nottingham in 2010. Mary Potter was a nun who devoted much of her life to working with the poor and destitute from a mission in Nottingham. Her remains are buried in a tomb in St Barnabas Cathedral.

✤ The Great Nottingham Bike Ride takes place in June each year and helps raise money for charity. In 2010 the event started and finished at the National Watersports centre at Holme Pierrepont, near Nottingham. Over 400 riders took part in a range of rides including a 75 sportive route, a 50-mile challenge ride, an 18-mile community ride and a family lap challenge.

✤ The glass house in Clumber Park is 450ft in length and provides cover for chrysanthemums, fuchsias and carnations as well as figs, grapes and peaches.

✳ Hucknall was the venue for the 1927 Kings Cup Air Race.

✳ A heliport opened at Lenton in July 1956. A helicopter service linking Nottingham with Birmingham and Leicester was planned with fares of £1 9s to Birmingham and 11s to Leicester. Despite initial enthusiasm financial problems and fuel shortages led to the service being suspended only a few months later. It was never resumed and the site was used as an off-road driving instruction area and later as a go-kart circuit.

✳ A livestock dealer in Nottingham was fined £1 in 1922 for being drunk in charge of a horse and cart, the latter containing a pig. When he was arrested a large crowd followed the cart to the police station.

✳ More than 5,000 Boots employees were taken to the British Empire Exhibition at Wembley in 1924. Workers were transported on eight specially hired trains. The earliest left Nottingham in 5.47am and all arrived at the exhibition before noon. An exclusive film of the occasion was made by Boots cameramen and shown later at the Elite cinema in the town.

✳ The Bishop and a Showgirl hit the headlines in 1970 when following a scandal, the Bishop of Southwell, Dr George Savage, resigned and became an Anglican chaplain in Tenerife.

✳ One of the top bands of the 1970s, Paper Lace, was discovered playing for £20 a night at the Grey Goose in Gedling. Showbiz manager Brain Hart was so impressed that he signed them up.

✳ The 16th Trades Union Congress was held at Nottingham in 1883. Delegates debated a number of issues including the training of steam engine drivers and the right of relatives of dead miners to be represented at coroners' inquests.

✳ Boys at the Mundella School raised funds to buy a husky for Captain Scott's ill-fated expedition to the South Pole. Scott named the dog Mundella.

✳ George Fox, the founder of the Quaker religion, was once imprisoned in the stocks at Mansfield Woodhouse for trying to preach the Gospel to people living in the area.

✳ The Pretty Polly brand of hosiery originated in Sutton in Ashfield around 1927 and was manufactured there until 2005.

✳ Francis Hacker of East Bridgford escorted King Charles I to his execution in Whitehall on 30 January 1649. After then Restoration he was declared a traitor and executed at Tyburn.

✳ The last passenger train pulled out of Nottingham's Victoria Station on the evening of Saturday 2 September 1967. Freight services continued for some time but the station was later demolished. The site is now the Victoria Shopping Centre.

✳ Nottinghamshire was supplied with natural gas for the first time in 1971.

✳ In 1785 Nottingham's ceremonial mace was stolen from the mayor's home on Beastmarket Hill. The thief, James Shirley, was caught and sentenced to seven years transportation to Nova Scotia.

✳ The authorities banned merry-go-rounds from the goose fair in 1813, insisting that they were 'disgraceful and dangerous machines'.

✳ Tourism became something of a problem in the Dukeries in the 1920s and in 1922 Nottingham County Council passed a bye-law ordering visitors not to 'blow a horn, use a noisy instrument or sing loudly'.

✳ Beeston has one of the highest concentration of pubs-per-person in the UK with 18 pubs (as of 2010) within a mile of the town centre.

✳ Sir Neil Cossons (Chairman of English Heritage) grew up in Beeston. One of his first jobs was working as a railway porter at Beeston Railway Station.

✳ Nottingham City Council looks after 136 parks and gardens across the city which range from attractions such as the impressive Arboretum through to smaller neighbourhood parks.

✳ Nottingham City Council manages over 3,000 allotment plots spread over 50 locations and boasts the largest and oldest site in Britain at the St Ann's Allotments.

✳ Biologists at Nottingham University's Spider Laboratory are studying a number of tarantulas including the Goliath Bird Eater, which can grow to 12in in size.

✳ Around Strelley and Cossall there are remnants of stone causeways known as monks or pilgrim paths. These may have been part of a 14th-century monastic trade network.

✳ West Bridgford used to be known as 'Bread and Lard Island' as Nottingham people suspected the inhabitants had no money to eat properly after spending all their income on grand houses and fur coats.

Select Bibliography

Beckett, J. (Ed) *A Centenary History of Nottingham* Chichester, 2006

Beckett, J. *The Book of Nottingham* Buckingham, 1990

Becket, J.V. *The East Midlands from AD 1000* London, 1988

Bowyer, C. *Albert Ball VC* London, 1977

Bryson, E. *Portrait of Nottingham* London

Chambers, D.J. *Nottinghamshire in the Eighteenth Century* London, 1966

Chapman, S. *Jesse Boot of Boots The Chemists* London, 1974

Christian, R. *Nottinghamshire* London, 1974

Davis, S. *Nottingham – City Beautiful* Derby 2009

Gray, D. *From Settlement to City* Wakefield, 1973

Hadfield, C. *The Canals of the East Midlands* Newton Abbott, 1981

Kaye, D. *A History of Nottinghamshire* Chichester, 1987

Marsden, K. *The County Books – Nottinghamshire* London, 1953

Mee, A. (Ed) *The King's England – Nottinghamshire*

Moore, H.T. and Morris W. *D.H. Lawrence* Over Wallop, 1988

Morris, J. (Ed) *Domesday Book – Nottinghamshire* Chichester, 1977

Palmer, M. and Neaverson P. *Industrial Landscapes of the East Midlands* Chichester, 1992

Pevsner, N. *The Buildings of England: Nottinghamshire*

Salter, M. *Castles of the East Midlands* Malvern, 2002

Smith, D.M. *The Industrial Archaeology of the East Midlands* Dawlish, 1966

Smith, M. *Castles and Manor Houses in and around Derbyshire* Derby, 1977

Smith, M.E. *Derbyshire Canals* Derby, 1987

Spencer, R. *D.H. Lawrence Country* London, 1979

Stocker, D. *England's Landscape – The East Midlands*, London 2006

Stone, R. *The River Trent*, Chichester 2005

Weir, C. *The Nottinghamshire Heritage* Chichester, 1991

Wood, A.C. *A History of Nottinghamshire* Nottingham, 1971

In my research I also made extensive use of a wide range of primary sources as well as newspapers, magazines and journals. A number of websites yielded useful information and local museums gave me valuable insights to a number of topics.